"This book is a must read for any practitioner. It is all here . . . everything you need to counsel and help a family who has lost a child of any age."

Daniel Roberts, DD, DMin, FT, coauthor
(with Melinda Moore) of *After the Suicide Funeral:
Wisdom on the Path to Posttraumatic Growth*

"Gamino poignantly captures the varieties of parental bereavement and the range of compassionate responses to them. His book will really speak to clinicians, and I have no doubt it will benefit all the people they serve."

Dale G. Larson, PhD, author of *The Helper's Journey:
Empathy, Compassion, and the Challenge of Caring, 2nd ed.*

"In this book, Gamino brings the full force of who he is as a clinician, scholar, educator, and most importantly—human being."

Heather L. Servaty-Seib, PhD, HSPP, coeditor of
Handbook of Thanatology, 3rd ed., and *We Get It:
Voices of Grieving College Students and Young Adults*

"Unerringly informed by his own parental grief, Gamino delivers workable approaches as he integrates theory and practice in readily accessible prose."

Helen Stanton Chapple, PhD, MA, MSN,
coeditor of *Handbook of Thanatology, 3rd ed.*

Working with Bereaved Parents

Working with Bereaved Parents is a thoughtful guide for frontline practitioners in mental health and medicine who face the daunting task of helping parents after the death of a child.

Within a culturally inclusive and respectful framework, chapters consider several psychosocial factors that complicate parental bereavement as well as helpful factors that facilitate adaptation. The author shows how contemporary theory and findings from evidence-based research can be artfully applied to clinical practice with bereaved parents. The book also shares a range of strategies for promoting parents' resilience and personal growth in the wake of devastating loss.

Louis A. Gamino, PhD, ABPP, FT, is a professor of psychiatry and behavioral sciences at Baylor College of Medicine and the director of the division of psychology for Baylor Scott & White Health in Temple, Texas.

The Routledge Series in Posttraumatic Growth
Richard G. Tedeschi and Bret A. Moore
Series Editors

The Routledge Series in Posttraumatic Growth includes authored and edited texts that identify and distill the most relevant information for students, practitioners, researchers, organizational leaders, and policy makers in the areas of psychological health, wellness, and growth. Volumes in the series focus primarily on concepts that guide discovery, development, and implementation of interventions that increase psychological strength and flexibility, facilitate health and recovery, and support responses of individuals, communities, and institutions in times of adversity and trauma.

Trauma, Resilience, and Posttraumatic Growth in Frontline Personnel
Edited by Jane Shakespeare-Finch, Paul J. Scully, and Dagmar Bruenig

Working with Bereaved Parents: A Practitioner's Guide
Louis A. Gamino

Working with Bereaved Parents
A Practitioner's Guide

Louis A. Gamino

Routledge
Taylor & Francis Group
NEW YORK AND LONDON

Designed cover image: Getty Images

First published 2025
by Routledge
605 Third Avenue, New York, NY 10158

and by Routledge
4 Park Square, Milton Park, Abingdon, Oxon, OX14 4RN

Routledge is an imprint of the Taylor & Francis Group, an informa business

© 2025 Louis A. Gamino

The right of Louis A. Gamino to be identified as author of this work has been asserted in accordance with sections 77 and 78 of the Copyright, Designs and Patents Act 1988.

All rights reserved. No part of this book may be reprinted or reproduced or utilised in any form or by any electronic, mechanical, or other means, now known or hereafter invented, including photocopying and recording, or in any information storage or retrieval system, without permission in writing from the publishers.

Trademark notice: Product or corporate names may be trademarks or registered trademarks, and are used only for identification and explanation without intent to infringe.

Library of Congress Cataloging-in-Publication Data
Title: Working with bereaved parents : a practitioner's guide / Louis A.
  Gamino.
Description: New York, NY : Routledge, 2025. | Series: Routledge series in
  posttraumatic growth | Includes bibliographical references and index. |
Identifiers: LCCN 2024045190 (print) | LCCN 2024045191 (ebook) |
  ISBN 9781032380896 (hardback) | ISBN 9781032380841 (paperback) |
  ISBN 9781003346883 (ebook)
Subjects: LCSH: Bereavement. | Grief. | Children—Death—Psychological
  aspects.
Classification: LCC BF575.G7 G36 2025 (print) | LCC BF575.G7 (ebook) |
  DDC 155.9/37—dc23/eng/20250113
LC record available at https://lccn.loc.gov/2024045190
LC ebook record available at https://lccn.loc.gov/2024045191

ISBN: 978-1-032-38089-6 (hbk)
ISBN: 978-1-032-38084-1 (pbk)
ISBN: 978-1-003-34688-3 (ebk)

DOI: 10.4324/9781003346883

Typeset in Helvetica Neue and Optima
by Apex CoVantage, LLC

Dedicated to my dear wife, Marla,
who enables me to follow my dreams . . .
and
. . . to all the bereaved parents whose stories
touched me
and inspired me to write this book.

Contents

Permissions	xiv
Acknowledgments	xv
About the Author	xviii
Series Editor's Foreword	xix
RICHARD G. TEDESCHI	
Foreword	xxi
WILLIAM G. HOY	
Preface	xxiii
Who Should Read This Book	xxiv
Cultural Context	xxv
Case Examples	xxv
References	xxvi
List of Tables	xxvii
List of Figures	xxviii

PART I

1. Introduction   3

Death Competence	4
Cultural Attunement	6
Scope of the Problem	9
Summary	10
References	10

2. What Makes Parental Grief So Difficult? — 11

Parent-Specific Factors — 12
    Off-Time Death — 12
    Empty Track — 14
    Loss of Legacy and Continuation — 15
    Loss of Self — 16
General Risk Factors — 17
    Unexpectedness — 17
    Traumatic Manner of Death — 17
    Perception of Preventability — 18
    Problematic Relationship — 19
    Lack of Social Support — 20
    Mourner Shortcomings — 21
    No Explanatory Framework — 22
Diagnostic Considerations — 23
Summary — 25
References — 26

3. Helpful Factors — 28

Inherent Strengths — 29
    Hardiness — 29
    Intrinsic Spirituality — 30
Adaptive Behaviors — 32
    Saying Goodbye — 32
    Focusing on Positive Memories — 33
    Engaging Rituals of Remembrance — 34
    Cultivating a Continuing Connection — 36
    Advocating for the Deceased Child — 37
    Finding Meaning — 39
    Embracing (Unsought) Positive Outcomes — 40
    Accessing Social Support — 41
    Personal Growth and Transformation — 42
Summary — 43
References — 44

4. Contemporary Treatment Approaches — 47

Evidence-Based Grief Treatment Models — 48
    Shear's Prolonged Grief Treatment — 48
    Lichtenthal's Meaning-Centered Grief Therapy — 51
    Rynearson's Restorative Retelling — 52
    Boelen's Cognitive Behavioral Therapy for Grief — 54

	Chochinov's Dignity Therapy	55
	Summary of Evidence-Based Models	56
	Cultural Limitations	59
	Contemporary Theoretical Models	60
	Kosminsky and Jordan's Attachment-Informed Grief Therapy	60
	Jordan and McIntosh's Suicide Bereavement Model	61
	Tedeschi and Calhoun's Expert Companionship Model	63
	Getting Started	65
	Summary	67
	References	68

PART II

5. Pregnancy Loss and Infant Death — 73

- Early Pregnancy Loss and Miscarriage — 73
- Stillbirth and Neonatal Death — 77
- Sudden Infant Death Syndrome — 83
- Grief Following Elective Abortion for Fetal Anomaly — 86
- Summary — 89
- References — 89

6. Death of a Younger Child or Adolescent — 93

- How Do Children Die? — 95
- What Do Bereaved Parents Need? — 96
- Parent Identity — 99
- Sibling Grief — 101
- Family Therapy — 103
- Child Bereavement Resources — 105
- Summary — 105
- References — 106

7. Death of an Adult Child — 109

- How Adult Children Die — 111
- Viewing the Body — 112
- Rituals of Remembrance — 113
- Life Rearranged — 115
- Converting Absence into Presence — 118
- Focused Techniques — 120
- Summary — 124
- References — 124

CONTENTS

8. Accidental Death — 127

Nature of Accidental Deaths — 130
Motor Vehicle Crashes — 131
Unintentional Overdoses — 136
Summary — 140
References — 140

9. Suicide — 143

Differences in Suicide Bereavement — 146
Victim-Perpetrator Paradox — 149
Inquest into the Death — 151
Retrospective Narrative — 153
Spiritual Considerations — 157
Summary — 159
References — 159

10. Homicide — 162

Importance of Language — 164
Anger and Reprisal Fantasies — 165
Guilt — 167
Criminal Justice System — 168
Social Disparities in Homicide — 171
Multiple-Victim Homicides — 174
Role of Forgiveness — 175
Timing Treatment Steps — 177
Summary — 179
References — 180

11. Military or Combat Death — 182

Military Culture and the Warrior Ethos — 184
Dying with Honor — 186
Military Protocol — 188
Military Suicides — 191
Summary — 194
References — 194

12. Non-Death Loss — 197

Ambiguous Loss — 198
Disenfranchised Grief — 199

Chronic Sorrow	200
Seven Types of Non-Death Loss Parents Grieve	200
Estrangement	200
Addiction	203
Incarceration	204
Missing or Kidnapped Children	205
Disability	207
Infertility	208
Adoption Loss	209
Gestalt-Based Chair Work	212
Summary	214
References	214

PART III

13. Long-Term Adaptation and Resilience — 219

Post-Bereavement Personal Growth	223
Posttraumatic Growth	225
Resilience	227
Summary	233
References	233

14. Practitioner Resilience — 236

Practitioner Self-Care	237
Practice Risks	239
Workaholism and Burnout	239
Helper Secrets	240
Compassion Fatigue	241
Personal Experience	242
Summary	243
Author's Loss of a Child	243
Anthony's Story	243
Epilogue	246
Statue 248	
Baptistry 249	
Tree 249	
References	250

Index — 252

Permissions

Haiku ("telegram in hand" "the autumn wind" "into the blinding sun . . ." "flag-covered coffin" "my gold star mother" "Thanksgiving dinner:") by Nick Virgilio, date unknown, Nick Virgilio Haiku Association. All rights reserved. Stanzas reprinted by permission.

Personal Growth items from Hogan Grief Reaction Checklist (HGRC), © 2010 Taylor and Francis Group. All rights reserved. Material reprinted by permission.

"Eye Has Not Seen" by Marty Haugen, © 1982 GIA Publications, Inc. All rights reserved. Lyric excerpt reprinted by permission.

Acknowledgments

No endeavor of any magnitude is accomplished alone, and this book project is no exception to that rule.

My first thanks go to Rich Tedeschi and Bret A. Moore at the Boulder Crest Institute for Posttraumatic Growth and to Anna Moore at Routledge for believing in me enough to support my proposal for inclusion in their Series in Posttraumatic Growth. Serendipity brought us together when their series was launching, and I was mulling a sequel of sorts to Rich's book (coauthored with Lawrence Calhoun) on helping bereaved parents. Writing a compendium of my accumulated knowledge and practice experience working with bereaved parents has been an enormous professional privilege. I express deep gratitude to these three individuals for giving me this career capstone opportunity.

Next, I acknowledge Radha "Krishna" Kambhampati, MD, chair of the Department of Psychiatry and Behavioral Sciences at Baylor College of Medicine–Temple and Baylor Scott & White Health Central Texas Division and our department director, Austin Taylor. These two men understand the importance of scholarship and academic activity for enhancing the vitality and effectiveness of our clinical mission to patients. I owe them a debt of gratitude.

I enjoy terrific relationships with all my professional colleagues and support staff in the Department of Psychiatry and Behavioral Sciences at Baylor Scott & White Health. I have never once doubted they "had my back" in good times and in bad. I thank them.

My colleagues in the Association for Death Education and Counseling (ADEC) have been incomparable in supporting me during this book project as well as in many other professional efforts over the decades. My attempt to list names will inevitably result in some omissions, so I apologize in advance to any individuals whom I fail to mention. Thanks go to ADEC members living and

ACKNOWLEDGMENTS

deceased (listed alphabetically) Greg Adams, Tom Attig, Sandy Bertman, Jane and Rick Bissler, Delpha Camp, Helen Chapple, MaryKatherine Clemons, Betty Davies, Ken Doka, Galen Goben, Fay Green, Earl Grollman, Chris Hall, Nancy Hogan, Jack Jordan, Phyllis Kosminsky, Dale Larson, Wendy Lichtenthal, Janet McCord, Jack Morgan, Rebecca Morse, Bob Neimeyer, Jon Reid, Jae Ross, Ted Rynearson, Gae Savino, Lara Schultz, Donna Schuurman, Heather Servaty-Seib, Kathy Shear, Harold Ivan Smith, Judy Stillion, Gordon Thornton, Becky Watkins, Howard Winokuer, Carol Wogrin, Ben Wolfe, Bill Worden, and many more.

Two other ADEC members deserve special recognition. Rabbi Danny Roberts offered to serve as a "content reader" for the entire manuscript in the last stages of editing before submission. His many insightful comments helped me improve the clarity and flow of the entire work and were much appreciated. No good deed goes unpunished so, if you like the outcome, tell me. If you don't like it, tell Danny!

ADEC friend and Texas neighbor Bill Hoy has been a superb supporter throughout this book project. He was there at the breakfast table when the vision for the book was hatched and has been tirelessly encouraging throughout the two years of writing. Bill sweated the small stuff and the big stuff with me and was kind enough to write a foreword for the book.

My friend and local editor Carla Hahn Clardy was instrumental in helping bring my initial drafts to the polished version readers find in this volume. I am grateful to her and Balaji Karuppana from Apex CoVantage for their copyediting.

The phenomenal staff of the Richard D. Haines Medical Library at Baylor College of Medicine–Temple was instrumental in enabling me to finish this book. Head Librarian Julie Bolin put the library's entire resources at my disposal and cheerfully accommodated my presence on "writing Fridays." Warm thanks go to Stephanie Fondy for book and article retrieval and to Carole Gruhn for research support. Good-natured assistance came from Amberlyn Phillips, Jodi Cowan, and Jonathan Pickle. Special thanks go to Jeff Swindoll for his masterful literature searches and constant flow of articles printed for my consumption. Like a skilled short-order cook, Jeff quickly delivered whatever was needed, always garnished with a sprig of sardonic humor.

My natural family and my in-laws cheered me on during this book project. I give thanks for my (deceased) parents, Joe and Mabel Rose Gamino, my mother-in-law Marilyn, and (deceased) father-in-law Frank Yarnell. I appreciate the support of my siblings Danny (Eloise, deceased), John (Jacque), Denise (Jay), Laura, Ray (Lisa), Helen, and Gary (Michelle), as well as my brother-in-law Kevin (Regina). Close friends Bill and Grace Becker, Steve Garrigan and Jeff Goodson, Jeff and Joan Schiller, Kenneth and Beth Sewell, Dave Lutz and Ellen McLean, Beryl Lawn, Christian Cable, my Saturday morning men's group, and many others also supported me.

My own children Gabriel, Claire, and Dominic, as well as my son-in-law, Andrew, lent the kind of support only your immediate family can and for which I am very grateful. I hope my deceased son, Anthony, is smiling as well because he had so much to do with this book's content.

Most of all, I pay tribute to my dear wife, Marla, who walked every step of the journey with me, and then some. She has been amazingly tolerant of my paper piles, nonstop prattling, long hours toiling at the computer, obsessive revisions, and neglected house chores. Not everyone gets issued a wife as wonderful as Marla. Her love humbles me. Any accolades this book may garner are as much hers as they are mine.

About the Author

Louis A. Gamino, PhD, ABPP, FT, is a professor of psychiatry and behavioral sciences at the Baylor College of Medicine–Temple and the director of the division of psychology for Baylor Scott & White Health (BSWH) in Temple, Texas. Dr. Gamino is a diplomate in clinical psychology through the American Board of Professional Psychology (ABPP) and a fellow in thanatology (FT) through the Association for Death Education and Counseling (ADEC).

Dr. Gamino is coauthor (with R. Hal Ritter) of *Ethical Practice in Grief Counseling* (Springer, 2009) and coauthor (with Ann T. Cooney) of *When Your Baby Dies through Miscarriage or Stillbirth* (Augsburg Fortress, 2002; translated into Italian and Mandarin). Dr. Gamino's research has focused on adaptive grieving after loss, with a special focus on working with bereaved parents.

Dr. Gamino is founder and program director of the Baylor Scott & White Biennial Bereavement Conferences, inaugurated in 1997 and endowed in his honor by the Volney A. Acheson Fund. He is former program director of BSWH's postdoctoral fellowship program in health service psychology-clinical (2011–2023) and former training director of the Scott & White Psychology Internship Program (2016–2019); both programs were accredited by the American Psychological Association.

Dr. Gamino served as ADEC president from 2018 to 2019. In recognition of excellence in care of the dying and the bereaved, Dr. Gamino was honored with ADEC's Clinical Practice Award in 2008.

Series Editor's Foreword

The Routledge Series in Posttraumatic Growth is a collaboration with the Boulder Crest Institute for Posttraumatic Growth and is designed to bring together theory, research, and intervention approaches to trauma that use a framework informed by the concept of posttraumatic growth. In this volume, Louis A. Gamino collects his decades of professional work in the realm of grief and bereavement to provide insight into the experiences of people who suffer from various losses and those who seek to comfort them.

One of the features of this book that will be most rewarding is the quotations and stories from bereaved people that richly describe their experiences. Dr. Gamino is a masterful clinician who has a heart for this work, and he has chosen the words of the bereaved persons themselves to show there is no replacing the understanding of lived experience to learn how to be effective as a clinician. At the same time, he is a producer and consumer of research on grief and bereavement. With these perspectives he is able to lead the reader through the emotional and intellectual processes that are involved in the most effective interventions. Readers will also note that there is a hopeful and constructive approach to grieving throughout his writing, as befits a volume in this series on posttraumatic growth.

When I first read Dr. Gamino's manuscript, I was struck by how his perspective on effective approaches to grieving people is applicable to all clinical work. I think that this book is one that is instructive for any clinician. That is because grief and loss are universal, and no matter what kind of clients you work with, you will come across loss. Think of the people you have seen in your practice and how often you find in their history or present circumstances a struggle with loss. But also, Dr. Gamino's approach to helping is applicable to all clinical work. In the very first chapter, he lays out the importance of being humble, culturally attuned, and determined to learn from the client while being well informed about these experiences based on study and research. To my mind, he describes the optimal clinical approach, one that never feels clinical but simply human.

The chapters that cover various kinds of losses show that there are nuances to be considered in approaching these different circumstances. It is clear that he has listened carefully to people who have been through these things, and he passes down the stories and the wisdom to us so we can better understand. Reading his accounts and perspective will equip the reader to enter into these terrible circumstances with more confidence but also provide a realization that every story is different, and that humble listening is always necessary, so we do not fall into assumptions that we know another person's story. Although there are differences in the circumstances of these losses, there are also similarities and, indeed, universalities. Professionals reading this book may be tempted to focus on chapters covering the types of losses they are familiar with, but it will be most instructive to learn from all the chapters in this volume, as the universalities will emerge in this reading.

The final chapter is particularly useful in helping practitioners find their way through the heart-wrenching experience of helping bereaved people. Dr. Gamino helps us see that there are rewards in this work that may on the surface seem to be full of only sadness. His writing is a demonstration of the satisfaction that comes from work with the bereaved. I believe that Dr. Gamino would say that his career in this area has brought him closer to the core of human experience and enriched his life. That richness is apparent in the empathy and compassion in his writing. I suggest that those of us working in this area recognize, sooner or later, that we experience vicarious posttraumatic growth as we learn how to live better when we are companions with those who struggle through grief. The self-care that Dr. Gamino describes in Chapter 14 helps in this regard, as we find ways to protect ourselves from becoming immersed in the repeated experiences of loss that are presented to us while remaining open to them with compassion and empathy.

I think that many of you will find that reading this book is breathtaking. Dr. Gamino honestly presents the horror of loss, and if you allow yourself to truly empathize, the feelings will be strong, and sometimes frightening. Then, when you learn from Dr. Gamino how you can respond in helpful ways, you will be heartened and eager to provide comfort to those suffering through these losses.

Richard G. Tedeschi, PhD
Boulder Crest Institute for Posttraumatic Growth
Bluemont, Virginia

Foreword

When Louis A. Gamino first reached out to me in 2008 to inquire about my interest in helping him and his cochair, Jon Reid, in planning the 2009 conference of the Association for Death Education and Counseling, he went to great lengths to introduce himself and his work. That introduction was quite unnecessary since my own mentor, J. William Worden, told me before leaving California for my new home in Texas, "Make sure you connect with Gamino in Temple!"

In truth, Louis's work was well known to me. I had read the research he and his colleagues had conducted through the Scott and White Bereavement Study and had utilized it in my own work with bereaved families in Long Beach, California. Many times, in fact, I had wished the research had been published when I was muddling through my own early fitful efforts with parents after a child's death. So, when Louis asked me to write the foreword for this book, the answer was an immediate and easy, "Of course!"

Louis has worked with thousands of bereaved individuals and families in his long career at Baylor Scott & White in Temple, Texas. Many of these troubled souls have been parents who have walked through the unimaginable experience of a child's death. So, as he promises in his introduction, his goals here are to provide a "practical compendium" of contemporary resources, demonstrate application to bereaved parents, and model how practitioners go about caring for ourselves in what is surely some of our most difficult work. He accomplishes those aims with aplomb.

Each chapter in this helpful book begins with a clinical case, and the book includes many others, generally taken from the author's own case files. These cases draw the reader into the book's contents and help put a personal face on what could otherwise be hard-to-understand perspectives. Then, with the deft of a skilled weaver, Louis stitches together contemporary research literature with practical ideas in caring for bereaved parents. These are not the philosophical musings of a theoretician, however. They are the practiced techniques he has honed through four decades of therapeutic work with bereaved families. In clinical encounters when the efforts did not go exactly as planned, Louis musters the bold courage to admit the failings and discuss what might have gone differently.

When reading the chapter on homicide, for example, I found myself several times wishing I had possessed this chapter decades ago when I shepherded my first family through the death of their teenager in the long-standing gang war on the streets of Long Beach. Though I have worked with thousands of bereaved individuals since that family, I have found in this volume dozens of ideas for better practice, all supported by the best our field of thanatology has to offer.

In addition to practical counseling guidance about parental grief in a diversity of circumstances, Louis also addresses issues of importance to every support professional: gaining professional competence, developing cultural attunement, and caring for self in what is arguably the hardest of all clinical settings—the care of bereaved parents.

Little could I have ever imagined that an invitation to join a project like the 2009 ADEC conference would result in one of the most fulfilling collegial relationships of my career. In the more than 15 years since Louis and I first met, we have shared the joys and challenges of teaching teenagers to drive; launched kids to college; married our daughters to wonderful men; cared for each other through the deaths of parents, siblings, and a host of other losses; and, together, faced the inevitable challenges that accompany our own aging. That is why it is, with confidence, that I recommend this book to all who work with bereaved families.

This book has delivered fully on its promises and will be a valuable contribution to the care of bereaved parents for years to come. These words reflect not only Louis's decades of experience in compassionately accompanying bereaved parents through the deaths of their children, but they are seasoned by the measure of the man who wrote them—a man whose own professional discernment has been sharpened on the whetstone of deep personal loss.

William G. Hoy, DMin, FT
Baylor University
Waco, Texas

Preface

I developed a soft spot for bereaved parents early in my professional career, long before I became a bereaved parent myself. I was struck by their extreme sadness and the immutable nature of their loss—a cherished child gone forever. Because the problem is irreversible, the only option is to figure how best to survive in the wake of unspeakable tragedy. I wanted to offer something of value to such heartbroken parents.

Plunging ahead without a specific treatment guide, I relied initially on curiosity and compassion while also reading the work of Dennis Klass (1988), an ethnography of bereaved parents' phenomenology and their efforts to cope. Therese Rando's (1986) impressive compilation of what was then known about parental loss of a child also proved most helpful. When I did not know what else to do, I listened intently.

Now, decades later, the prospect of working with bereaved parents is no less daunting. But the tools available to health-care professionals and others in a position to help bereaved parents have increased greatly. The model of "expert companionship" articulated by Tedeschi and Calhoun (2004) introduced a respectful yet engaged approach to helping bereaved parents cope with loss of a child. Their notion of posttraumatic growth among bereaved parents changed the treatment landscape from a singular focus on distress relief to a binocular consideration of growth and meaning as well.

In addition, newer theoretical models and the emergence of evidence-based grief treatment protocols give practitioners a variety of possibilities for crafting interventions. My primary intentions in writing this book are to a) provide readers a practical compendium of these contemporary resources and b) show how they may be applied when working with parents grieving the loss of a child, at various ages and in different circumstances. Finally, how practitioners can care for themselves while taking care of bereaved parents is addressed in the final section on resilience.

My own experience of losing an infant son in 1997 certainly changed me as a person and inevitably influenced my clinical work with bereaved parents. Now forcibly enrolled in "the club no one wants to join," I sometimes use selective self-disclosure to convey understanding or offer hope. However, one does not have to be a bereaved parent to know how to help bereaved parents. The tools offered in this volume can be learned and effectively employed by anyone who encounters bereaved parents in a professional role and cares enough to learn something about the terrain.

WHO SHOULD READ THIS BOOK

Have you found yourself in an exam room or clinic office caring for a bereaved parent, hoping to say something beyond, "I'm sorry for your loss"? Have you conducted a hospital consult only to discover the patient is a bereaved parent whose medical distress is inseparable from grief over their missing child? Have you tried to bring calm to the chaos when faced with a panicked family in the emergency department after their young adult child has died tragically? Have you stood with sobbing parents at the NICU bedside of a dying infant, wondering how to help? Have you made a hospice home visit to grief-stricken parents, attempting to be a comforting presence while their child is dying in the next room? Have you participated in a funeral planning conference with an elderly mother or father saddled with the burden of burying a middle-aged child, wondering what to suggest that would be meaningful? Have you sat with bereaved parents who, months or even years after the death of their child, are still struggling to find answers or questioning whether there even is a God? If you answered yes to any of the these questions, this book is for you.

My primary audiences are health-care practitioners of any specialty, mental health clinicians, clergy, and funeral personnel actively engaged in professional work with bereaved parents. The work is a great privilege and an immense responsibility. Equipping oneself with the best knowledge available fulfills part of that professional obligation. The material in this book is organized to inform the practice of these professionals when encountering bereaved parents.

Others may benefit from reading this book as well. This list includes educators and mentors from any discipline who train future professionals for the fields mentioned earlier; volunteers who work with bereaved parents in hospices, community-based bereavement centers, or special programs like grief camps or family retreats; and even bereaved parents themselves who may be curious about the professional literature. Information empowers the ability to help and heal.

CULTURAL CONTEXT

None of us can change the family into which we were born, the place(s) where we were raised, or the circumstances in which we grew up. We are all subject to blind spots and biases. Yet, all of us can continually strive to learn more about our multicultural world and appreciate the nuances and differences embedded in others' experiences. Understanding the worldview of others begins with acknowledging one's own grounded history in a geographic location, a cultural context, and a point in time, while also seeking to be open to the diverse experiences of others. Throughout this book, practitioners will be urged to practice in a culturally attuned manner that begins with cultural humility and requires them to be culturally informed.

In the interest of full disclosure, I identify my roots in the southwestern United States, from Hispanic and German parents, in a monolingual English household, from a middle-class neighborhood, with Catholic Christian values and the benefits of higher education. My entire professional career has been spent working in a large health-care system in a medium-sized Texas city populated primarily by White European, Hispanic/Latinx, and African American people. I treasure my wife, my three living children, my relatives, and many friends.

CASE EXAMPLES

One of the great rewards of my professional career in clinical psychology is the connections I have forged with the many bereaved parents I have met. Listening to their stories—pain and triumph, sadness and regeneration, tragedy and forgiveness—has been an honor. These bereaved parents graced me by sharing some of the most intimate aspects of their emotional lives. I consider it a professional privilege to work with them. Fortunately, several of them have allowed me to retell their stories here so that others may also learn how best to do this work. The idea that something beneficial and educational can emerge from the aftermath of a child's death can lend significant meaning to their loss experience and contribute to their child's legacy, some of the most precious outcomes available to bereaved parents.

Case illustrations employed throughout the book orient readers to the context of parents' grief—such as how recently the child died and under what circumstances—enabling caregivers to truly understand and best help. All case examples have been de-identified and altered in some aspects to preserve confidentiality and protect the privacy of the individuals involved. Pseudonyms have been employed throughout the book, except in those instances where the bereaved parents specifically requested that their child's given name be used to honor their memory. (Readers will not be informed as to which cases these are.) I owe a tremendous debt to these bereaved parents for assisting me in this endeavor, and that is why the book is dedicated to them.

REFERENCES

Klass, D. (1988). *Parental grief: Solace and resolution.* Springer Publishing Company.

Rando, T. A. (1986). *Parental loss of a child.* Research Press.

Tedeschi, R. G., & Calhoun, L. G. (2004). *Helping bereaved parents: A clinician's guide.* Brunner-Routledge.

Tables

4.1	Ten Key Therapeutic Elements Drawn from Evidence-Based Models of Grief Therapy (Adapted for work with bereaved parents)	57
4.2	Getting the Patient's Stories	65
13.1	Post-Bereavement Personal Growth Subscale Items (n = 12) from the Hogan Grief Reaction Checklist	225

Figures

14.1 Theory-Research-Practice Triangle with Personal Experience   242

Part I

CHAPTER ONE

Introduction

> At a critical moment, he let me tell what it was like to be wading through a grief I had not volunteered for.
> —Harold Ivan Smith (personal communication, 2024)

CASE 1.A

Dana's daughter, Amber, collapsed and died at a party. Nine months pregnant with her first child, Amber was the guest of honor at a shower hosted by her friends. Excitement turned to horror when she fell unconscious. Emergency medical services rushed Amber to a nearby hospital, where resuscitation efforts continued, and surgeons operated immediately to save the baby. In the end, Amber never regained consciousness, and her baby sustained a period of oxygen deprivation during the ordeal. Even though the baby survived, she suffered extensive brain damage and existed in a vegetative state of nonresponsiveness.

Months later, Dana and her husband, Roger, attended a support group meeting for bereaved parents. She became distraught recounting the story of Amber's sudden death and the tragic outcome for their granddaughter. Dana's extreme emotional state so alarmed the other participants that they urged her to seek psychological help. Roger, an outgoing salesman with an unflappable disposition, fully supported the idea even though he remained stoically composed.

> Dana and Amber had experienced a contentious relationship during Amber's teenage years. Amber dated boys of whom they did not approve and eventually married instead of finishing college. However, with a baby coming, mother and daughter had started to draw closer, and their relationship improved. Because of Amber's congenital heart condition, her pregnancy was considered high risk, but she made weekly visits to her obstetrician and all seemed well.
>
> Coming from a difficult childhood with an abusive father, Dana had experienced periods of depression earlier in life. Yet nothing compared to the massive sadness crushing her now. With her daughter gone and the grandchild's prospects bleak, Dana felt deep despair. Roger focused on the injustice of it all and targeted his anger at the obstetrician. The grieving parents had an extensive circle of friends who rallied around them and a younger son to finish raising. They continued to practice their Christian faith.

Helping bereaved parents move from tragedy to resilience is the goal of professional intervention. Besides general clinical acumen, two crucial practitioner attributes—death competence and cultural attunement—are needed for effective intervention with bereaved parents.

DEATH COMPETENCE

Stories such as Dana's reveal what can await practitioners who work with bereaved parents. Descriptions of their losses can be gut wrenching and emotionally shocking. Buckling one's professional seatbelt is essential because the ride is bumpy. Doing this work requires keen self-awareness and tolerance for strong emotions. Likewise, countertransference feelings of fear, sadness, anger, guilt, or even disgust may emerge. In short, working with bereaved parents can be overwhelming and exhausting. So how does a professional or volunteer know if they have what it takes to do this work?

Gamino and Ritter (2009, 2012) proposed the construct of *death competence*, defined as specialized skill in tolerating and managing clients' problems related to dying, death, and bereavement. Death competence starts with a bedrock of cognitive competence—what one knows intellectually from study, training, supervision, and life experience. That knowledge is bolstered by emotional competence—the capacity to endure the emotional rigors of the therapy process, especially remaining fully present and engaged during graphic descriptions of conflict, trauma, loss, anguish, and suffering. Death competence builds on this foundation of cognitive knowledge and emotional fortitude to develop specialized skills in the domain of dying, death, and bereavement. Additionally, possessing death competence means practitioners must understand and accept their own loss histories, emotionally integrate those experiences, and accurately monitor their interior responses. Only then can practitioners operate with effective use of self as a therapeutic agent while maintaining professional objectivity and clinical perspective.

When children die, death competence includes the capacity to sit with shell-shocked mothers and fathers as they try to regroup and sort through the aftermath of their personal disaster (cf. Raphael, 1986). That means being fully present to communicate authentic empathy while at the same time maintaining perspective on what can help and how to assist. It means *listening from the heart while hearing with the mind* so that a workable plan can be developed for helping bereaved parents move forward from their place of pain and dejection.

When dealing with bereaved parents, any number of challenges to death competence can arise. Wogrin (2013) emphasized how responsible practitioners must be willing to "get close" to intense and difficult emotions expressed by the griever, a stance that may generate uncomfortable feelings and reactions in the practitioner. Unmanaged personal emotion can lead to unfavorable outcomes when practitioners do not handle their own reactions responsibly.

For example, when a bereaved parent's loss or trauma is similar to something the practitioner has experienced in life, or has imagined or feared could happen, an identification process occurs. Identification can arise from similarities between the practitioner's own children or loved ones and the deceased child's age, gender, personality, occupation, or station in life. It could come from similarity between the circumstances or cause of death for the deceased child and what the practitioner has personally experienced. It could come from similarity between the practitioner and the bereaved parent in terms of attitudes, reactions, feelings, choices, sensibilities, stage of life, or relationship dynamic with the deceased child. Any of these similarities could be a source of uncomfortable feelings and reactions for practitioners working with bereaved parents.

Try answering the following questions as a brief personal experiment with identification and death competence. What was your immediate reaction to reading Dana's story of loss? What emotions stirred in you? Or did you find yourself feeling nothing at all? If you are a parent, how did Dana's story touch you? Has one of your children died or experienced a close brush with death? Have you ever fantasized about a dreaded "call in the night" informing you that your son or daughter has died? If you have never lost a child or are not a parent, how did Dana's story parallel losses you have experienced personally or known vicariously through the lives of people important to you? What type of death do you fear most?

Hopefully this exercise illustrates how personal feelings and fears can surface when working with bereaved parents and how important integrating one's own loss history is for practicing with death competence. Practitioners are people, too. We carry both actual experiences and imagined realities that can lead to identification with bereaved parents. Such deeply personal feelings can be beneficial when they lead to greater understanding and empathy. Alternately, such discomfort can cause the unprepared or ill-equipped practitioner to create distance through self-protective aloofness or avoidance.

Gamino and Ritter (2009) offered a simple inventory for practitioners to assess their level of death competence. Imagine a clinical encounter with a bereaved parent such as Dana and see how many of the following characteristics you can confirm as part of your professional demeanor.

- Contemplate the prospect of your own death.
- Recall or visualize the death of an important loved one, without undue sadness or overwhelming emotion.
- "Steer into" Dana's narrative about the death and her affective experience.
- Possess the capacity to empathize with Dana.
- Tolerate the graphic descriptions of Amber's demise and the condition of her baby.
- Monitor and manage your own emotions in response to Dana's story.
- Remain nonjudgmental about any suicidal thoughts, feelings, or behaviors expressed by Dana.
- Accept diverse ways of grieving.
- Unwind from work in healthy ways.
- Maintain a professional will to take care of patients in the event of your own untimely death or medical event precluding continued practice.

Ideally, practitioners should be able to endorse all ten characteristics of death competence. If you could endorse eight or nine, your footing is solid. If you claimed fewer than eight, some additional preparation is likely needed on the points you missed before you are ready for this work.

CULTURAL ATTUNEMENT

Hoskins (1999) introduced cultural attunement as an aspirational goal for educators, administrators, and practitioners when encountering individuals different from oneself on important cultural and ethnic dimensions. She identified five major processes designed to enhance mutual understanding and facilitate cooperative activity among individuals from diverse backgrounds, particularly when the educator or practitioner represents the dominant or majority culture. These processes include acknowledging the pain of oppression, engaging in acts of humility, acting with reverence, engaging in mutuality, and maintaining a position of "not knowing."

Cultural attunement is a pragmatic construct defining how practitioners can respond adroitly to culturally diverse individuals in mental health settings (Oakes, 2011), including bereaved parents. As a construct, cultural attunement subsumes principles of cultural humility and culturally informed practice.

Cultural humility originated with Tervalon and Murray-Garcia (1998). These authors sought to supplant the myth of cultural competence, which no practitioner can conscientiously claim. They decried cultural competence as an illusion based on "an easily demonstrable mastery of a finite body of knowledge [about generalizations]" (p. 118). Instead, cultural humility requires practitioners to acknowledge personal limitations in understanding the lived experiences of others whose backgrounds and sensibilities differ from them. It means a commitment to lifelong learning and critical self-reflection. Cultural humility is the foundation for establishing trusting, respectful relationships and managing differences and conflicts. It demands advocacy for personal and institutional transformation whereby cultural differences are not only accepted but also embraced.

Culturally informed practice goes beyond basic curiosity about the other person, no matter how politely that curiosity is expressed. The "not knowing" stance articulated by Hoskins (1999) means openness to the experience of others but not exclusive reliance on what is sometimes called the student position—assuming a posture of willingness to learn from the other person, as the expert, about their cultural practices or traditions. The student position is exemplified by inquiries such as, "In your tradition, what is supposed to be done at the time of death?" or "Help me understand more about your [group's] customs for funerals and burial," as well as, "How do you think about the concept of the afterlife in your cultural framework?"

The student position is a fundamental stance in qualitative research where the phenomenon being studied is discovered and understood through in-depth interviews with individuals who have experienced it (Glaser & Strauss, 1999), such as studying the experience of child loss by interviewing bereaved parents. Yet a subtle downside of the student position is placing the burden of educator on the bereaved person who is seeking help (Gamino & Ritter, 2009). Imposing such a burden is not only presumptive but also insensitive. If practitioners assume patients can teach them whatever needs to be understood about their cultural experience, it effectively exonerates practitioners from any further responsibility for self-education and development. That position is not one of humility but rather arrogance. Furthermore, it is unrealistic to expect bereaved parents in the throes of acute grief and emotional vulnerability to shift gears into executive mode to educate their caregivers about cultural considerations, even if they wanted to do so.

While the student position may be an acceptable starting point, culturally informed practice involves more than passive curiosity. Seeking additional information outside of the clinical encounter is part of self-education and lifelong learning. Typical avenues for becoming more culturally informed include reading material about the group or culture in question, seeking supervision from another practitioner knowledgeable in the area, consulting with experts or elders within a particular cultural group (without breaching confidentiality), or attending training sessions or workshops to learn more. Admittedly, some emergent situations may not afford the time or opportunity to seek outside information. Yet the discipline of self-education can hone a practitioner's sensitivity when asking questions, create a richer context for understanding, and enhance one's ability to navigate within the patient's cultural frame of reference.

Culturally attuned practitioners focus on each bereaved parent as a unique person whose lived experience of losing a child is influenced by both their cultural heritages and their individual history. Even when learning more about specific cultural groups, astute practitioners keep in mind that group membership is not a monolithic entity and intra-group differences are not only possible but also quite common. Everyone is seen as multidimensional, with a complex cultural identity derived from a matrix of diverse influences. This mindset incorporates the aphorism, "Each person is like all other persons, like some other persons, and like no other person."

Cultural attunement means paying close attention to the continual interplay of cultural influences and individual differences that each bereaved parent embodies in a dynamic that may shift and evolve. Working in a culturally attuned manner results in more accurate empathy, more incisive questioning, and a stronger therapeutic alliance. Cultural attunement encompasses a nimble-footed readiness on the part of practitioners to honor the values, traditions, language, rituals, customs, and sensibilities of the bereaved parents seeking care. That obligation includes translating and adapting the interventions described in this book to best address the unique bereavement needs of each parent grieving the loss of a child.

CASE 1.A (Continued)

Dana and Roger both came from White European backgrounds. They endorsed strong Christian beliefs in a harmonious afterlife featuring union with God and reunion with deceased loved ones. These beliefs powered their hope for a future where they would see Amber again.

> Cultural attunement by their practitioner involved sensitivity to the tenets of their Christian beliefs and an openness to incorporating those ideas within the therapeutic dialogue. In addition, Dana and Roger were devoted to philanthropic activities supporting regional children's hospitals. They helped arrange compassionate care for Amber's baby until she died from natural complications several months later. Subsequently, Dana and Roger assumed a leadership role in the bereaved parents' support group that had welcomed them and vowed to assist other bereaved parents through the heartache of child loss. They found these altruistic activities to be important legacy work (see Chapter 3, "Helpful Factors"). Esteeming these cultural values and affiliations enabled the practitioner to encourage Dana and Roger's efforts, recognizing the potentially salutary effect of these activities for their ongoing bereavement adjustment.

SCOPE OF THE PROBLEM

Everyone who dies is someone's child. The vital question for this book is whether the parents of the deceased person are still alive. Therefore, the true extent of parental bereavement cannot be readily calculated through the usual government statistics on mortality. As life expectancy rates increase, the phenomenon of older or elderly parents outliving their children increases as well. In addition, when accounting for the experiences of bereaved grandparents, stepparents, and foster parents, the problem expands even more.

Mortality data for 2020 in the United States revealed that 19,582 children less than age 1 died (i.e., infant mortality) and 3,529 children between ages 1 and 4 died (Kochanek et al., 2023). These figures do not include untold numbers of miscarriages (defined as pregnancy loss before 20 weeks of gestation and estimated to occur in 15% or more of all pregnancies) that go unreported, even though many potential parents grieve these events as child deaths. U.S. 2020 mortality data showed 41,439 deaths for young people between ages 5 and 24. Death totals in 2020 for persons aged 25 to 54 may be pertinent as well, reasoning that some younger and middle-aged adults predecease their older parents. Thus, at least some of the 369,118 deceased individuals in the United States from those age ranges left behind grieving parents (and sometimes grandparents).

Considering that each deceased child has two biological parents and four grandparents, and possibly stepparents or other surrogate parental figures, extrapolation from these data reveal an enormous bereavement toll likely close to a million people a year in a developed country in North America. Given that the United States makes up about 4% of the global population of more than eight billion people (United States Census Bureau, 2024), one can see that millions of parents across the world are bereaved each year due to the death of a child.

SUMMARY

Working with bereaved parents is demanding and difficult. Practitioners undertaking this clinical challenge must exhibit death competence and cultural attunement—two key attributes for working effectively with the agony of child loss and encountering bereaved parents from diverse backgrounds. The statistical scope of the problem is significant and even more prevalent as the population ages and older parents (and grandparents) experience the deaths of their young adult and middle-aged children.

REFERENCES

Gamino, L. A., & Ritter, R. H., Jr. (2009). *Ethical practice in grief counseling*. Springer Publishing Company.

Gamino, L. A., & Ritter, R. H., Jr. (2012). Death competence: An ethical imperative. *Death Studies*, *36*, 23–40. https://doi.org/10.1080/07481187.2011.553503

Glaser, B., & Strauss, A. (1999). *Discovery of grounded theory: Strategies for qualitative research*. Routledge.

Hoskins, M. L. (1999). Worlds apart and lives together: Developing cultural attunement. *Child & Youth Care Forum*, *28*(2), 73–85. https://doi.org/10.1023/A:1021937105025

Kochanek, K. D., Murphy, S. L., Xu, J. Q., & Arias, E. (2023). Deaths: Final data for 2020. *National Vital Statistics Reports*, *72*(10). National Center for Health Statistics. https://dx.doi.org/10.15620/cdc:131355

Oakes, K. E. (2011). Health care disparities and training in culturally competent mental health counseling: A review of the literature and implications for research. *International Journal of Humanities and Social Science*, *1*(17), 46–57.

Raphael, B. (1986). *When disaster strikes: How individuals and communities cope with catastrophe*. Basic.

Tervalon, M., & Murray-Garcia, J. (1998). Cultural humility versus cultural competence: A critical distinction in defining physician training outcomes in multicultural education. *Journal of Health Care for the Poor and Underserved*, *9*(2), 117–125. https://doi.org/10.1353/hpu.2010.0233

United States Census Bureau. (2024). *U.S. population estimated at 335, 893, 238 on Jan. 1, 2024*. www.census.gov/library/stories/2023/12/happy-new-year

Wogrin, C. (2013). Professional issues and thanatology. In D. A. Meagher & D. E. Balk (Eds.), *Handbook of thanatology: The essential body of knowledge for the study of death, dying and bereavement* (2nd ed., pp. 395–409). Association for Death Education and Counseling, The Thanatology Association.

CHAPTER TWO

What Makes Parental Grief So Difficult?

> Grief is the tax on loving—the price we pay for our attachments.
> —Thomas Lynch (2000)

CASE 2.A

Reyna received a call in the wee hours of Christmas morning that her adult son Jude was missing. Several hours later, rescuers discovered him in his crashed vehicle off the side of a mountain road more than 100 miles from his house. Jude was airlifted to a hospital and placed in intensive care. Reyna rushed to his bedside only to find him intubated and unresponsive. Details were sketchy, but apparently there had been a dispute between Jude and his wife. He had stormed out of the house and driven away angry. It was unclear if Jude had been drinking, had been driving recklessly, or had intentionally crashed.

After five days, Jude's doctors advised his wife that his injuries were too extensive for him to recover. They suggested withdrawing life support. The next day—Reyna's wedding anniversary—Jude's wife gave permission to turn off the machines, and he died without ever regaining consciousness. Reyna said her goodbyes but could not bear to stay in the room when life support was removed.

Reyna's marriage to Jude's father, when they were both in their early 20s, lasted only a short time. She raised Jude as a single parent for several years. As a result, mother and son were always close. Reyna remarried when Jude was about 12 years old. Her new husband accepted Jude amiably, so the stepfamily was stable, and Reyna's close connection with Jude continued into his adulthood.

However, when Jude planned to marry, Reyna had serious misgivings about compatibility between him and his fiancée. She expressed those concerns to him. That disclosure damaged the relationship with her future daughter-in-law, and tensions had simmered ever since then. In her mind, Reyna blamed the daughter-in-law for the couple's marital problems and for "running Jude out of the house" the night he died. To make matters worse, the ill feelings between them led the daughter-in-law to exclude Reyna and her husband from the lives of the three grandchildren after Jude's death. That entire branch of the family seemed lost.

Already predisposed to clinical depression, Reyna fell into prolonged grief over Jude's death. She felt chronically restless and sorrowful. Antidepressant medicines had limited effect. She wondered why Jude did not reach out to her in his distress, thinking she could have "talked him down" as she always had in times of trouble. She was haunted by awful images of Jude in intensive care. Alienation from her beloved grandchildren gnawed at Reyna, adding insult to injury. She became distant from her husband. Reyna's doctor referred her for grief therapy, where she told the clinician, "I just want him [Jude] back."

Practitioners who work with grief and loss can attest that bereaved parents are among their saddest and most difficult cases, as illustrated by Reyna's tragic story. Thomas Lynch's (2000) quote at the beginning of this chapter contains an immutable truth—bereaved parents pay a high grief tax because of great love for their deceased children. Findings from research and scholarly literature help explain the psychological dynamics that create so much suffering. Factors making parental grief difficult can be considered from two different angles— parent-specific factors and general risk factors for complicated grief.

PARENT-SPECIFIC FACTORS

Off-Time Death

The phrase "assumptive world" is sometimes invoked to convey the idea that people carry all kinds of expectations about how the world operates and what should happen in life. Assumptions help us make sense of the world and give it order and predictability. Some expectations may be explicit and consciously acknowledged, such as expecting the sun to come up in the morning or positing that adults should work to support themselves. Other expectations may be implicit and unspoken, such as believing that good citizenship somehow shields a person from random acts of violence or misfortune or anticipating that children will outlive their parents.

Yet many people may not be completely aware of what they believe, or assume, about the world until something happens that violates one or more of their implicit assumptions. Janoff-Bulman (2002) explored some of these implicit assumptions that can shatter when a traumatic event—such as losing a child—intrudes on a person's life. She identified three critical dimensions of the assumptive world, generally held by individuals fortunate enough to be reared in secure environments with loving caregivers. These assumptions include beliefs that a) the world is a safe and benevolent place, b) actions have logical consequences, and c) good behavior is rewarded while bad behavior is punished.

The expectation that children will outlive parents is an implicit assumption in modern society. In previous centuries, when human civilizations were more agrarian, this expectation was not always held. Families tended to be larger, and it was more accepted that some offspring may not survive, just as seen in their animal herds. Yet advances in medical science and declining infant mortality rates, especially in more developed countries, have entrenched this expectation deeply among contemporary parents. Even when parents do not explicitly state it or allow themselves to consciously ponder it, this belief remains. "I always thought the child should bury the parent, not the other way around," lamented one bereaved father whose middle-aged son died from heart disease. The unforeseen turn of events elicited the father's implicit belief that was always present but never articulated prior to his son's death.

Developmental psychologist Bernice Neugarten (1979) coined the phrase "off time" to describe events that do not occur according to life-cycle expectations of *when* they are "supposed" to happen. People find such incongruity in timing to be jarring and unsettling. For parents, anytime a child predeceases them is the wrong time in the life cycle. Death of a child is always out of season. It violates the assumption of generational succession. It shatters implicit beliefs in an orderly universe where things make sense and happen in a predictable order. The experience of losing a child sends bereaved parents reeling into a "foreign country," a journey for which they are utterly unprepared and that they reflexively resist (Tedeschi & Calhoun, 2004). As Rabbi Harold Kushner (2004), himself the bereaved father of a young son who died from progeria (advanced aging), so famously advised: Bad things can and do happen to good people. In

Reyna's case, she certainly endorsed the idea that her son's death was something she never wanted to witness in her lifetime.

Empty Track

Most parents imagine themselves doing a variety of things for and with their children over the course of a lifetime. With infants, it may be holding, feeding, changing, bathing, guarding. With toddlers, it may be playing, teaching, reading, training, correcting. With school-age children, care shifts more to guiding, coaching, showing, doing, disciplining. With teens, it may become directing, exhorting, watching, disputing, hoping. With adult children, parents shift yet again to supporting, encouraging, befriending, celebrating, grandparenting. Some of these functions are physical, and some more cerebral. Yet in all these activities, parents express their love and realize incredible joy (and sometimes pain). Death of a child interrupts this imagined progression of interaction.

The concept of empty track, first identified by Klass and Marwit (1988–1989), describes the experiences of bereaved parents whose aspirations and dreams to perform all these various functions are suddenly dashed. As one bereaved mother put it after her son died in a car wreck, "My job description got eliminated." All the parenting roles that she wanted to perform, and that brought so much meaning and satisfaction, suddenly were no longer needed, no longer in demand. That is how Reyna felt. She was no longer able to fulfill the roles of mother-confidante, advice giver, and grandmother deluxe.

Bereaved parents often feel that they have been benched in the game of life and banned from child-rearing. Observing other adults parenting their children and celebrating their accomplishments brings pangs of jealousy, envy, and even resentment. While other parents actively participate in their children's lives, bereaved parents find themselves on an empty developmental track, devoid of the opportunity to perform these desired functions. Their sense of loss may be felt most acutely at what would have been developmental milestones or highlight moments: walking, talking, first day of school, mastering the bicycle, recitals, ball games, livestock competitions, religious ceremonies, graduations, driving lessons, marriages, first jobs, childbirths, promotions, new houses, holiday reunions, vacations together. The empty track leaves empty arms, empty hands, empty spirits, and empty hearts.

Existential problems of meaninglessness and missing purpose associated with empty track affect grieving grandparents as well. Their dreams of caring for a grandchild and reveling in the vitality of a new generation get short-circuited too. Reed (1999) emphasized how "grandparents cry twice" over the death of a grandchild. They mourn their own lost relationship with the precious grandchild, but they also hurt from seeing their adult child—the bereaved parent—sustain great pain and distress, knowing the wound is one they cannot remedy.

Loss of Legacy and Continuation

Deeply embedded in the consciousness of parents is the prospect of legacy and continuation. Children function as an extension of their parents in so many ways. At a biological level, children carry the DNA of both parents and thus ensure their genes will somehow survive and continue to impact the world. Parents extend their own lives and spheres of influence through their children. Parents continue to "live on" through their children and grandchildren, even after their own deaths, perhaps acquiring a proxy sense of immortality along the way.

Legacy and continuation are not just about biology. Parents' hopes and dreams are often expressed through what they want for their children, envisioning an experience of the world that exceeds or improves on their own, exemplified by the sentiment, "I want something better for my children." Parents' achievements and acquisitions are also part of this picture. Legacy can involve keeping the family business, family farm, or family fortune intact to be enjoyed or even expanded by the next generation. Legacy can encompass a multitude of continuities: practicing a craft, playing a sport, speaking a native language, working a similar occupation, pursuing a profession, continuing a line of training, cultivating an avocation, developing a particular trait or talent, valuing certain choices, following a faith tradition, or affiliating with a particular political party, fraternal organization, or social club. Conveying family heirlooms or keepsakes is another expression of legacy.

The parental quest for legacy and continuation gets short-circuited by the death of a child. It hits a brick wall. There may be no one to carry on the family line or family name, no one to continue endeavors or causes important to the parents, no one to care for the parents in their old age or remember the parents after their deaths. In Reyna's case, she believed deep in her heart that Jude would always be there for her if she ever became widowed, infirm, or terminally ill. With his death and the subsequent alienation from her grandchildren, Reyna felt despair and loneliness. Her prospects for legacy and continuation were dashed: "That's it—the end of the line."

One poignant example of loss of legacy and continuation is the case of Chinese *Shidu* parents—couples who have lost their only child and have not given birth again or adopted another child. The one-child policy enforced by the Chinese government from 1979 to 2015 was meant to slow population growth and promote economic development, yet it increased the risk of one-child households becoming childless (Xiong et al., 2023). In traditional Chinese culture, influenced by Confucianism, lacking descendants to continue the family bloodline means *Shidu* parents may be stigmatized as facing extinction. Children are seen not only as a biological lineage but also as a source of well-being, affectional bonds, and vital caregiving for their elderly parents. Therefore, *Shidu* parents may suffer low self-esteem, social discrimination, and worries about economic support and physical assistance as they age (Zheng et al., 2017). Yet Xiong's findings indicated that robust social support for *Shidu* parents can counteract the liabilities of childless status and reinforce a healthy sense of belonging and self-worth despite losing an only child (see Chapter 3, "Helpful Factors").

Loss of Self

Who am I without my child? What am I without my child? There's nothing left of me, why should I go on? These questions nag at bereaved parents. So much identity in contemporary society derives from one's activities and roles. The opportunity to be mother or father to one's children may be among the most cherished of roles, if not the most important role, in a parent's life. Death of a child strikes bereaved parents at the core of their identity, leaving them emotionally eviscerated. Feelings of helplessness, worthlessness, and emptiness ensue. Even when bereaved parents have other children to raise and love, parenting after the death of a child can prove to be enormously challenging—a task often fraught with doubt and second thoughts (Buckle & Fleming, 2011; see Chapter 6, "Death of a Younger Child or Adolescent").

The despairing nihilism that many bereaved parents experience after losing a child makes others uncomfortable. Family and friends often fall into the trap of attempting to reassure bereaved parents or focus them away from identity angst, offering platitudes such as, "Your other children need you," "You still have your work," "You're important to me," or "God has other plans for you." Usually, bereaved parents experience these admonitions as hollow and not at all comforting. Despite the good intentions of others, such remarks trade in a false currency devoid of material value when a child is dead. Pointing out to bereaved parents that they still bear responsibility for their surviving children may only intensify guilt rather than relieve it.

Practitioners need to recognize that loss of self connected to bereaved parents' loss of identity cannot be easily restored. Any authentic sense of self develops on the inside. Identity cannot be created by someone else's pronouncement. Rather, identity grows like a field crop that takes a full season to mature. That is why parents who lose an only child, or parents who suffer an early pregnancy loss before a transactional bond builds, often feel particularly devastated. Not only are they no longer parents, but they may also feel as if they are nobody at all once their child has died. Practitioners need to take a "slow growth" approach to restoration of parental identity. Acute grief feelings must subside before most bereaved parents are receptive to rethinking their lost identity and reconfiguring how they still fit into the world.

GENERAL RISK FACTORS

Unexpectedness

The concept of unexpectedness differs from the notion of off-time deaths where children die before their parents in violation of life-cycle assumptions about the natural order of mortality. Unexpectedness refers to sudden and abrupt deaths, ones with a did-not-see-it-coming quality. Unexpected deaths can be shocking and psychologically unsettling. Deaths occurring unexpectedly pose greater difficulties for mourners and make assimilating the loss more problematic (Parkes & Weiss, 1983; Rando, 1993; Worden, 2018).

When children die, unexpectedness compounds the grief already present because their deaths occurred off time chronologically. Classic examples of unexpected child deaths include miscarriages, unforeseen birth complications, sudden infant death syndrome (SIDS), fatal car wrecks, accidental drownings, sudden cardiac events, suicides, homicides, and many other possibilities. In Reyna's case, Jude's death was not instantaneous but occurred within a few days of sustaining injuries that were ultimately fatal, rendering his death abrupt and unexpected. An important point to remember is that unexpectedness exists in the eye of the beholder. What may seem like an expected death to professional caregivers or hospital staff may be unexpected in the eyes of family members and friends. When consulting with bereaved parents who saw their child's death as unexpected, practitioners should take their cue from the parents and acknowledge their perception as a starting point.

However, not all child deaths are unexpected, as in sudden and abrupt. Some newborns may struggle for months on touch-and-go status before finally dying from their medical problems. Some children die after lengthy battles with cancer or eventually succumb to a congenital or developmental disorder years after diagnosis. Deaths among middle-aged adults with older parents can be the result of decades-long bouts with heart conditions, neurological disorders, genetic anomalies, organ failures, or blood diseases. Even though their child is dead, parents in these situations have had more opportunity to prepare mentally and brace emotionally for the unwanted outcome.

Traumatic Manner of Death

From his work with individuals whose loved ones died violently, Rynearson (2001) described how deaths that occur in a traumatic manner impact survivors at different levels. He distinguished *separation distress*—anguish over the reality that the loved one is *gone*—from *trauma distress*—anguish over *how* the loved one died. The presence of trauma distress adds to the misery grievers experience.

Unfortunately, when children die traumatically, bereaved parents may contend with the horrible consequences of their child's disfigured or mutilated body. Or they deal with the awful realization that their child died violently or incurred painful injuries at the time of death. Awareness that their deceased child suffered greatly haunts bereaved parents. Visualizations and thoughts can replay endlessly in their minds, a particular form of rumination Rynearson (2018) called reenactment imagery.

Like unexpectedness, traumatic manner of death is a perception based on what the parents view as traumatic. Practitioners need to proceed carefully when children die in a traumatic way. Trauma treatment protocols do not push survivors to retell gruesome accounts of death, a process that can be emotionally triggering and retraumatizing. Rather, initial steps focus on ensuring that bereaved parents learn to moderate and reduce the intensity of their emotional responses before ever addressing details of what happened and how. These techniques are described in Chapter 4, "Contemporary Treatment Approaches."

Perception of Preventability

Preventable deaths are ones that might not have happened if the actors involved had exercised better judgment, used more caution, been more careful, or taken less risk. Perception of preventability can be dicey. Sometimes an outside party was negligent or reckless, resulting in the death of an innocent victim. When a child playing on the sidewalk in front of a suburban home is struck and killed when a motor vehicle operated by an intoxicated driver jumps the curb, there is little controversy over who is at fault. In legal terms, such deaths are classified as manslaughter—directly resulting from the perpetrator's actions, albeit unintentional—and subject to criminal prosecution.

On the other hand, sometimes children put themselves in harm's way or take undue risks, wittingly or unwittingly. In those cases, the deceased child becomes both responsible party and victim. One instance involved a teenager fatally hit by a freight train at night. The young man and his friends were seeking thrills through a stunt called "training" where they deliberately stationed themselves within the iron framework of a trestle so they could experience a rush from the train speeding by within inches of where they stood. Lamentably, the son lost his footing and was crushed by the train. Who was to blame for such a needless outcome? Their son? His friends? Both? Assigning appropriate blame for a child's preventable death is not always clear cut.

One of the cardinal rules for practitioners working with bereaved parents comes from dealing with deaths deemed to be preventable: *It is not the place of professional caregivers to criticize the behavior of the deceased child.* Even if there is every indication that the child was partly or fully at fault, criticizing the deceased child will alienate bereaved parents and damage rapport, sometimes irreparably. Bereaved parents do not want to hear that "he caused it" or "she should have known better." Such attributions, if ever acknowledged in a constructive way during therapeutic work, can only come from the parents themselves. With appropriate timing and sensitivity, practitioners may sometimes explore potential attributions of responsibility with gently probing questions such as, "Knowing [Tommie] as only you could, what do you suppose he was thinking at that moment?" Yet great care must be taken to avoid any inference of blaming the child for a death the parents perceive as preventable.

Sadly, sometimes bereaved parents themselves play a role in a preventable death, such as backing the car over a young child not seen behind the vehicle or faulty supervision at a pool party where an unattended child drowns (see Chapter 8, "Accidental Death"). Even when there is no criminal culpability, a parent's guilt may seem unforgivable. Tension and accusations between the grieving parents may appear insurmountable. Considerable diplomacy is required by practitioners assisting in such difficult cases. Similar to instances where the child may have contributed to their own demise, practitioners should refrain from assigning responsibility to a bereaved parent who may have unwittingly played a role in the preventable death of their child. Those parents already blame themselves, so it is more advantageous to work toward modifying guilt through reframing and self-forgiveness strategies (see Chapter 9, "Suicide").

Problematic Relationship

More than a century ago, Freud (1917/1957) identified how a problematic or ambivalent relationship between the griever and decedent can complicate mourning, an insight as pertinent today as it was then. For Freud, the essence of an ambivalent relationship was one that embodied elements of love and hate at the same time. Certainly, not every parent-child relationship reflects textbook ideals. Families can experience conflicts, cutoffs, and ruptures due to addiction, avarice, personality clashes, opposing value systems, criminal acts, or many other reasons. Despite such problematic situations and the negative feelings they engender, most parents retain some degree of familial love for children who may have hurt them deeply or failed to respond at all.

When parents were embroiled in a problematic relationship with the child who died, the emotional consequences can be disastrous. Gone forever is hope for the parent-child relationship to improve. Gone forever is the chance to repair the rupture, to seek and extend forgiveness. Gone forever are unrealized dreams. Instead, those bereaved parents are left holding a bag of mixed feelings that can be difficult to sort. In the case of losing a child with whom there was significant conflict, many bereaved parents are reticent to admit the hostile emotions they harbor. They feel more guilty than ever about the complaints, resentments, disappointments, and grudges they carry. Suppressing such negativity takes considerable psychological and emotional energy, one explanation for the prolonged depression and sense of depletion many bereaved parents report.

Winning the confidence of bereaved parents is essential to creating a therapeutic atmosphere where shameful or unflattering feelings toward the deceased child can be safely aired and examined. The psychological benefits of doing so (e.g., unburdening, reevaluating, coming to terms) can be well worth the effort. At the same time, practitioners must remain vigilant to the fact that any relationship problems between the bereaved parents and the deceased child could be largely the result of parental shortcomings. Should this dynamic prove to be the case, it means bereaved parents will have to confront their own blind spots and the focus of any therapeutic work will have to shift in the direction of forgiving themselves rather than forgiving their child.

Lack of Social Support

Retaining the support and love of loyal family and friends can make a world of difference to a grieving person. Social support can take many forms: informational (advising or planning), logistical (decision-making or coordinating), physical (assisting with activities of daily living), financial (helping with expenses), cognitive (processing grief), emotional (being present, caring), or spiritual (connecting with faith beliefs or rituals). Better health outcomes during bereavement for grievers acknowledging interpersonal support have been well documented in social science research on African American (Boulware & Bui, 2016), Chinese (Li et al., 2022), White (Cacciatore et al., 2021), and diversified U.S. populations (Chen, 2022). Conversely, when interpersonal support is lacking or when bereaved parents become socially isolated, grieving a deceased child becomes even more difficult.

Any griever can feel temporarily alienated following a difficult loss when no one else in their social circle shares a similar experience or knows fully what the griever has endured. However, this sense of alienation can be even more pronounced for bereaved parents. First, loss of a child is a statistically less common occurrence, despite the prevalence figures noted in Chapter 1, "Introduction," so there will be fewer individuals who can empathize experientially with loss of a child. That is why many bereaved parents turn to organizations such as Bereaved Parents of the USA (www.bereavedparentsusa.org) or The Compassionate Friends (www.compassionatefriends.org) for support. Second, because many parents develop friendships with people who have children at similar ages, awkwardness may ensue because of "empty track" comparisons described earlier in this chapter. Rather than face uncomfortable feelings brought on by the presence of other people's children, some bereaved parents distance themselves from potential support networks. Ironically, the path of isolation that seems less irksome in the short run can prove more burdensome in the long run for parents grieving a deceased child.

Mourner Shortcomings

Sometimes bereaved parents struggle with personal shortcomings that complicate grieving. Rando (1993) called such characteristics mourner liabilities. Liabilities or shortcomings can encompass a wide range of personal problems. Basically, any factor that makes life adaptation more difficult in general will make grieving a significant loss more challenging. Mourner shortcomings that hinder bereaved parents' efforts to cope with child loss include a history of adverse childhood events (e.g., abuse, neglect, or trauma), preexisting mental health problems, chemical abuse or addiction, insecure attachment styles, concomitant life stressors, socioeconomic pressures, or history of previous losses that have not been handled well. Practitioners who detect mourner shortcomings when working with bereaved parents need to be prepared to address those factors.

CASE 2.B

One bereaved father's alcoholism constituted his shortcoming. Upon learning of his daughter's death in a car crash, the father relapsed and went on a bender. All communication from him stopped. Finally, a friend located him at a hunting cabin and persuaded him to come home for his daughter's funeral and burial. By "finding his comfort in a bottle," he was absent when funeral arrangements were made and "checked out" during the daughter's services. The father was not emotionally available to support his wife or the other children as they grieved. His drinking subsequently jeopardized his job performance and put the family's financial standing at risk during a time of high emotional vulnerability. For the practitioner, helping the father confront his alcohol problem and enter a recovery program was prerequisite to addressing parental grief over his daughter's death.

No Explanatory Framework

Most explanatory frameworks for understanding death as part of the human condition are forged from religious beliefs, life philosophies, cultural practices, scientific paradigms, collective wisdom, an individual credo, or some combination of these elements. However, comments such as, "God doesn't give you more than you can handle," "Everything happens for a reason," "God needed another angel in heaven," "Maybe [child's name] will come back in a better life," or "We all die sometime" rub bereaved parents the wrong way. Individuals who say such things mean well, but they overlook the fact that explanatory frameworks are a highly personal matter. Sympathizers, no matter how well intentioned, cannot simply impart to a grieving parent their own beliefs about death, the life cycle, or the concept of an afterlife. Attempts to do so are presumptive. Such efforts might make the sympathizing person feel better about the child's death, but they usually leave bereaved parents feeling discounted and their grief minimized.

Having an explanatory framework for death can help bereaved parents regain some semblance of equilibrium following the loss of a child. The key points are a) whether the bereaved parents' belief system can explain and accommodate a tragic event such as the death of a child and b) whether the parents can activate those beliefs during their time of grief. Some disillusioned bereaved parents have said things such as, "I always thought there was a God, but now I don't know because how could a loving God allow something like this to happen?" Whatever explanatory framework they had collapsed under the weight of the tragedy. Bereaved parents without a durable explanatory framework for death often feel adrift and rudderless in their search for coherency and meaning following their child's death.

Exploring a bereaved parent's explanatory framework requires deft maneuvering. Sometimes bereaved parents spontaneously self-disclose their explanatory framework or give important clues to their worldviews or practices pertaining to death or the afterlife. Those clues contextualize the subsequent therapeutic interchange so practitioners can respond with cultural sensitivity. Conversely, some bereaved parents may endorse no explanatory framework at all, and their position should be respected as well. When information about an explanatory framework is not readily apparent, culturally attuned practitioners can gently inquire about bereaved parents' beliefs. A question such as, "Does faith or spirituality enter into how you view things like this [loss]?" may open the door to fruitful discussion (cf. Gamino et al., 2003). Some parents may express doubts or misgivings about what they thought they believed, as discussed in the previous paragraph, and need help re-scaffolding their explanatory framework. In these instances, practitioners should "lead from one step behind" and avoid proselytizing or patronizing bereaved parents who are uncertain and searching for answers. Knowing the extent of a bereaved parent's explanatory framework, and identifying important cultural considerations connected with it, helps practitioners provide customized care while honoring parental diversity.

DIAGNOSTIC CONSIDERATIONS

How and when practitioners assign a psychiatric diagnosis to a grieving person has stirred much controversy in recent decades (Prigerson et al., 2021; Zachar et al., 2023). While some grieving parents find reassurance in knowing that their suffering has a name and a defined set of symptoms, others resent the medical establishment adding to their pain by imposing a psychiatric label as they try to cope with the catastrophe of losing a child. Thieleman et al. (2023) found a clear majority of bereaved parents (68%) viewed assignment of a psychiatric diagnosis as unhelpful. Yet some practitioners operate in clinical settings where service provision is contingent upon identifying a treatable medical or psychiatric condition. When required, accurate diagnosis is a professional responsibility (Gamino & Ritter, 2009). The current status of diagnostic nomenclature is summarized in this section for practitioners requiring information and guidance in this area.

Diagnosis is as much art as science. When it comes to the psychological and emotional state of bereaved parents, a categorical approach to diagnosis may not be very informative. The complicating factors examined in this chapter illustrate how complex and nuanced parental grief can be, something not easily encapsulated in a discrete diagnostic designation. Certainly, all bereaved parents do not exhibit the same symptoms or levels of distress. The diagnostic term *complicated grief* is descriptive and flexible, often preferred by practitioners working in clinical settings (Gamino & Ritter, 2009), and one that still appears in the professional literature (Champion & Kilcullen, 2023). This description qualifies the fact that some grief cases are more complex, thus predicting a more difficult clinical course and a more likely need for professional treatment. It can work well when practitioners document in their records a granular account of specific complicating factors.

Studies from around the world (Australia, China, Denmark, Germany, Japan, Netherlands, and the United States) pooled into a meta-analysis demonstrated that a consistent percentage of bereaved persons, approximately 10% overall, showed a constellation of diagnostic features indicative of a condition now called Prolonged Grief Disorder (Lundorff et al., 2017). This finding means a consistent minority of grievers can be expected to struggle in the aftermath of a major loss. At the same time, data from Thieleman et al. (2023) and a literature review conducted by Morris et al. (2019) suggest the diagnostic rate may be much higher among bereaved parents. The International Classification of Diseases (ICD-11) developed by the World Health Organization (2022) listed Prolonged Grief Disorder (6B42) among stress-related conditions. It can occur following the death of a person close to the bereaved, such as a son or daughter. The ICD-11 describes Prolonged Grief Disorder as follows:

> A disturbance in which . . . there is a persistent and pervasive grief response characterized by longing for the deceased or persistent preoccupation with the deceased accompanied by intense emotional pain . . . for an atypically long period of time following the loss (more than 6 months at a minimum) and clearly exceeds expected social, cultural or religious norms for the individual's culture and context.

The condition must be severe enough to cause significant impairment in personal, family, social, educational, occupational, or other important areas of functioning. Many bereaved parents will meet criteria for this specific diagnosis.

In the United States, the American Psychiatric Association (2022) included the diagnosis of Prolonged Grief Disorder in its *Diagnostic and Statistical Manual of Mental Disorders*, 5th edition, text revision (*DSM-5-TR*). Its criteria are similar to ICD-11, with the exception that the diagnosis cannot be assigned until 12 months following the death of a person close to the bereaved, rather than after six months. Otherwise, the diagnosis requires either intense yearning or longing for the deceased person or preoccupation with thoughts or memories of the deceased, or both. A minimum of three of eight symptoms of emotional distress (i.e., identity disruption, disbelief about the death, avoidance of reminders, intense emotional pain, difficulty reintegrating into life, emotional numbness, meaninglessness, or intense loneliness) must be observed. While many bereaved parents could read these symptoms as a checklist of what they experience, they still manage to function and meet their duties and obligations. For a diagnosis to be assigned, the condition must cause clinically significant distress or impairment in social or occupational functioning. Like ICD-11, the duration and severity of symptoms must exceed social, cultural, or religious norms for the griever's culture and context.

Besides considerations of how to diagnose parental grief, the question of *when* to diagnose presents a dilemma for practitioners. Some evidence suggests that grief trajectories for bereaved parents may last three to five years or longer following the death of their child before some semblance of emotional equilibrium is reestablished (Klass, 2001; Lannen et al., 2008). Therefore, it might be argued that parental grief constitutes a unique social and cultural phenomenon and that its prolonged nature is not atypical within its own norm group. Many bereaved parents find it validating to know their grief process could extend much longer than people grieving other losses or than diagnostic systems assume.

In the final analysis, questions about diagnosis and when it is clinically appropriate to treat a bereaved parent may be answered in a pragmatic way—*provide help when it is requested or when parents accept such an offer.* Allow bereaved parents to make their own determination on whether their distress is too severe or their functioning too impaired to manage without professional help. Application of a basic two-question tool recommended by Gamino and Ritter (2009) can be useful. Are you having trouble dealing with [son or daughter's] death? Would you like to see someone for help? Two affirmative answers merit referral to a practitioner. At that point, the clinical status of the bereaved parent seeking help will most likely satisfy the requisite criteria for Prolonged Grief Disorder.

SUMMARY

As a review of this chapter's contents, the parent-specific and general risk factors complicating parental grief can be applied to Reyna's case. Jude's death as a young adult was certainly *off time*, developmentally speaking. Reyna suffered from *empty track* feelings, not only from loss of the relationship with Jude but also from loss of contact with the grandchildren. Her sense of *legacy and continuation* was severely disrupted by Jude's death. Her *identity* as a mother and grandmother evaporated almost completely afterward. Furthermore, Jude's death was *unexpected*, totally out of the blue. It occurred in a *traumatic manner* with his extensive injuries and brief ICU stay. Reyna definitely saw Jude's death as *preventable* because the couple could have addressed their marital problems more maturely. Worse yet, the ambiguity of the circumstances left Reyna wondering whether reckless behavior by Jude may have contributed to the crash. While blaming the daughter-in-law was convenient, holding anger toward her son for endangering himself would prove harder to release. *Relationship disruption* was present because Reyna's formerly close connection with her son became compromised after his marriage and he did not reach out to her about his current troubles. *Mourner shortcomings* applied in the form of Reyna's previous depression problems, which intensified and prolonged her grief. Finally, Reyna endorsed *no explanatory framework* or systematic worldview that provided perspective on why tragedies occur or what happens after death. Thus, there was little basis for deriving potential comfort from a sense of continuing connection with Jude. The presence of almost every possible risk factor applying in Reyna's case certainly compounded her grief. Given the length of time Reyna struggled with Jude's death and her constellation of symptoms, severe even among bereaved parents, a diagnosis of Prolonged Grief Disorder was warranted.

REFERENCES

American Psychiatric Association. (2022). *Diagnostic and statistical manual of mental disorders, text revision DMS-5-TR* (5th ed., text revision). American Psychiatric Association.

Boulware, D. L., & Bui, N. H. (2016). Bereaved African American adults: The role of social support, religious coping, and continuing bonds. *Journal of Loss and Trauma, 21*(3), 192–202. https://doi.org/10.1080/15325024.2015.1057455

Buckle, J. L., & Fleming, S. J. (2011). *Parenting after the death of a child: A Practitioner's Guide*. Routledge.

Cacciatore, J., Thieleman, K., Fretts, R., & Jackson, L. B. (2021). What is good grief support? Exploring the actors and actions in social support after traumatic grief. *PLoS One, 16*(5), e0252324. https://doi.org/10.1371/journal.pone.0252324

Champion, M. J., & Kilcullen, M. (2023). Complicated grief following the traumatic loss of a child: A systematic review. *OMEGA—Journal of Death and Dying*. Advance online publication. https://doi.org/10.1177/00302228231170417

Chen, R. (2022). Social support as a protective factor against the effect of grief reactions on depression for bereaved single older adults. *Death Studies, 46*(3), 756–763. https://doi.org/10.1080/07481187.2020.1774943

Freud, S. (1917/1957). Mourning and melancholia. In J. Strachey (Ed.), *The standard edition of the complete psychological works of Sigmund Freud, Vol. XIV (1914–1916)* (pp. 237–260). Hogarth Press and the Institute of Psycho-Analysis.

Gamino, L. A., Easterling, L. W., & Sewell, K. W. (2003). The role of spiritual experience in adapting to bereavement. In G. R. Cox, R. A. Bendiksen, & R. G. Stevenson (Eds.), *Making sense of death: Spiritual, pastoral, and personal aspects of death, dying and bereavement* (pp. 13–27). Baywood.

Gamino, L. A., & Ritter, R. H., Jr. (2009). *Ethical practice in grief counseling*. Springer Publishing Company.

Janoff-Bulman, R. (2002). *Shattered assumptions: Towards a new psychology of trauma*. New York: Free Press.

Klass, D. (2001). The inner representation of the dead child in the psychic and social narratives of bereaved parents. In R. A. Neimeyer (Ed.), *Meaning reconstruction and the experience of loss* (pp. 77–94). American Psychological Association.

Klass, D., & Marwit, S. J. (1988–1989). Toward a model of parental grief. *OMEGA—Journal of Death and Dying, 19*, 31–50. https://doi.org/10.2190/BVUR-67KR-F52F-VW35

Kushner, H. S. (2004). *When bad things happen to good people*. Anchor.

Lannen, P. K., Wolfe, J., Prigerson, H. G., Onelov, E., & Kreicbergs, U. C. (2008). Unresolved grief in a national sample of bereaved parents: Impaired mental and physical health 4 to 9 years later. *Journal of Clinical Oncology, 26*(36), 5870–5876. https://doi.org/10.1200/JCO.2007.14.6738

Li, J., Li, M., & Reid, J. K. (2022). Social support in bereavement: Developing and validating a new scale. *International Journal of Psychology, 57*(2), 306–313. https://doi.org/10.1002/ijop.12816

Lundorff, M., Holmgren, H., Zachariae, R., Farver-Vestergaard, I., & O'Connor, M. (2017). Prevalence of prolonged grief disorder in adult bereavement:

A systematic review and meta-analysis. *Journal of Affective Disorders, 212,* 138–149. https://dx.doi.org/10.1016/j.jad.2017.01.030

Lynch, T. (2000). From interview in *On our own terms: Moyers on dying.* American Archive of Public Broadcasting: Bill Moyers Collection. https://billmoyers.com/series/on-our-own-terms-moyers-on-dying/

Morris, S., Fletcher, K., & Goldstein, R. (2019). The grief of parents after the death of a young child. *Journal of Clinical Psychology in Medical Settings, 26,* 321–338. https://doi.org/10.1007/s10880-018-9590-7

Neugarten, B. (1979). Time, age, and the life cycle. *The American Journal of Psychiatry, 136,* 887–894. https://doi.org/10.1176/ajp.136.7.887

Parkes, C. M., & Weiss, R. S. (1983). *Recovery from bereavement.* Basic Books.

Prigerson, H. G., Kakarala, S., Gang, J., & Maciejewski, P. K. (2021). History and status of prolonged grief disorder as a psychiatric diagnosis. *Annual Review of Clinical Psychology, 17,* 109–126. https://doi.org/10.1146/annurev-clinpsy-081219-093600

Rando, T. A. (1993). *Treatment of complicated mourning.* Research Press.

Reed, M. L. (1999). *Grandparents cry twice: Help for bereaved grandparents.* Routledge.

Rynearson, E. K. (2001). *Retelling violent death.* Routledge.

Rynearson, E. K. (2018). Disabling reenactment imagery after violent dying. *Death Studies, 42*(1), 4–8. https://doi.org/10.1080/07481187.2017.1370411

Tedeschi, R. G., & Calhoun, L. G. (2004). *Helping bereaved parents: A clinician's guide.* Brunner-Routledge.

Thieleman, K., Cacciatore, J., & Frances, A. (2023). Rates of prolonged grief disorder: Considering relationship to the person who died and cause of death. *Journal of Affective Disorders, 339,* 832–837. https://doi.org/10.1016/j.jad.2023.07.094

Worden, J. W. (2018). *Grief counseling & grief therapy: A handbook for the mental health practitioner* (5th ed.). Springer Publishing Co.

World Health Organization. (2022). *6B42 prolonged grief disorder.* International Classification of Diseases (ICD 11) for Mortality and Morbidity Statistics. https://icd.who.int/browse11/l-m/en#/http://id.who.int/icd/entity/1183832314

Xiong, J., Ma, H., Ma, R., Xu, T., & Wang, Y. (2023). The relationship between perceived stress and prolonged grief disorder among Chinese Shidu parents: Effects of anxiety and social support. *BMC Psychiatry, 23,* 714. https://doi.org/10.1186/s12888-023-05206-9

Zachar, P., First, M. B., & Kendler, K. S. (2023). Prolonged grief disorder and the DSM: A history. *The Journal of Nervous and Mental Disease, 211*(5), 386–392. https://doi.org/10.1097.NMD.0000000000001618

Zheng, Y., Lawson, T. R., & Anderson Head, B. (2017). "Our only child has died"—A study of bereaved older Chinese parents. *OMEGA-Journal of Death and Dying, 74*(4), 410–425. https://doi.org/10.1177/0030222815612285

CHAPTER THREE

Helpful Factors

> The energy of love is not erased because a loved one dies.
> —Nancy S. Hogan (personal communication, 2024)

CASE 3.A

Leslie and John never imagined life would turn out the way it did for their middle son, Ritchie. In his 20s, he came out as gay. Steeped in conservative values, they found his disclosure difficult to accept. Nonetheless, Leslie and John continued to love and support Ritchie even when he contracted HIV. In his 30s (and prior to the development of current life-sustaining antiretroviral therapies; Bekker et al., 2023), Ritchie was diagnosed with AIDS and declared terminally ill. They chose to care for him at home. Leslie described her thinking this way: "I brought him into this world, and I'm going to be there when he goes out. I may scream and cry, but I am going to be strong."

Leslie and John's two other children were not so tolerant. They remained judgmental and distant toward Ritchie, refusing to endorse his homosexual lifestyle. They disapproved of their parents' loyalty to Ritchie. Leslie explained to the hospice nurse, "There's lots of ways you can lose your children besides death, so you need to try to support them and understand." The couple stayed on good terms with their other children, despite their criticism. They took care of Ritchie until his death. Leslie was present at his bedside during his final moments.

Around the first anniversary of Ritchie's death, Leslie and John found themselves struggling and consulted a grief therapist. John also started a jigsaw puzzle around that time, a new activity for him. Muddling through the jigsaw, he pondered how life happens: "Sometimes you can fit the pieces together, sometimes you can't. Sometimes you just have to walk away from it. Come back later and keep trying to put everything together." The therapist discussed how working the jigsaw paralleled their search for meaning and a sense of coherency in the aftermath of Ritchie's untimely death.

John later reported with some dismay that he had finally finished the jigsaw puzzle only to discover there was a single piece missing, so the final image was incomplete. The therapist continued working with the metaphor by suggesting that perhaps Ritchie himself was the missing piece. The incomplete puzzle accurately reflected the reality of their current life—Ritchie was no longer in the picture, and therefore an irreplaceable element was missing. Leslie added that, with Ritchie's mischievous sense of humor, he would probably be laughing at John for trying to "put it all together." The therapist ventured that maybe Ritchie even held the missing piece himself, just to tease!

Leslie and John found this exchange to be oddly comforting. Paradoxically, a focus on the missing puzzle piece made it seem as if Ritchie were still present in some way, still an active influence in their lives. It enabled them to better accept Ritchie's physical absence as permanent. This intervention also illustrated how the grief therapist and the bereaved parents worked together in co-constructing the new narrative with which they would live, how all the different dimensions of life and death interrelate, and how meaning can be assigned to loss events in a way that promotes healing.

Sometimes called protective (from distress) factors, helpful factors promote the adaptation of bereaved parents. Helpful factors can be inherent strengths parents possessed prior to the loss of their child or adaptive behaviors they practice that reduce distress and aid coping. Helpful factors promote parental resilience following the tragedy of child loss.

INHERENT STRENGTHS

Hardiness

Psychologists have long recognized that some individuals adapt to life better than others. Individual differences in adaptability can be seen among bereaved parents as well. Some parents seem to find a way to cope with the tragedy of a child's death while other parents languish. This generic trait of adaptability and perseverance has been assigned various names: hardiness (Campbell et al., 1991; Kobasa et al., 1982; Maddi, 2006; Mund, 2016), ego strength (Vaillant, 1993), self-efficacy (Bandura, 1977, 1982), psychological flexibility (Doorley et al., 2020; Hayes et al., 2011), hope (Snyder et al., 1991), and grit (Duckworth et al., 2007; Duckworth & Quinn, 2009; Panigrahi & Suar, 2021). *Hardiness* may be the most translatable term for describing what comprises this source of personal strength that can buffer the painful aftermath of losing a child.

Initial research by Kobasa et al. (1982) found that individuals who displayed features of personal hardiness responded differently to life stress compared with their less-hardy peers. Hardy individuals maintained good physical health and showed overall better performance on work tasks, even under strain. Kobasa et al. identified three specific mental attitudes that comprise hardiness: commitment, control, and challenge. *Commitment* means involving oneself in life activities, engaging vigorously, and showing curiosity about the surrounding world. *Control* means believing and acting as if one's own efforts can influence events surrounding the person, sometimes called a sense of personal agency. *Challenge* means expecting change, rather than stability, to be the norm in life and viewing change as an opportunity for growth instead of a threat to security. Practitioners whose recommendations leverage attitudes of commitment, control, and challenge can guide bereaved parents toward better outcomes and transformative personal growth.

In the case example, Leslie declared that she was going to "be there" when her son Ritchie died. She pledged to be intimately involved in Ritchie's final decline rather than shy away from his deathbed. Those resolutions showed an attitude of commitment. Leslie also intended to "be strong" and stand tall when Ritchie died, rather than falling apart, displaying an attitude of control. Her vow to "support and understand" her children, even in the face of difficulties and conflict, connoted the element of challenge. Leslie anticipated hurdles in the process of raising and loving her children, knowing that it would not always be easy. Her remarks implied that she would adjust to changes and find a way to deal with difficulties required of her as a parent. Leslie's stance robustly reflected the dimensions of hardiness.

Intrinsic Spirituality

Intrinsic spirituality is a culturally relative attribute. Societies throughout human history have embraced an array of belief systems and cultural practices that reflect internal convictions concerning the spiritual realm. As just one example of the myriad ways people understand spirituality, the U.S. armed forces officially recognize scores of faith affiliations in distinct emblems featured on grave markers for veterans, including the Christian cross, Jewish star of David, Muslim crescent and star, Hindu Om, Wiccan pentacle, Bahia star, atheist symbol, and Shinto torii gate, among many others (National Cemetery Administration, & United States Department of Veterans Affairs, 2023). Furthermore, even within a particular faith affiliation or cultural group, wide variation can be expected in the degree to which a given individual adheres to or deviates from any system of beliefs. Idiosyncratic forms of spirituality, or no spirituality at all, can manifest as well. Practitioners working with bereaved parents should be prepared for a multitude of expressions when it comes to intrinsic spirituality.

Researchers at Harvard University attempted to define intrinsic spirituality apart from identification with any specific faith group or denominational affiliation (Kass et al., 1991). They focused on how individuals conceptualize the idea of a "higher power," supreme being, or transcendent force. They conceived of intrinsic spirituality as internal to a person, rather than a function of external religious rituals, worship styles, or cultural patterns. Their measurement tool asked questions such as the following: "How often do you spend time on religious or spiritual practices?" "How often have you felt as though you were very close to a powerful spiritual force that seemed to lift you outside yourself?" "Have you experienced a feeling of unity with the earth and all living beings?" These items probe how individuals perceive spirituality and the extent to which they endorse a personal relationship with divine or transcendent elements in their worldview. Kass et al.'s intrinsic spirituality scale performed well compared to other psychometric scales intended to measure similar constructs (Newberg et al., 2019). Furthermore, an individual's intrinsic spirituality is often manifested by personal practices performed outside the scope of group worship or prescribed rituals. Gamino et al. (2000a) showed that intrinsic spirituality, more than attendance at formalized worship, was associated with the lowest distress levels exhibited by grievers in general.

With bereaved parents, intrinsic spirituality can form the basis of an explanatory framework for how they think about their child's death, while lacking such a framework can be a liability (see Chapter 2, "What Makes Parental Grief So Difficult?"). Intrinsic spirituality can impart several potentially beneficial results: insulating a bereaved parent from feeling alone, providing comfort from a relationship with a higher power or supreme being, imparting hope for reunion in the afterlife, and informing other adaptive coping practices, as discussed in the next section of this chapter, such as rituals of remembrance, continuing connection with the deceased child, finding meaning, and openness to growth and transformation.

ADAPTIVE BEHAVIORS

Saying Goodbye

As simple as it seems, saying goodbye can be incredibly difficult. Many grieving people back away from final leave-taking because they do not want to let go of their loved one. They avoid directly acknowledging the reality and inevitability of death. The emotional intensity of saying goodbye forever feels like a pitch point too extreme to tolerate. As a result, final goodbyes go unsaid. One salient aspect of funeral and memorial services is providing formal, ritualized ways to accomplish leave-taking, sometimes by "walking out" a final goodbye for which no words are adequate (Hoy, 2025).

Byock (2004) wrote eloquently about the importance of saying goodbye as death approaches and codified it as one of the essential things that matter most at the end of life. Empirical research (Gamino et al., 2000b) supported this assertion, finding that grievers who said goodbye fared better during post-loss adjustment. One clear benefit of saying goodbye is that it precludes or diminishes regret. Those who muster the courage to say goodbye know they heeded the moment, regardless of fear or sadness, and bade farewell to their dying loved one in a manner that honored the significance of their relationship. Leslie's story certainly captures that kind of courage.

A straightforward assessment question such as, "Did you have the chance to say goodbye?" can help practitioners determine whether this all-important step occurred between bereaved parents and their dying son or daughter (Gamino et al., 2000a). Perhaps at the bedside or in an emergency department. Perhaps at the funeral or memorial service. Perhaps during a private moment or in a personal way only the two parties understood. When bereaved parents confirm they said goodbye to their deceased child, a sensitive review of when and how the goodbye happened is often cathartic and comforting. It reinforces a conclusion that the grieving parents did all they could when their child was dying.

Sometimes bereaved parents cannot bring themselves to say goodbye to their dying son or daughter. Sometimes circumstances of sudden or unexpected death deprive them of that opportunity. Sometimes bereaved parents avoid saying a final goodbye even during funerals or memorial services. Much therapeutic benefit can be gained from assisting bereaved parents in saying goodbye, even after the child's death, when a goodbye did not occur spontaneously. Two options exist—surrogate and symbolic.

A goodbye message bereaved parents did not convey can still be verbalized in conversation with someone who serves as a surrogate or proxy for the deceased child. A surrogate may be a relative or friend who knew the child well and can function as the "receiver" of the message by listening to the parent's goodbye statement and affirming it. Bereaved parents may wonder why they should say the undelivered goodbye out loud. Neurolinguistic research has shown that mechanisms of recited speech are more powerful than merely hearing or reading silently for developing enduring neural pathways as the basis of memory (Forrin & MacLeod, 2018). In other words, the exercise of saying goodbye out loud makes the message more impactful and long lasting.

Symbolic goodbyes can be orchestrated in numerous ways: talking to the child at the cemetery or columbarium, writing and reading a goodbye letter to the child, visiting a location special to the child, releasing balloons or doves (sometimes with messages attached), or spreading cremains. Creative possibilities are endless. Symbolic goodbyes with high personal involvement by the bereaved parents can be meaningful and healing. They constitute behaviors of control and commitment observed among psychologically hardy individuals.

Focusing on Positive Memories

When children die, their physical life stops, but their story continues in memory. Some bereaved parents ruminate on reenactment imagery (Rynearson, 2018) or cannot stop thinking about what happened to their deceased child. Sometimes, finally worn down by the seemingly endless replays, they feel "numb-ified," as one bereaved mother put it.

Practitioners can acknowledge the suffering of these bereaved parents but not leave them stuck in their misery. Reprocessing reenactment imagery is possible (see Chapter 4, "Contemporary Treatment Approaches"). Also helpful is reminding bereaved parents that their children's lives were about so much more than what happened in their last few moments. While nothing can change how their child died, some relief and balance can be restored by consciously shifting attention to the treasure trove of positive memories parents carry about their children. Even during a single therapy session, bereaved parents can move from ruminating over death circumstances to recalling highlight moments. Tears can give way to smiles, even laughter, as positive or humorous memories are revisited. When the mood in the room shifts this way, hope appears as a beacon. Bereaved parents begin to recognize they can survive and somehow go on with their lives. They see how important perspective is in keeping their child's memory alive through positive recollections.

> ### CASE 3.B
>
> One bereaved father lost his mentally ill son to suicide. The father found himself preoccupied with recurring mental images of his son in the intensive care unit, intubated, with a head wrap over the gunshot

> wound. That was not how he wanted to remember his son. With the practitioner's encouragement, the father combed through his collection of family photos and selected images illustrating the best sides of his son's personality, including one photo of him grinning in his unique, quirky way. The father made that image the centerpiece of a photo collage he framed and displayed prominently at home to emphasize positive memories of his deceased son.

Today's digital technology makes remembering more vivid. Many funeral homes prepare slide shows of the deceased person's life using photos supplied by the family. Such a recording can become an important keepsake for bereaved parents. Many families archive their positive memories in self-published photo books or digital picture frames displaying a series of images that can be updated or modified with new entries. Video clips can be merged into files showing dynamic events in the life of the deceased child in a movie-like fashion.

Engaging Rituals of Remembrance

Milestones in children's lives bring parents immense joy: birthdays, graduations, weddings, the arrival of grandchildren, family trips, reunions, and holidays. As noted in Chapter 2, "What Makes Parental Grief So Difficult?," bereaved parents often experience the empty track phenomenon when these special occasions occur after a child has died. Adaptive grievers engage rituals of remembrance at these times to express their feelings. Even though they could not control the cause of death, rituals give bereaved parents a sense of "symbolic mastery" when they intentionally determine how their child's death is observed or remembered (Doka, 1984–1985). Research shows that active participation in grief rituals is associated with better overall grief adjustment (Gamino et al., 2000b).

When considering how best to promote the use of rituals when working with bereaved parents, a multicultural lens is imperative. Many religious traditions prescribe defined mourning intervals, such as the 40-day grief observance in Islam or Buddhism's 49-day observance. Specific anniversary dates may be designated for remembrance, such as Judaism's lighting of the yahrzeit candle on the anniversary of the death or Catholicism's annual observance of All Soul's Day in November, also recognized in Hispanic cultures as Dia de los Muertos, or Day of the Dead.

CASE 3.C

One bereaved mother dreaded what would have been the next birthday of her deceased adult son. Rather than feel morose, she opted to host a dinner for her other children and some of her deceased son's friends. She prepared traditional ethnic foods her deceased son would have savored. After the meal, they gathered on her back patio, where she lit a traditional Japanese lantern as the sun went down. The guests told stories and anecdotes about her son, relishing his role in their lives. Some stories were funny, some complimentary, some tender, and some the mother had never heard. She could sense her deceased son's spirit during the proceedings. Once everyone had taken a turn, she blew out the lamp, indicating the end of the evening and signifying her son's departure from their lives. The idea for the dinner party was entirely her own and left her with a sense of satisfaction over remembering her son the best way she could.

Because anniversaries and holidays occur throughout the year, bereaved parents frequently ask questions during therapy about how to handle these occasions when they arise. The Dual Process Model of grief (Stroebe & Schut, 1999, 2010) offers a theoretical framework that can assist bereaved parents in structuring their rituals of remembrance. The model suggests the everyday lived experience of bereavement consists of both loss-oriented (i.e., grieving) and restoration-oriented (i.e., going on with life) activities. Grievers typically shift back and forth from one domain to the other as they mourn their loved one. Meaningful remembrance rituals usually incorporate both elements, just as many funeral or memorial services (i.e., formalized grieving) are followed by a bereavement meal intended to physically sustain and emotionally support mourners after the work of grieving (i.e., going on with life). Thus, practitioners can suggest a combination of the two elements—a ritual to honor or remember the deceased child paired with a ritual to affirm that life goes on for the survivors, usually in that order.

In the example just given of the bereaved mother hosting a dinner party on her deceased son's birthday, both aspects of the Dual Process Model were evident that evening. Affirming that life goes on occurred with the meal featuring her son's favorite foods, where guests nourished themselves and enjoyed one another's company. Honoring and remembering occurred in a deliberate but natural way with the storytelling circle around the lantern. The bereaved mother's wisdom and creativity were rewarded with a memorable event where guests reminisced about her deceased son and celebrated his influence in their lives.

Cultivating a Continuing Connection

Dennis Klass and colleagues (Klass et al., 1996; Klass & Walter, 2001) championed post-death continuing bonds between grievers and their deceased loved ones and dispelled the notion prevalent in Western societies, promulgated by Freud (1917/1957), that relinquishing the bond was required for healthy mourning. Continuing bonds can manifest as a) sensing the presence of the deceased, b) speaking to the deceased, c) taking the deceased as a moral guide, or d) talking about the deceased. Many Asian cultures and Eastern religions embrace the notion of an ongoing, even interactive, connection between the living and their deceased ancestors (Benore & Park, 2004; Chan et al., 2005; Hsu et al., 2009; Liang et al., 2024). Bereaved parents who ascribe to such possibilities can benefit from deliberate efforts to cultivate a continuing connection with their deceased son or daughter.

Continuing connections can also occur when creatures or features of the natural world are interpreted as communications from the deceased. Consider the following example.

CASE 3.D

An African American mother's mentally ill son was shot and killed by police officers during an episode of agitated psychosis. Several months later, when shopping for groceries, the mother returned to her vehicle and found a large bird perched conspicuously on the hood. Viewing the bird as a pest, she slammed the car door to scare it away but to no avail. She honked the horn and started the windshield wipers, again with no effect. She slammed the door a second time. The bird never winced. Instead, it peered directly at her through the windshield for several seconds. Finally, the bereaved mother gasped in recognition, "My God, it's Tony!" Her tack changed from shooing to welcoming. She began speaking softly to the bird, "Hello, son . . ." After a bit of monologue, the bird flew away, leaving the mother with a sense of serenity that her murdered son was okay in the next world. At the Thanksgiving holiday some weeks later, the bereaved mother set an honorary place at the table for Tony, adorning his plate with a decorative paper bird as a symbol.

Many bereaved parents hold conversations with their deceased children, as suggested by Klass and Walter (2001), especially when it is consistent with their cultural and religious beliefs. Even though the child is gone, they maintain an ongoing connection by speaking aloud to them and trusting that their messages are heard. Some bereaved parents long to connect in this way with their deceased child but hesitate for fear they will be labeled crazy or insane. By normalizing such behavior among bereaved parents—within the scope of their cultural context—practitioners can encourage this healthy form of continuing connection. In addition, practitioners should note whether bereaved parents who talk to their deceased children leave the opportunity for something to come back in return. An interval of contemplative silence and attentiveness is needed. Something may register through the physical senses (e.g., sight, sound, scent, sensation), thoughts (e.g., image, memory, idea, word, phrase, song), or feelings that renders the conversation a bilateral connection. Such "return channel" experiences can be very powerful.

Besides natural phenomena and verbal conversations with or about the deceased child, there are many other ways to experience a sense of connection with a deceased son or daughter. Mitima-Verloop et al. (2019) found several meaningful ways Dutch grievers cultivated a connection with their lost loved ones: creating an altar or memory space in the home with photos, visiting the gravesite or place where the deceased's ashes were scattered, lighting a candle, carrying an item or wearing clothing of the deceased as a reminder, listening to music or watching a movie the deceased would have liked, visiting a place special to the deceased, or journaling or writing a letter or poem to the deceased. Mitima-Verloop et al. found these activities were most often practiced by individuals grieving a high-salience loss, such as the death of a child. These suggestions resonate with many bereaved parents because they reinforce the underlying parent-child bond as ongoing and permanent.

Advocating for the Deceased Child

Most often, advocating for a deceased child follows a wrongful death, such as drunk-driving crashes, avoidable accidents, medical malpractice, or even homicides (see Chapter 8, "Accidental Death"; Chapter 9, "Homicide"; Chapter 10, "Suicide") by seeking accountability from responsible parties. Many bereaved parents make it their mission to advocate for their deceased child in criminal justice systems or in their community, to be their child's voice that would not otherwise be heard. The process of serving the deceased child, even after death, provides an avenue for bereaved parents to continue parenting as well as satisfy their own needs for justice in cases of wrongful death.

CASE 3.E

One bereaved father's two young boys were killed when a motorist under the influence of alcohol crossed the highway center line and struck their vehicle at high speed. The boys' mother, who was driving at the time, was also seriously injured. The defense team intended to argue that the mother was at fault for falling asleep at the wheel, so she was precluded from testifying. Only the father could speak at the manslaughter trial. During the father's emotional testimony about the crash and finding his sons' bodies among the wreckage, the defense team repeatedly requested a recess (ostensibly to allow emotions to cool and the jury not to be swayed). Yet the father insisted to the judge that he could continue his witness, not wanting the unheard cries of his deceased sons to be silenced by a procedural ploy. Vindicated, the bereaved father believed he had spoken out valiantly on behalf of his two sons who could not represent themselves.

CASE 3.F

A bereaved mother lost both her young daughter, Marlee, and her own mother (the child's grandmother) in a regrettable car crash. The vehicle driven by the grandmother sometimes did not shift gears properly. It stalled momentarily while she was attempting to cross a four-lane highway, and an oncoming car struck them broadside at high speed. The highway patrol investigation found the deceased grandmother at fault and exonerated the other driver. When the bereaved mother discovered there had been two other serious injury crashes at the same intersection, she appealed to the state's department of transportation to build an overpass. Such a project involved considerable cost, so the agency took its time evaluating the situation. Nonetheless, the mother campaigned tirelessly with government officials, pleading that no more lives be lost at the dangerous crossing. The state eventually conceded the risk and built an overpass approximately three years after her daughter's death. Although too late to save her own child (and mother), advocacy for making the roads safer gave the bereaved mother a cause her deceased daughter would have enthusiastically endorsed. The bereaved mother privately referred to the new structure as "Marlee's overpass."

Some bereaved parents may be hesitant to testify in court or speak out publicly on behalf of their deceased children. Their reluctance may come from natural shyness or fear of breaking down with emotion or a desire to keep their grief private. Practitioners can encourage such advocacy efforts, when indicated, knowing the potential benefit for long-term coping. While always respecting a bereaved parent's right to choose, sometimes a gentle nudge is needed.

One potential strategy is to ask bereaved parents how they would react if someone directly threatened their child in their presence. Invariably, parents describe actions to defend their child or warn them of danger. Practitioners can transition from those descriptions to discussing how that protectiveness might be converted into advocacy.

CASE 3.G

A bereaved mother's preschool-aged daughter died in a lake mishap when a boat operator steered his vessel too close to a designated swimming area. Reticent by nature, the bereaved mother did not plan to give a victim impact statement during the sentencing phase of the offender's trial. Yet when the practitioner emphasized that this moment was her best opportunity to address the offender or tell publicly the story of her daughter's life, the bereaved mother changed her mind and decided "to let the world know what a wonderful girl she was." (See Chapter 10, "Homicide," for more details about this case.)

Finding Meaning

Children carry incalculable worth to their parents, and their lives become an endless source of reflection and meaning. Parents are renowned for telling stories about how their children both delight and dismay them. Even when children die, their stories continue as parents talk their way through grief. Finding meaning in a child's life—and death—can serve a protective function for bereaved parents.

The vignette about Leslie and John that opened this chapter is about finding meaning. John tried to piece together the disparate aspects of Ritchie's life into a coherent story. Working the jigsaw puzzle provided an analogue for that meaning-making process. While some aspects of Ritchie's life were tragic, other parts seemed admirable, charming, redemptive, humorous, or even vexatious. Leslie's meaning making suggested that parental elements of loyalty and love were the glue that held it all together. Finding meaning in the deceased child's life and death, in the form of a narrative encompassing all the principal elements of a complex, textured life (Walter, 1999), can give bereaved parents some solace in the aftermath of losing their child.

However, finding meaning after a loved one's death does not happen for every griever. A fascinating study of the families of Canadian miners who perished in a cave-in illustrated this fact (Davis et al., 2007). All surviving families suffered the tragic death of a loved one in the same calamity. Yet researchers found stark differences in their grief trajectories. Some grieving family members saw no meaning in the senseless disaster and simply lived with that bitter reality. Others searched for a sense of meaning but could not find any. A third group was able to derive meaning about their loved one's life or come to an understanding of what happened. Not surprisingly, those grievers who found no meaning showed the most extreme distress scores on psychological measures taken eight years after the cave-in, while grievers who did manage to find meaning in the stories of their loved ones' lives fared much better in their emotional recovery.

These results remind practitioners that finding meaning after the death of a child, even if helpful and adaptive for grieving parents such as Leslie and John, may elude some bereaved parents. Also, practitioners should gauge bereaved parents' receptivity because ideas about "making sense" of the loss could be heard as implying the child's death was somehow acceptable, an assertion bereaved parents would universally reject as ludicrous. Instead, listen for inclinations toward meaning making, as in the case of Leslie and John, and build upon them. Alternatively, help bereaved parents explore for potential meaning while keeping in mind that some may never find it.

Embracing (Unsought) Positive Outcomes

Positive outcomes following the death of a child can and do occur, depending on the perspective of the viewer. One example that surfaces with some regularity is prosocial changes by bereaved parents in how they relate to other people, including surviving children. The death of a son or daughter may serve as a wake-up call, reminding bereaved parents that life issues no guarantees. Realizing how precious life is can trigger an existential realignment of values, such as reprioritizing family relationships often taken for granted in the process of leading busy lives. Gamino et al. (2000a) described how some bereaved families resolved to stay in closer touch and check on each other more diligently after the death of a prominent family member. They began expressing love and care more freely and made sure to follow through with commitments. When bereaved parents redouble their efforts to nurture important relationships after the death of a child, it usually comes with forlorn regret that they had to sustain such a profound loss to realize what is truly important in life.

Improved interpersonal relationships signal personal growth after sustaining trauma, according to the work of Tedeschi and Calhoun (1995; Calhoun &

Tedeschi, 2006). Their model, and how it applies to resiliency among bereaved parents, is discussed in more detail in Chapter 13, "Long-Term Adaptation and Resilience." Research based in constructivist psychology found that unsought benefits identified in the aftermath of tragic loss were associated with better emotional and psychological adjustment among grievers in general (Davis et al., 1998; Gamino et al., 2000a) and for bereaved parents specifically (Keesee et al., 2008; Lichtenthal et al., 2010). Sensitive practitioners acknowledge the tragedy of a child's death while also reinforcing any unsought positive outcomes resulting from it.

Some bereaved parents may take offense at the notion that anything good came from their child's senseless death. Parents already know they are changed forever. That some beneficial changes result from their grief struggles could feel like a betrayal of their deceased child. Practitioners and sympathizers alike need to proceed carefully in discussions around unsought positive outcomes and how they affect bereaved parents.

Accessing Social Support

Finding social support that comforts can be a real asset for bereaved parents. Securing social support highlights the interactive nature of how support is offered and received. For example, isolating or turning away from available sources of social support becomes an avoidance response that negates potential help others could provide. On the other hand, when bereaved parents either reach out to trusted family and friends for help or graciously accept help when it is proffered, salutary results can happen.

Lack of social support happens for many reasons. Some bereaved parents are isolated within sparse or disengaged interpersonal networks. Other bereaved parents voice a wish not to burden others with their heavy sorrow or express a desire to spare others from the immense pain of their grief. Instead, they bear the load alone. They often do not realize others would gladly lend support and feel good about doing so. Still other bereaved parents may feel considerable shame or guilt about their child's death and do not want anyone seeing their vulnerability. Thus, they eschew support, sometimes rationalizing that "they would not understand." Sometimes potential supporters hold back because they are unsure whether broaching the subject of the child's death would be unwelcome or too painful for the grieving parents. Many sympathizers would rather say nothing than inadvertently say something insensitive. These various disconnects can create a conspiracy of silence, depriving bereaved parents of much-needed social support.

Practitioners can encourage bereaved parents to exercise emotional leadership within their interpersonal circles by taking the initiative to mention the deceased child. That step signals to others that the topic can be safely discussed.

When potential supporters recognize permission to talk about the deceased child—either explicitly, such as, "It's okay to talk about Janie," or implicitly, such as, "Janie would sure enjoy a concert [or meal, or event] like this"—they typically follow the parent's lead and respond in kind. This simple maneuver may be enough to initiate dialogue and establish a pathway for others to provide comfort and support. Exercising emotional leadership is completely at the discretion of bereaved parents. They decide *when* and *where* and *with whom* to share. No obligation exists for bereaved parents to open themselves to busybodies or emotional voyeurs.

The death of a child can also cause significant changes in the social network of bereaved parents. A common lament heard is the "changed address book" whereby some family members and friends from whom bereaved parents would have anticipated support turn out to be absent or distant. Anger over such disappointments is further isolating. Conversely, individuals not necessarily on the bereaved parents' social radar may emerge to play helpful roles in their moment of need. Remaining open to new social possibilities is highly adaptive. Normalizing these social changes for bereaved parents can be empowering. It encourages them to seek support where it may be found and not waste precious energy waiting on certain people to respond or pursuing support where it is not forthcoming.

Some bereaved parents may protest that "no one's there for me" or "I have nobody to support me." Such statements can be understood as a commentary on how the bereaved parents perceive their situation, not a definitive appraisal that ends the inquiry. In these instances, it is wise to patiently review who was there for them in the past. Often, with reflection, bereaved parents can identify individuals they have overlooked or discounted. Sometimes dormant social relationships can be revived to good effect for both parties. Also, nascent or budding relationships sometimes develop into deeper ties when bereaved parents take the risk of disclosing more about their loss. Practitioners should continue encouraging bereaved parents to seek the social support they need.

Personal Growth and Transformation

CASE 3.H

I don't like it. I can't fix it. I'll never get over it, but hopefully it won't turn me into a hateful, bitter old soul. I didn't lose the whole future because of [my other children]. I feel pretty grateful about a lot of things. Eventually, I'm gonna be okay. I'll never be the same. [I] do have suicidal thoughts sometimes, but I'm not gonna do it.

> A bereaved mother spoke these words to her grief therapist approximately five years after her young adult son was killed by a freight truck traveling at high speed. Getting to that point of reflection had not been easy.
>
> Ambiguity surrounded the son's death. He had walked away from the house in the middle of the night after a quarrel with his mother. He met some associates at an all-night restaurant and left with them. Shortly thereafter, he exited their vehicle for unknown reasons. As a shortcut, he attempted to cross an interstate highway and may have been swept into the truck's path by the force of the undertow as it sped past. The driver claimed the young man jumped in front of the truck in an apparent suicide. The bereaved mother never believed the trucker's account, insisting her prideful son was "too vain" to ever risk personal harm or detriment to his appearance. Even with the benefit of professional help, it took a long time for the bereaved mother to come to terms with her son's untimely death.

Bereaved parents frequently declare they will "never be the same" following the death of a son or daughter, a turning point from which there is no going back. Bereaved parents cannot revert to when their child was still alive; therefore, life cannot proceed on the same trajectory. The critical question is whether the altered trajectory incorporates personal growth and transformation. In Case 3.H, the mother's statement rejecting the stance of a "hateful, bitter old soul" revealed her desire to rise above the grief and remain open to living as fully as possible. Detecting growth potential and promoting transformative resilience is part of the mission for practitioners who undertake this work.

SUMMARY

Professional consultation with bereaved parents is as much about helping them grow toward a revised, post-loss version of themselves as it is about reducing symptomatic distress. This chapter catalogued helpful factors that promote adaptation, many of which were apparent with Leslie and John. Personal hardiness and intrinsic spirituality characterized Leslie's response to Ritchie's death. She stayed highly involved, accepted the inevitability of change, and maintained her faith. Leslie was there to tell her son goodbye when he died. John grappled with meaning making, reflected in his musings about life as he attempted to complete the jigsaw puzzle. The insoluble outcome to the puzzle—the missing piece—led Leslie and John to focus on positive memories of Ritchie's personality and solidify a continuing connection with their treasured son even after his death. Treatment approaches recommended throughout this book utilize bereaved parents' inherent strengths of hardiness and intrinsic spirituality and incorporate the adaptive behaviors described in this chapter.

REFERENCES

Bandura, A. (1977). Self-efficacy: Toward a unifying theory of behavioral change. *Psychological Review*, *84*(2), 191–215. https://doi.org/10.1037//0033-295x.84.2.191

Bandura, A. (1982). Self-efficacy mechanism in human agency. *American Psychologist*, *37*(2), 122–147. https://doi.org/10.1037/0003-066X.37.2.122

Bekker, L. G., Beyrer, C., Mgodi, N., Lewin, S. R., Delaney-Moretlwe, S., Talwo, B., Masters, M. C., & Lazarus, J. V. (2023). HIV infection. *Nature Reviews Disease Primers*, *9*(1), 42. https://doi.org/10.1038/s41572-023-00452-3

Benore, E. R., & Park, C. L. (2004). Death-specific religious beliefs and bereavement: Belief in an afterlife and continued attachment. *International Journal for the Psychology of Religion*, *14*(1), 1–22. https://doi.org/10.1207/s15327582ijpr1401_1

Byock, I. (2004). *The four things that matter most: A book about living*. Simon & Schuster.

Calhoun, L. G., & Tedeschi, R. G. (Eds.). (2006). *Handbook of posttraumatic growth: Research and practice*. Routledge.

Campbell, J., Swank, P., & Vincent, K. (1991). The role of hardiness in the resolution of grief. *OMEGA—Journal of Death and Dying*, *23*(1), 53–65. https://doi.org/10.2190/QVHR-5FWW-74LA-F884

Chan, C. L. W., Chow, A. Y. M., Ho, S. M. Y., Tsui, Y. K. Y., Tin, A. F., Koo, B. W. K., & Koo, E. W. K. (2005). The experience of Chinese bereaved persons: A preliminary study of meaning making and continuing bonds. *Death Studies*, *29*(10), 923–947. https://doi.org/10.1080/07481180500299287

Davis, C. G., Nolen-Hoeksema, S., & Larson, S. (1998). Making sense of loss and benefiting from the experience: Two construals of meaning. *Journal of Personality and Social Psychology*, *75*, 561–574. https://doi.org/10.1037/0022-3514.75.2.561

Davis, C. G., Wohl, M. J. A., & Verberg, N. (2007). Profiles of posttraumatic growth following an unjust loss. *Death Studies*, *31*, 693–712. https://doi/abs/10.1080/07481180701490578

Doka, K. J. (1984–1985). Expectation of death, participation in funeral arrangements, and grief adjustment. *OMEGA—Journal of Death and Dying*, *15*, 119–129. https://doi/abs/10.2190/HG24-EBR1-503H-C69V

Doorley, J. D., Goodman, F. R., Kelso, K. C., & Kashdan, T. B. (2020). Psychological flexibility: What we know, what we do not know, and what we think we know. *Social and Personality Psychology Compass*, *14*(12), 1–11. https://doi/abs/10.1111/spc3.12566

Duckworth, A. L., Peterson, C., Matthews, M. D., & Kelly, D. R. (2007). Grit: Perseverance and passion for long-term goals. *Journal of Personality and Social Psychology*, *92*(6), 1087–1101. https://doi.org/10.1037/0022-3514.92.6.1087

Duckworth, A. L., & Quinn, P. D. (2009). Development and validation of the Short Grit Scale (GRIT-S). *Journal of Personality Assessment, 91*(2), 166–174. https://doi/abs/10.1080/00223890802634290

Forrin, N. D., & MacLeod, C. M. (2018). This time it's personal: The memory benefit of hearing oneself. *Memory* (Hove, England), *26*(4), 574–579. https://doi.org/10.1080/09658211.2017.1383434

Freud, S. (1917/1957). Mourning and melancholia. In J. Strachey (Ed.), *The standard edition of the complete psychological works of Sigmund Freud, Vol. XIV (1914–1916)* (pp. 237–260). Hogarth Press and the Institute of Psycho-Analysis.

Gamino, L. A., Sewell, K. W., & Easterling, L. W. (2000a). Scott & white grief study—Phase II: Toward an adaptive model of grief. *Death Studies, 24*, 633–660. https://doi/abs/10.1080/07481180050132820

Gamino, L. A., Sewell, K. W., Easterling, L. W., & Stirman, L. (2000b). Grief adjustment as influenced by funeral participation and occurrence of adverse funeral events. *OMEGA—Journal of Death and Dying, 41*(2), 79–92. https://doi/abs/10.2190/qmv2-3nt5-bkd5-6aav

Hayes, S. C., Strosahl, K. D., & Wilson, K. G. (2011). *Acceptance and commitment therapy: The process and practice of mindful change*. Guilford.

Hoy, W. G. (2025). *Creating meaning in funerals: How families and communities make sense of death*. Routledge.

Hsu, C., O'Connor, M., & Lee, S. (2009). Understandings of death and dying for people of Chinese origin. *Death Studies, 33*(2), 153–174. https://doi.org/10.1080/07481180802440431

Kass, J., Friedman, R., Leserman, J., Zuttermeister, P. C., & Benson, H. (1991). Health outcomes and new index of spiritual experience. *Journal for the Scientific Study of Religion, 30*, 203–211. https://doi.org/10.2307/1387214

Keesee, N. J., Currier, J. M., & Neimeyer, R. A. (2008). Predictors of grief following the death of one's child: The contribution of finding meaning. *Journal of Clinical Psychology, 64*(10), 1145–1163. https://doi.org/10.1002/jclp.20502

Klass, D., Silverman, P. R., & Nickman, S. L. (Eds.). (1996). *Continuing bonds: New understandings of grief*. Taylor & Francis.

Klass, D., & Walter, T. (2001). Processes of grieving: How bonds are continued. In M. S. Stroebe, R. O. Hansson, W. Stroebe, & H. Schut (Eds.), *Handbook of bereavement research: Consequences, coping and care* (pp. 431–448). American Psychological Association.

Kobasa, S. C., Maddi, S. R., & Kahn, S. (1982). Hardiness and health: A prospective study. *Journal of Personality and Social Psychology, 42*, 158–167. https://doi.org/10.1037/0022-3514.42.1.168

Liang, H.-J., Xiong, Q., Remawi, B. N., & Preston, N. (2024). Taiwanese family members' bereavement experience following an expected death: A systematic review and narrative synthesis. *BMC Palliative Care, 23*(1), 14. https://doi.org/10.1186/s12904-024-01344-3

Lichtenthal, W. G., Currier, J. M., Neimeyer, R. A., & Keesee, N. J. (2010). Sense and significance: A mixed methods examination of meaning making after the loss of one's child. *Journal of Clinical Psychology, 66*(7), 791–812. https://doi.org/10.1002/jclp.20700

Maddi, S. R. (2006). Hardiness: The courage to grow from stresses. *The Journal of Positive Psychology, 1*(3), 160–168. https://doi.org/10.1080/17439760600619609

Mitima-Verloop, H. B., Mooren, T. T. M., & Boelen, P. A. (2019). Facilitating grief: An exploration of the function of funerals and rituals in relation to grief reactions. *Death Studies, 45*, 1–11. https://doi/full/10.1080/07481187.2019.1686090

Mund, P. (2016). Kobasa concept of hardiness. *International Journal of Engineering, IT & Scientific Research, 2*(1), 34–40.

National Cemetery Administration, & United States Department of Veterans Affairs. (2023). *Emblems of belief*. Retrieved November 12, 2024, from https://www.cem.va.gov/hmm/emblems.asp

Newberg, A., Wintering, N., & Waldman, M. (2019). Comparison of different measures of religiousness and spirituality: Implications for neurotheological research. *Religions, 10*(11), 637. https://doi.org/10.3390/rel10110637

Panigrahi, G. S., & Suar, D. (2021). Resilience among survivors in the aftermath of the 2018 Kerala flood: An avenue toward recovery. *International Journal of Disaster Risk Reduction, 64*, 102477.

Rynearson, E. K. (2018). Disabling reenactment imagery after violent dying. *Death Studies, 42*(1), 4–8. https://doi.org/10.1080/07481187.2017.1370411

Snyder, C. R., Harris, C., Anderson, J. R., Holleran, S. A., Irving, L. M., Sigmon, S. T., Yoshinobu, L., Gibb, J., Langelle, C., & Harney, P. (1991). The will and the ways: Development and validation of an individual-differences measure of hope. *Journal of Personality and Social Psychology, 60*(4), 570–585. https://doi.org/10.1037//0022-3514.60.4.570

Stroebe, M., & Schut, H. (1999). The Dual Process Model of coping with bereavement: Rationale and description. *Death Studies, 23*, 197–224. https://doi/abs/10.1080/074811899201046

Stroebe, M., & Schut, H. (2010). The dual process model of coping with bereavement: A decade on. *OMEGA—Journal of Death and Dying, 61*, 273–289. https://doi/abs/10.2190/OM.61.4.b

Tedeschi, R. G., & Calhoun, L. G. (1995). *Trauma and transformation*. Sage.

Vaillant, G. E. (1993). *The wisdom of the ego*. Harvard University Press.

Walter, T. (1999). *On bereavement: The culture of grief*. Open University Press.

CHAPTER FOUR

Contemporary Treatment Approaches

> If I can stop one heart from breaking, I shall not live in vain.
> —Emily Dickinson [1995] (1830–1886)

CASE 4.A

When Vickie answered the late-night phone call, she heard her son's girlfriend shouting frantically, "Bubba's been shot!" Rushing to the scene, Vickie could not get clear information about Bubba's condition from law enforcement personnel. Only by reaching out to a family friend in the local sheriff's office did Vickie confirm that her son, Bubba, was "a fatality." A bystander guided Vickie to a visual angle of the crime scene from which she could see her son on the ground, face down, wearing a distinctive jacket. An ambulance arrived, and they waited until Bubba's body had been taken before leaving. Later her husband (Bubba's stepfather) went to the hospital to identify Bubba's body while Vickie elected to stay home. She recalled being numb and disbelieving—frozen in her recliner, clutching a photo of her son.

Vickie saw a reputable local therapist biweekly for about a year regarding her grief. That supportive care bolstered her during the subsequent trials and convictions of the two assailants. However, about three years after Bubba's murder, Vickie became so despondent that she was hospitalized for depression. She began antidepressant medicine and was referred for specialized grief therapy. Vickie spent most of her day

> sitting in her recliner, curtains closed, replaying in her mind the events of her son's murder. She described, "I'm still waiting for him to walk through the front door, but I know he's not." Vickie asked pleadingly, "What can I do to make it better?"
>
> Vickie dreaded every holiday without Bubba. When his birthday or the anniversary of his death occurred, she felt paralyzed with sadness and grief. Whenever the parole board contacted her about the assailants, Vickie relived the trauma. She did not feel safe in her own community and wanted to relocate, but her husband's family lived nearby and he was unwilling to move. The only thing that brought Vickie joy was visiting her daughter's home and interacting with her young grandson. Otherwise, she just existed in a state of aimless, unrelenting melancholy.

Evidence-based grief treatment models as well as contemporary theoretical models have much to offer practitioners working with bereaved parents. In this chapter, several prominent models are explained and their key treatment maneuvers highlighted.

EVIDENCE-BASED GRIEF TREATMENT MODELS

Shear's Prolonged Grief Treatment

Shear's Prolonged Grief Treatment (PGT; Shear et al., 2005) launched from a landmark randomized controlled trial demonstrating its efficacy over Interpersonal Psychotherapy (IPT; Klerman et al., 2004) when treating individuals with complicated grief. These findings were replicated with a sample of elderly adults (Shear et al., 2014). She initially published an instruction manual entitled *Complicated Grief Treatment* (Shear, 2015) explaining the rationale for her model and detailing how to conduct the 16-session treatment sequence. When the *DSM-5-TR* (American Psychiatric Association, 2022) included Prolonged Grief Disorder as a diagnostic entity, Shear renamed her protocol Prolonged Grief Treatment.

PGT prioritizes helping the bereaved individual accept the reality of the loss and the necessity for a changed relationship with the deceased person. At the same time, PGT promotes regaining the ability to function and finding a sense of purpose in life. For Shear, the treatment goal is reaching a state of integrated grief when the bereaved individual adapts to the changes necessitated by the loss and recaptures the capacity to thrive. In addressing dimensions of both loss and restoration, PGT borrows significantly from the Dual Process Model (Stroebe & Schut, 1999, 2010), which characterized the everyday experience of bereavement as one of oscillating between the grief work of mourning and the challenge of going on with life. In addition, Shear's model is heavily influenced by trauma treatment methods featuring prolonged exposure (cf. Foa et al., 2019). Although PGT was not developed specifically for work with bereaved parents, it has much to offer practitioners who do.

PGT begins with psychoeducation about the nature of grief and teaches self-calming techniques (sessions 1–2). A key support person is invited to a session to ensure that the patient has needed interpersonal support throughout the treatment protocol (session 3). Repeated exposure to the death scenario is conducted through a procedure called imaginal revisiting (sessions 4–9). With eyes closed to enhance neural imaging, the patient visualizes and recounts first learning of the death while employing self-calming measures. The narration is recorded, and the patient listens to it several times at home between sessions. The therapist helps the patient process the experience and address emotional hot spots, that is, aspects of the recounting that trigger intense distress. Imaginal revisiting is designed to progressively reduce the emotional distress induced by problematic recollections and help the patient rethink the loss to gain new perspective. One question Shear poses is, "Death is but one event in a lifetime of events, so how does the death fit into the bigger picture of the deceased's life?" The therapist must be adroit in managing such reprocessing work with bereaved parents when their child may have lived only a short time.

PGT features several other components. Places, people, or activities associated with the deceased person that have been avoided are gradually reintroduced through situational revisiting (sessions 5–15). At the same time, emphasis is placed on learning how to enjoy life again, building social connections with others, and setting aspirational goals for the future (sessions 5–15). Holding an imaginal conversation with the deceased person (sessions 11–12) and systematically reviewing both positive and negative memories (sessions 6–15) help foster a continuing connection. As the protocol progresses, the patient is guided toward developing an acceptable story of the death and learning to live with inevitable reminders (sessions 11–15). Reviewing progress, consolidating strengths, and finalizing termination conclude the protocol (session 16).

CASE 4.A (Continued)

Because Vickie seemed stuck in her grief and preoccupied with ruminations about Bubba's death, the therapist adopted key elements of PGT during treatment. Some convincing was required before Vickie agreed to undertake the protocol, mainly due to reluctance about engaging traumatic memories. She had some trouble learning self-regulation methods such as diaphragmatic breathing. Her husband was included intermittently both to apprise him of what Vickie was doing in treatment and to enlist his support for her enjoying life again, such as traveling together or eating at a favorite barbecue restaurant. Vickie completed four sessions of the imaginal revisiting procedure and partially followed through on listening to the recordings at home. As she progressed through the imaginal revisiting, her subjective distress about those events steadily declined and she felt less trapped by rumination.

The most resistance to the program occurred with situational revisiting. Vickie remained hesitant about returning to avoided places that had once been part of her life. She reclaimed some pleasurable activities such as cooking favorite foods, spending time with siblings, and taking short trips. When a cousin's son died tragically in a murder-suicide, Vickie declined to attend the funeral, fearing it would be too painful. However, she later met privately with her cousin to offer support. Also, Vickie agreed to speak at a hearing for one of Bubba's assailants and felt vindicated when his parole was denied. By the six-year anniversary of Bubba's death, Vickie's choices reflected the program's twin goals of accepting the loss and learning to live again—she placed flowers at the site of the murder and then cooked Bubba's favorite meal of beef tips and rice for the family.

Program objectives of enjoying life again and connecting with others were evident through real events in Vickie's life. She and her husband moved to a smaller residence, prompting her to give away the recliner in which she had been trapped for so long. Vickie ventured out to a grandson's basketball game, which was forfeited when a fight broke out between the teams. While there, Vickie encountered another woman wailing about the violence as reminiscent of how her own son had died. Vickie started to walk past the grieving mother, then returned to comfort her, saying, "I know how that feels, I lost a son too." Later, a family friend contacted Vickie when a relative's son was murdered and asked her to speak to that bereaved mother. Vickie initially responded, "I just cannot do it." With encouragement from the therapist, she reconsidered and reached out to the newly bereaved mother.

By the time Vickie's therapy ended almost seven years after Bubba's murder, most of the major components of PGT had been incorporated. She credited the imaginal revisiting with substantive changes. She felt considerably stronger and freer to live life. Vickie endorsed the viewpoint of many bereaved parents in concluding that Bubba's death was resolved as much as it would be. Even though her life was permanently different without him, Vickie regained the ability to experience joy with her friends and family—especially her grandchildren—and feel gratitude in many ways. She reflected, "I am truly blessed." A sense of mastery returned to her outlook on life: "I take my time, one day at a time."

Lichtenthal's Meaning-Centered Grief Therapy

Lichtenthal's Meaning-Centered Grief Therapy (MCGT) has the advantage of being developed specifically to help parents grieving the death of a child to cancer (Lichtenthal & Breitbart, 2015; Lichtenthal et al., 2019; Lichtenthal et al., 2017). Inspired by the existential work of Viktor Frankl (1959) and based on meaning-centered psychotherapy for cancer patients (Breitbart & Poppito, 2014a, 2014b), MCGT emphasizes a bereaved parent's ability to choose their own attitude toward suffering in the aftermath of losing a child. A meaning-rich framework for contextualizing the loss can make all the difference in how bereaved parents cope. Enhanced meaning following the tragedy of child loss can be realized in several ways: making sense of the child's life and death, examining the legacy one was given, realizing (unsought) benefits such as personal growth accrued along the way, reconciling one's sense of identity, or finding new purpose in living. These various meaning sources overlap, creating multiple entry points where practitioners may access the attributional world of bereaved parents and promote healthy changes.

MCGT is intended to help bereaved parents learn to coexist with their grief and tolerate their pain. Lichtenthal's approach capitalizes on any emerging discussion of the child's specialness, or unique ways that the son or daughter touched the world, to assuage the sadness of losing that child. To uncover important meaning-related content, Lichtenthal's program employs higher-order philosophical concepts based on Friedrich Nietzsche's teaching that someone who has a "why" to live can find a "how" to survive. Her protocol requires participants to write several reflections in response to various prompts. As a result, MCGT can be slightly more cerebral than other approaches. Just as journaling is not for everyone, the program's focus on writing tasks may not appeal to all bereaved parents. Practitioners should bear in mind these considerations when planning a treatment approach for a particular bereaved parent.

Lichtenthal's 16-session program starts with the bereaved parent relating the child's cancer story, receiving psychoeducation about grief, and learning mindfulness (sessions 1–2). Next, the child's legacy is explored for its impact on the bereaved parent and the world at large—first through a guided two-way conversation exercise in which the parent communicates with the deceased child (session 3), followed by writing a letter to the child and writing the child's imagined response (session 4). In sessions 5–8, bereaved parents embark on reflective writing exercises about personal identity and sources of meaning *before* the child became ill, *during* the child's illness, *after* the child's death, and in the *future* as envisioned by their aspirations. Lichtenthal compares sources of meaning to "lighthouses in the distance," beacons that provide direction to bereaved parents. Focusing on those beacons of hope helps bereaved parents navigate the storms of grief and transcend suffering.

MCGT continues with inclusion of a key support person for a facilitated exchange (session 9). In sessions 10–12, the bereaved parent is challenged to discover personal meaning through their attitude, creativity, and life experiences. Bereaved parents are further urged to revise their story of child loss, directly address "stuck points" carrying residual negative emotions, and extend compassion toward self just as a friend might do (session 13). Creating significance through a living legacy project—photo album, video, music compilation, involvement in a cause important to the child, choosing a new activity—helps move the bereaved parent on a forward path (sessions 14–15). MCGT concludes with an emphasis on hope and gratitude (session 16).

Initial empirical support for MCGT came from a small, open trial study (without a control group) showing robust decreases in grief-related distress together with substantial increases in positive psychological functioning, findings still observed up to three months following treatment (Lichtenthal et al., 2019). Even though developed for parents whose children died from cancer, MCGT's methods promise wide applicability with bereaved parents whose children die from other causes.

Rynearson's Restorative Retelling

Restorative Retelling (RR; Rynearson et al., 2015) is a group-based, 11-session treatment model designed specifically for grievers whose loved ones died violently, such as in homicides, suicides, and motor vehicle crashes. It is patterned on the recovery process experienced by the first author following the suicide death of his wife. Rynearson argued that violent deaths generate not only separation distress from losing the deceased but also trauma distress because of *how* the loved one died (see Chapter 2, "What Makes Parental Grief So Difficult?"). Both aspects of the loss experience must be addressed in treatment. RR targets obsessive "reenactment imagery" about the death scenario itself, which frequently haunts survivors of violent deaths (Rynearson, 2018).

The constant ruminations about Bubba's death reported by Vickie are a prime example of such reenactment imagery and show its possessive force.

RR promotes psychological resilience of the griever by instilling three capacities: self-soothing (*pacification*), maintaining detachment from the trauma (*partition*), and reclaiming a story of the deceased's life that supersedes the traumatic dying (*perspective*). Similar to Shear's PGT, RR incorporates direct imaginal exposure to the death imagery. However, the exposure unfolds in a carefully choreographed sequence, enabling participants to confront their reenactment imagery and reprocess events in a therapeutic way. Results from an open trial of RR (without a control group) suggested this treatment modality was effective in reducing distress among survivors of violent loss (Rheingold et al., 2015). Practitioners interested in this model can readily access the RR treatment manual online (Rynearson et al., 2015).

Initially (sessions 1–4), RR includes psychoeducation on trauma as well as practicing relaxation methods for self-calming (pacification). Group members in turn share their loss experience, which helps develop mutual understanding and build group cohesion. Next (sessions 5–6), they intentionally celebrate the lives and significance of their deceased loved ones through sharing "reunion" stories, photos, and memorabilia. Reconnecting with positive pre-death memories builds a firm foundation before attempting detachment from the trauma imagery (partition).

At the heart of RR (sessions 7–8), participants produce a drawing of their reenactment scene, intended to replicate how the brain visually stores trauma material. Alternately, participants may choose to verbally describe their reenactment as if narrating what they see on an imaginary movie screen or write an account. They may also use news media or police reports to convey the imagery. Their portrayal is then reprocessed to facilitate the griever's ability to separate from the actual events (partition) rather than emotionally fusing with them. Deconstructing and revising the death imagery—including fantasized elements of rescue, retaliation, caregiving, and relinquishment—involve altering attributions and assigning new meaning to what happened (perspective). Facilitators provide ample support and crucial expertise during the exposure exercise. They elicit how participants might have provided care to their loved one if they had the chance and suggest the deceased person would want to release them from entrapment in the scene. RR concludes with a family member or friend attending a meeting to ensure support (session 9) and helping participants reconnect to joy and meaning as they terminate treatment (session 10). A group reunion is held one month later to reflect on the treatment's impact (session 11). Readers can see how RR offers yet another option for helping bereaved parents change reenactment imagery and revise their death narrative.

Boelen's Cognitive Behavioral Therapy for Grief

Paul Boelen and colleagues in the Netherlands brought the theory and tools of Cognitive Behavioral Therapy (CBT) to bear on the problem of complicated grief. Boelen's Cognitive Behavioral Therapy for Grief includes cognitive restructuring, exposure techniques, and behavioral activation. CBT proved to be superior to supportive counseling in reducing symptoms of complicated grief and general psychiatric distress (Boelen et al., 2007). Of the three components, exposure techniques appeared to be the most impactful treatment intervention (cf. Boelen et al., 2006, 2011; Eisma et al., 2015).

Understanding how Boelen operationalizes exposure as a therapeutic intervention can enable practitioners to adapt this element in their own work with bereaved parents. After explaining the rationale that confrontation with painful aspects of the loss can facilitate bereavement adjustment, grievers are asked to list situations, places, people, objects, or memories related to the loss they tend to avoid in daily life (e.g., never entering the deceased's room, not associating with the deceased's friends, staying away from photos or reminders of the deceased). In addition, grievers are asked to list any behaviors in which they regularly engage to maintain a bond with the deceased (e.g., visiting the gravesite, sorting clothes or possessions of the deceased, thinking about the deceased person).

In a gradual and systematic manner, grievers are then directed to purposely expose themselves to those very aspects of the loss they tend to avoid. For example, in Vickie's case, she would be encouraged to attend sporting events that remind her of Bubba, such as the basketball game, or even go grocery shopping (which she avoided for fear of encountering someone she knew who might want to talk about Bubba). Alternately, grievers are also instructed to intentionally reduce or restrain behaviors that keep them riveted on the loss, sometimes called response prevention. Again, in Vickie's case, she would be encouraged to deliberately spend time each day away from her recliner where she perched and ruminated. Or, when her thoughts spontaneously reverted to the night of Bubba's murder, she would be encouraged to divert her attention to some other compelling activity so as not to dwell on the horror. These dual strategies of exposure and response prevention were condensed neatly in a dictum offered by hospital chaplain Judy Hoelscher, "Sometimes you 'lean in' to the pain; sometimes you 'lean out' of the pain" (personal communication, 2022).

CBT's cognitive restructuring involves actively challenging negative attributions about life ("Everything is meaningless since [child's name] died"), irrational diminution of self ("I am nothing if I'm not a parent anymore"), or catastrophic misinterpretations of grief reactions ("If I told you what I really thought, you'd lock me up as crazy"). Practitioners familiar with CBT will easily identify such faulty cognitions and quickly move to dispute and reformulate them: "Some parts of your life are still worth living." "You may not be able to parent [child's name] anymore, but parenting your other children can still bring joy." "We may have lots of extreme thoughts we would never act on; knowing the difference is the key to good adjustment."

CBT is not unique in promoting behavioral activation, which is part of many psychotherapy models, including Shear's PGT. Behavioral activation is consistent with the restoration-related domain of the Dual Process Model (Stroebe & Schut, 1999, 2010) and can be applied in a variety of ways with bereaved parents. For example, branching out from confining or unhealthy routines and moving beyond passive inactivity can promote a positive mood and enhance a sense of well-being. The goal is increasing the number of meaningful and fulfilling activities the bereaved person undertakes, based on their own values and interests.

CASE 4.A (Continued)

During Vickie's treatment, when the therapist brought up doing something besides languishing in her recliner, her immediate response was, "How?" Because it was a temperate spring day, the therapist suggested taking a short walk together outside the building for some fresh air and sunshine while they talked. That simple activity helped Vickie see how behavioral activation could start small yet generate new outcomes. She remarked afterward, "That felt good."

Chochinov's Dignity Therapy

Dignity Therapy (DT), designed by Harvey Chochinov, was intended to help medical patients with end-stage disease reduce psychosocial suffering and improve their quality of life (Chochinov et al., 2005). In a randomized controlled trial across sites in Australia, Canada, and the United States, DT was shown to achieve better outcomes when compared with either standard palliative care or client-centered therapy when all treatment conditions allocated the same amount of personal attention from an empathic listener. Study participants receiving DT showed favorable advantages on factors such as sense of personal dignity, spiritual well-being, communicating important life reflections and perspectives to their families, and realizing meaning and legacy at the end of life (Chochinov et al., 2011).

DT consists of a guided interview based on standardized questions about the most important aspects of a person's history—when they felt most alive, their greatest accomplishments, hopes and dreams for their loved ones, what they have learned worth passing on to others, and how they want to be remembered (Chochinov, 2012). Patient interviews are recorded, then transcribed, edited, and read back to patients for confirmation or modification. Patients are encouraged to give their life stories a thematic title. The revised transcript is presented to the patient and their family as a legacy document. Throughout the process, great emphasis is placed on *care tenor*, a compassionate attitudinal stance adopted by the caregiver that conveys honor, respect, and esteem.

Although developed for work with dying patients, Chochinov's (2012) protocol offers practitioners some additional tools when working with parents grieving the death of a son or daughter. His list of questions guiding the DT interview can be transposed for a deceased child, giving practitioners guidelines for talking to bereaved parents about their deceased child's legacy. Consider the following examples of transposed DT questions: "Are there particular things you would want others to know about [child's name], or particular things for which you want [child's name] to be remembered?" "What were [child's name] most important accomplishments?" "What do you feel most proud of when it comes to [child's name]?" "Are there particular things that need to be said to [child's name] or things you want to say again?" Practitioners will find it useful to study the entire list of DT questions to augment and refine their repertoire of inquiry during clinical encounters with bereaved parents.

Summary of Evidence-Based Models

Professionals working with bereaved parents often face clinical realities that make it impractical to implement grief treatment protocols in a strictly manualized manner. Most practitioners routinely customize care to meet the unique needs of the bereaved parents they serve, in a sequence and timeframe adjusted for each family and the circumstances of their loss. Understanding the key therapeutic elements embedded in these models enables practitioners to borrow from various approaches when tailoring a treatment plan for a particular grieving parent. Because several commonalities exist among the evidence-based models described here—particularly the Shear, Lichtenthal, and Rynearson protocols—delineating those key elements helps identify the most important takeaways for clinical practice. Table 4.1 contains a list of ten elements, each of which appears in one or more of the evidence-based models described in the previous section.

Many of these elements can be seamlessly woven into the ongoing therapeutic work with bereaved parents, even when working within a general treatment model such as Acceptance and Commitment Therapy (ACT), Dialectical Behavior Therapy (DBT), trauma therapy, or psychodynamic psychotherapy. In subsequent chapters, numerous examples illustrate how these key elements from evidence-based grief treatment models can be usefully applied.

TABLE 4.1 Ten Key Therapeutic Elements Drawn from Evidence-Based Models of Grief Therapy (Adapted for work with bereaved parents)

1. **Educating** about the nature of parental grief and trauma
2. **Teaching distress-reduction** methods (e.g., diaphragmatic breathing, mindfulness, and imagery)
3. **Utilizing a key support person** to ensure interpersonal support
4. **Revisiting the death scenario** to reduce its emotional hold or reconstruct its meaning, or both
5. **Developing a narrative** of the child's death, and life, that has personal meaning and significance for the bereaved parent
6. **Finding ways to honor and remember** the deceased child, affirming their legacy
7. **Communicating symbolically** with the deceased child to enhance continuing bonds or resolve unfinished business (e.g., saying goodbye, expressing remorse, extending forgiveness), or both
8. **Reversing avoidance** of activities, places, or people associated with the deceased child
9. **Reclaiming a sense of self-worth and identity** despite the child's death
10. **Envisioning hope** for the future and enjoying life again

However, as important as these ten elements may be, they are not just ingredients in a cookbook recipe for treatment. Psychotherapy is not a lockstep endeavor. It requires tactful skill in managing not only the *presenting problems* but also the *people* experiencing those problems. All health-care professionals have an ethical obligation to conduct treatment in a manner responsive to and respectful of the individuals involved (Gamino & Ritter, 2009). With bereaved parents, that means accounting for the risk factors outlined in Chapter 2, "What Makes Parental Grief So Difficult?," as well as parent assets outlined in Chapter 3, "Helpful Factors." It means adjusting the pace and flow of treatment to account for individual differences while still maintaining fidelity to a treatment plan and proven therapeutic principles. It means being flexible in the face of unexpected developments and finding ways to adapt protocols to achieve the best therapeutic outcomes. Never a cookie-cutter process, working with bereaved parents demands clinical acumen and creative expertise.

For example, consider the element of including an important support person during the treatment sequence. Shear (2015) does so early, wanting to ensure support for the patient before imaginal revisiting begins. Lichtenthal and colleagues (Lichtenthal & Breitbart, 2015; Lichtenthal et al., 2019; Lichtenthal et al., 2017) include the support person midway through the treatment, once bereaved parents have wrestled with difficult questions of identity and can relate their progress. Rynearson et al. (2015) involve the support person late in the sequence, as a pretermination step to help the patient bridge back to regular life. The practitioner's choice of when, or whether, to include a support person in the treatment of a bereaved parent may hinge on many factors such as the parent's willingness, the support person's availability, the presence of family conflict, or the parent's sense of emotional immobility. Keeping in mind how valuable such visits can be, practitioners should schedule them when most beneficial to the therapy work. Also, sensible practitioners take advantage of such opportunities when they present themselves spontaneously, such as suggesting the participation of a family member or close friend who drove the bereaved parent to the appointment that day (contingent on the strategic importance of that person and the parent's consent, of course).

All treatment approaches assume that practitioners can establish a welcoming, reassuring, nonjudgmental atmosphere, embodying the all-important care tenor described by Chochinov (2012). Care tenor is a priority because many bereaved parents engage in punitive self-judgment and relentless second-guessing, or they perceive society has judged them faulty or defective as parents. Practitioners create a safe harbor where bereaved parents can unburden themselves without fear of recrimination or blame, where they can lower their defenses to convey doubts, fears, or misgivings. Bereaved parents need a therapeutic space where they can speak frankly about what happened to their deceased son or daughter and explore their own roles and responses, relying on the guidance of an objective, empathic professional.

Research has shown overwhelmingly that the therapeutic relationship between patient and practitioner is a cornerstone of any form of psychotherapy (Norcross & Wampold, 2011). Norcross and VandenBos (2018) emphasized that mental health practitioners are not merely technicians who perform psychological repairs consisting of discrete steps, regardless of complexity. Rather, the *person* of the therapist is an essential ingredient in the enterprise and arguably the most important element in the room. Most practitioners choosing to work with bereaved parents already possess the warmth and empathy needed for the task. Learning contemporary treatment models is necessary as well. Yet every treatment model depends on a human practitioner to carry it out. The adage "They don't care what you know until they know that you care" speaks to the patient's need to experience the caring presence of a practitioner fully engaged in the therapeutic dialogue. No matter what school of psychotherapy is the biggest influence or which evidence-based grief treatment model is preferred, the ability of the practitioner to form a working alliance with the bereaved parent supersedes any specific technique or intervention.

Cultural Limitations

Cautions concerning cultural relevance arise from a critique of the five evidence-based treatment models explained previously. Quite simply, there is a striking lack of cultural diversity among the study samples. The individuals who participated in the various randomized controlled trials and open trials that authenticated these models were overwhelming female (except Chochinov's study), White, middle-aged, and highly educated compared to the general populations in the countries where the research occurred. Furthermore, bereaved parents were a clear minority in the study samples, except in Lichtenthal's small study where all participants had lost a child. Time since death varied widely but averages ranged from two to three years since death. One can infer from these data that males, people of color, individuals of lower socioeconomic standing, those with less formal education, and grievers whose loss may have occurred several years prior were clearly underrepresented. As Tedeschi and Calhoun (2004) so wisely observed, "Clinicians do not work with averages, they work with individual people, couples, and families" (p. 25).

In some ways, these biases are not surprising. From the earliest systematic studies of bereaved persons (cf. Parkes & Weiss, 1983), research samples have disproportionately included White widows from developed countries. This bias has not gone unnoticed, and critics have called for more diversity in bereavement-related investigations (Stroebe et al., 2008). However, disadvantaged and marginalized groups can be difficult to identify and recruit into bereavement research.

Several reasons likely influence why non-Whites and socioeconomically disadvantaged persons do not typically enter grief research cohorts. Often research studies advertise for participants online, in newspapers, or through publicity outlets associated with universities and medical centers. Such efforts may not reach people of color or individuals from lower socioeconomic strata. Also, inherent distrust of medical research may exist in some non-White communities so that only an Indigenous spokesperson may be able to effectively recruit. Economically disadvantaged people generally have less access to computers or may have less facility with completing the forms or handling the paperwork required in any psychosocial research. Regarding gender, males may be less inclined than females to enroll in studies focused on their thoughts and feelings about loss. My own bereavement investigations necessitated special efforts to diversify research samples beyond White female participants (Gamino et al., 1998, 2000, 2010).

In the final analysis, practitioners should be aware that the cohorts on which evidence-based grief treatment models were developed may vary in gender, ethnicity, education level, and socioeconomic standing from the demographics of the bereaved parents whom they serve. When such disparities exist, flexibility in applying these models is needed. Many of the ten key therapeutic elements may still be applicable and useful. But if bereaved parents express hesitation or doubt, their viewpoints should be respected, and practitioners should employ their best judgment on how to proceed, always taking care to maintain trust and operate with a spirit of constructive collaboration.

CONTEMPORARY THEORETICAL MODELS

Kosminsky and Jordan's Attachment-Informed Grief Therapy

Phyllis Kosminsky and John "Jack" Jordan's (2024) Attachment-Informed Grief Therapy drew on decades of attachment research as well as advances in neuroscience to generate their theoretical model for grief therapy. Bereavement among adults is understood as having direct parallels to distressed children deprived of their principal caregiver or attachment figure. Observed differences in response are thought to be a function of attachment style—secure versus insecure. Knowing the patient's attachment style can be enormously helpful when addressing problems with grief. Adults with a secure attachment style predominantly feel sadness when someone close to them dies, but they weather the loss naturally and find ways to go on living.

In contrast, adults with insecure attachment styles are more likely to struggle with bereavement. For example, anxiously attached individuals may demonstrate extended hyperarousal responses such as yearning, pining, preoccupation with the deceased, or prolonged grief. Their treatment often prioritizes self-regulation of emotion. They must learn to tolerate distress while developing a new personal narrative about the loss. Avoidantly attached individuals may show persistent deactivating responses—diminished overt grief, suppression of reminders, limited emotional awareness, compartmentalizing, and delayed or absent grief. Their treatment intentionally reverses avoidance of grief triggers, in a graduated fashion, to accommodate remembering and develop a more integrated form of emotional mastery.

Individuals with disorganized or mixed attachment styles may express contradictory and confusing response patterns. They may become easily overwhelmed and flooded with emotion that severely undermines their executive processes. Or they may shut down altogether as a hard stop against further emotional pain. Their vacillation and unpredictability require practitioners to negotiate various approach and avoidance behaviors while patiently assisting these individuals to steady themselves during the aftermath of loss.

Kosminsky and Jordan (2024) proposed that bereaved parents operate according to a crucial behavioral system called the *caregiving system*. Parents' caregiving behaviors are biologically rooted in an evolutionary need to protect their offspring and ensure their survival. Such caregiving generates an intense affective bond between parent and child. Essentially, the parents' caregiving system is the reciprocal of the child's attachment behaviors. In times of distress or difficulty, parents serve as a secure base and safe haven for their children. The parent's caregiving system calls for proximity seeking with a distressed child with the goal of protecting a dependent child rather than preserving oneself. This caregiving system is the basis of much satisfaction and provides a sense of purpose for parents.

Recognizing the presence and operation of this caregiving system enables practitioners to better understand the grief of bereaved parents. The parent specific factors discussed in Chapter 2, "What Makes Parental Grief So Difficult?" (e.g., off-time death, empty track, loss of legacy, and loss of self), arise from frustration when the parental caregiving system is disrupted by a child's death. Much of the pain experienced by bereaved parents comes from a subjective sense of failure to protect the deceased child and keep that child safe from harm. Even when such feelings do not seem entirely rational—as in cases of manslaughter, murder, and even suicide—many bereaved parents continue to second-guess themselves for failing to adequately guard their child's life. Klass and Marwit (1989) refer to these feelings of abject failure as a loss of parental competence. Correspondingly, several interventions described in the following chapters are intended to help restore a sense of parental competence by providing alternate outlets for bereaved parents to express their caregiver strivings.

Finally, Kosminsky and Jordan's (2024) Attachment-Informed Grief Therapy helps explain the extended trajectory of parental grief. Even with the cognitive realization that their child is dead, bereaved parents' caregiving system may activate, and remain activated for a considerable period after the child's death, reflecting their protector role and their strong attachment to the child as the recipient of caregiving efforts. Understanding this dynamic clarifies why bereaved parents' grief may persist much longer than expected timelines following other losses, such as death of a parent or spouse.

Jordan and McIntosh's Suicide Bereavement Model

Suicide bereavement has similarities to and differences from other types of bereavement (Jordan & McIntosh, 2011; Jordan, 2020). While details about the specific psychological dynamics affecting parents whose children die by suicide are addressed in Chapter 9, "Suicide," some of the principles gleaned from working with suicide survivors bear mention here as part of a more omnibus approach to helping bereaved parents.

Jordan (2011) promoted the idea that grief counseling relies on practitioners using both head and heart when working with suicide survivors. Imparting knowledge about grief and trauma, teaching distress reduction, and using techniques such as imaginal revisiting from evidence-based protocols constitute symptom-focused interventions characteristic of what health-care clinicians do. At the same time, the heart (and soul) of grief counseling employs a concentrated form of empathically accurate and skillfully applied social support that is less characteristic of medical treatment. Jordan observed, "Grief counseling from this point of view is primarily person focused, rather than symptom focused, and intervention is primarily relationally focused rather than technique focused" (p. 188). Effective work with grieving individuals, where loss of a relationship is the presenting problem, requires practitioners to do both things interchangeably and fluidly, especially with bereaved parents such as Vickie. In her case, specific interventions of imaginal revisiting and situational revisiting were conducted from the stance of a clinical expert and seamlessly combined with ample empathic support and relational presence from the stance of an engaged, compassionate helper.

Another useful concept championed by Jordan (2011) is *dosing*. Dosing refers to the bereaved person actively managing their exposure to grief triggers or trauma imagery only at the level they can handle at a given moment, consistent with protocols used in trauma treatments such as Cognitive Processing Therapy (CPT; Resnick et al., 2010). Over time and with treatment, grievers can develop tolerance for greater levels of emotional intensity and learn how to hold competing emotions simultaneously, for example, sadness over the absent loved one as well as joy with important others still living. Part of Shear's (2015) situational revisiting and Boelen et al.'s (2011) exposure methods is structuring a plan to revisit avoided places, activities, or people according to a hierarchy where targets inciting lower levels of emotional distress are approached first. The griever gradually works up to targets stirring more intense distress. For example, Vickie declined attending the funeral of her cousin's son killed in a murder-suicide because she deemed that situation too emotionally charged for her. Instead, she met privately with her cousin to offer support and condolences, a less intense encounter she felt prepared to handle based on the progress made to that point in her own recovery. Learning how to dose one's exposure is a valuable coping skill for bereaved parents.

Jordan (2011) found that contact with other suicide survivors was an important part of the healing process for many individuals after losing a loved one to suicide. While the idea of peer support for bereaved parents is not new, its importance as a healing agent or as an adjunct to professional intervention cannot be emphasized enough (see Chapter 3, "Helpful Factors"). Supportive contact with others living the same saga of child loss—who have "been there" in that tragic space—can afford a kind of encouragement and inspiration like no other. Bereaved parents and survivors of violent deaths (e.g., accidents, suicide, or homicide) often feel out of place in general grief support groups populated by a preponderance of widowed people. Inevitable social comparisons in these groups, whether overt or implicit, can leave bereaved parents feeling like outsiders even among other grievers. Support groups specific to the cause of death are often the most helpful.

Tedeschi and Calhoun's Expert Companionship Model

Tedeschi and Calhoun (2004) advocated for a therapeutic approach they call *expert companionship*. Their heuristic model was based on extensive clinical experience working with bereaved fathers and mothers, thus lending it a from-the-trenches authenticity and a pragmatism grounded in what has proven helpful. Using an exile metaphor, Tedeschi and Calhoun described bereaved parents as unfortunate individuals banished against their will to a foreign land of loss. They think of the practitioner not as someone who knows firsthand that forlorn "country" but rather as someone who journeys alongside bereaved parents as a companion, lending knowledge and perspective when applicable, while the parents slowly explore the unwanted terrain and learn how to adapt.

The notion of expert companionship embodies several important corollaries (Tedeschi & Calhoun, 2004). First, expert companions *stick with it*, even if that means working with bereaved parents over the long haul, perhaps much longer than practitioners using time-limited models are accustomed to doing. Many bereaved parents feel they have worn out their welcome with friends or family who are weary from the lingering nature of their grief. Practitioners stay the course for as long as necessary.

Second, expert companions consider every life or death to be different, so it is imperative to *get to know the deceased child* through the parent's eyes to truly appreciate and fathom what they have lost. An excellent option is asking bereaved parents to bring in photographs of their deceased child, preferably from a range of ages (cf. Gamino, 2012). Much can be learned from viewing the child's expressions and postures, as well as from stories that emerge spontaneously during the parents' commentary. The deceased child's artwork, journals, or other memorabilia can be revealing as well.

Third, expert companions *practice cultural attunement*. They strive to understand how cultural influences and socialization impact bereaved parents, always taking care to consider unique dimensions rather than making assumptions based on group membership. They pay attention to the language bereaved parents use when speaking about their deceased child and echo their terminology when appropriate. They consider how family traditions, cultural practices, religious beliefs, or spiritual thinking may determine a parent's sensibilities regarding the afterlife, continuing bonds, or the role of God or deities. They avoid imposing a worldview on bereaved parents but rather work respectfully within the parent's cultural frame.

Fourth, expert companions *rely on bereaved parents as the real experts in their own experiences*, much the way qualitative researchers approach the subjects of their inquiry. Therefore, when introducing ideas or suggestions, Tedeschi and Calhoun (2004) frequently use the following format: "Some [Many] bereaved parents have told me [thus and so]. . . . Has that been the case for you?" (p. 51). In posing the interrogative this way, credibility comes from conveying what has been learned from other bereaved parents. Even if the practitioner happens to be a bereaved parent also, assumptions are never made regarding the other parent's experience.

The art of gently *steering the therapy conversation from the passenger seat* is well illustrated by how Tedeschi and Calhoun (2004) handle the phenomenon of counterfactual thinking. Counterfactuals are thought constructs or ruminations about what might have been done differently or potential actions that could have been taken so that the child did not die (cf. Neimeyer et al., 2021). For example, one bereaved mother speculated that her adult son would still be alive if she had not canceled the family dinner scheduled that evening due to her migraine headache. Had the family gone out as planned, she reasoned, her son would not have attended the party where he was shot and killed during an argument about drugs (see Chapter 10, "Homicide," for more details about this case).

Tedeschi and Calhoun do not directly dispute counterfactual thinking but instead caution parents about the biases of hindsight, that is, judging events based on what they know now rather than what they knew at the time. Instead, they ask parents to return to the scenario as it unfolded, play out their imagined responses in the present tense, and consider the likely results as realistically as possible. Often bereaved parents will conclude that the imagined action may not have precluded the child's death, as they would like to believe. The bereaved mother whose son was murdered at the party was finally able to acknowledge, given her son's headstrong nature, that he most probably would have repelled any efforts by her to keep him from leaving the house that evening with questionable friends. The practitioner's role is not to dissuade bereaved parents from their counterfactual thinking but rather to patiently assist them in processing it more objectively.

Finally, having pioneered the concept of posttraumatic growth following a difficult life crisis, Tedeschi and Calhoun (2004) encourage expert companions to *operate from a growth perspective*. Salutary personal growth can happen with bereaved parents, not because of the loss itself but as a function of struggling with the aftermath of the child's death. Expert companions listen and watch for indicators of personal growth and always encourage them (see Chapter 13, "Long-Term Adaptation and Resilience").

Getting Started

Given these evidence-based and theoretical treatment models, how does a practitioner start when working with bereaved parents? Conducting a thorough assessment usually comes first. Some of the ten principal interventions summarized earlier, specifically educating about grief and trauma as well as teaching distress reduction, may begin as early as the first clinical encounter. However, exigent circumstances might call for prioritizing immediate intervention over standard assessment questions, such as when practitioners initially encounter parents in emergency departments, neonatal or pediatric intensive care units, medical-surgical hospitals, or hospice settings when child deaths have just occurred or are imminent. In these situations, "reading the room" to rapidly assess clinical priorities is crucial. Generally, providing a non-anxious presence, offering comfort, encouraging caring ministrations to the child (where possible), and facilitating goodbyes supersedes taking a formal history.

When bereaved parents come to an office setting for grief therapy, a more deliberate assessment process can be employed. Practitioners who display a welcoming demeanor and promote interpersonal safety through an earnest, engaged manner have the best chance of gaining parents' trust. Remember, impressions form rapidly, so the first few minutes are critically important for developing rapport and laying a foundation for further therapeutic work.

Bereaved parents often feel helpless, powerless, and completely defeated in the aftermath of child loss. Therefore, simply giving options as you guide them through the consultation can begin restoring a sense of personal control. One way is allowing bereaved parents to choose where to begin—either with their *grief story* or with their *life story* (see Table 4.2).

Some parents are ready to plunge right in retelling what happened to their deceased child. Other parents need time to acclimate to the consultation environment, take stock of the practitioner, and gauge their readiness before

TABLE 4.2 Getting the Patient's Stories

Life Story	*Grief Story*
Symptoms/complaints	What happened?
Medical status	Complicating factors
Psychiatric history	Tasks of grieving/current functioning
Family of origin	Relationship with deceased child
Education/occupation	Other grievers
Partner/own family	Funeral/memorial
"Turning points"	Growth factors
General adaptation	Directions for treatment

divulging intimate information about their personal grief. Bereaved parents will appreciate the practitioner's sensitivity in offering this choice. Handling the initial phase of the interview this way also conveys the practitioner's confidence and mastery with the subject matter, helping to reassure anxious parents.

Most practitioners with mental health training or medical credentials recognize the main components of the life story displayed in Table 4.2 as part of a comprehensive biopsychosocial history. The idea of "turning points" is a developmental construct based on the notion that everyone's life story features critical events that change their destiny in significant ways, such as a career-making job opportunity or meeting one's life partner. Death of a child becomes one of those major turning points. Likewise, a profound change in the bereaved parent's grief journey may also signal a turning point.

Pragmatically, whether starting with the life story or the grief story, information about both threads emerges because the inquiry often shifts back and forth between the two domains. In cases where bereaved parents are hesitant and seem to focus exclusively on life story material, practitioners can gently announce their intention to shift the dialogue to the grief story (e.g., "I'm hoping you can also tell me something about what happened to [child's name]") and ascertain whether the bereaved parent is ready to "go there."

Another important way to promote parental agency is delegating control over the level of disclosure about the child's death circumstances to the parents themselves. Not only is this approach personally respectful, but it is also consistent with the concept of *dosing* described earlier (Jordan, 2011). In one case where the bereaved parents were seen conjointly following the death of their adult son in a motorcycle crash, the father and mother showed different tolerances for describing the fatal collision. The mother excused herself while the father explained how the son's bike skidded beneath the bed of a truck that had pulled out on the highway in front of him without sufficient space for his son to brake. She returned when the inquiry progressed to subsequent topics.

Part of the grief story is discovering what risk factors complicate the parent's grief, as outlined in Chapter 2, "What Makes Parental Grief So Difficult?" Knowing these pressure points directs the practitioner to where attention is needed. Worden's (2018) task-based model of grief—accepting the reality of the loss, working through the pain of the grief, adjusting to an environment in which the deceased is missing, and emotionally relocating the deceased and moving on with life—helps practitioners see where progress has already been made and where therapeutic work needs to be concentrated. It also enables them to "map" the trajectory of parental grief as treatment proceeds. Many practitioners entering the field start by learning Worden's model. Once familiar with it, they can augment how they use it by incorporating the advances provided by evidence-based protocols and important theoretical contributions.

The nature of the parents' relationship with the deceased child is a huge consideration in how their grief manifests. Practitioners should carefully note any data pertaining to attachment styles as well as any evidence of conflict or contention. Other grievers in the parents' social network may be influential in their experience. Reviewing what funeral or memorial arrangements occurred, or are planned (if any), helps the practitioner assess to what extent the bereaved parent has said goodbye. If no formal farewell has happened, suggestions for such rituals may become part of the treatment plan.

The initial assessment of a bereaved parent usually concludes with a summary by the practitioner regarding the impact of the child's death and the specific challenges faced in grieving the loss. The parent's chief assets and resiliencies are noted as well. Recommendations for treatment or follow-up care will incorporate principles and techniques from the models described in this chapter.

Finally, practitioners must always instill hope. While nothing can bring back the deceased child and some aspects of pain and missing will be permanent, the practitioner's message is twofold: help is available, and life can improve. In the end, bereaved parents will decide for themselves whether working with a professional caregiver has tangible prospects for making a positive difference in their lives.

SUMMARY

From reviewing current evidence-based protocols for grief therapy and end-of-life treatment, ten principal interventions emerge as mainstays for work with bereaved parents. These interventions include educating about grief and trauma, teaching distress reduction, including supportive individuals, revisiting the death scenario, developing a narrative account of the child's death and life, honoring the child's legacy, communicating symbolically with the deceased child, reversing avoidance, reclaiming self-worth and identity, and envisioning hope for the future. Other contemporary theoretical models also offer practitioners valuable perspectives and tips for working with bereaved parents. Readers are encouraged to go to the primary sources to gain more information on models of interest that complement their theoretical orientation and therapeutic style. Having completed this review, Part II of this volume considers the problem of child loss at various points in the life cycle and under various circumstances to show how these methods may be applied.

REFERENCES

American Psychiatric Association. (2022). *Diagnostic and statistical manual of mental disorders, text revision DMS-5-TR* (5th ed., text revision). American Psychiatric Association.

Boelen, P. A., de Keijser, J., van den Hout, M. A., & van den Bout, J. (2007). Treatment of complicated grief: A comparison between cognitive-behavioral therapy and supportive counseling. *Journal of Consulting and Clinical Psychology, 75*(2), 277–284. https://doi.org/10.1037/0022-006X.75.2.277

Boelen, P. A., de Keijser, J., van den Hout, M. A., & van den Bout, J. (2011). Factors associated with outcome of cognitive-behavioral therapy for complicated grief: A preliminary study. *Clinical Psychology & Psychotherapy, 18*(4), 284–291. https://doi/full/10.1002/cpp.720

Boelen, P. A., van den Hout, M. A., & van den Bout, J. (2006). A cognitive-behavioral conceptualization of complicated grief. *Clinical Psychology: Science and Practice, 13*(2), 109–128. https://doi.org/10.1111/j.1468-2850.2006.00013.x

Breitbart, W. S., & Poppito, S. R. (2014a). *Individual meaning-centered psychotherapy for patients with advanced cancer: A treatment manual.* Oxford University Press.

Breitbart, W. S., & Poppito, S. R. (2014b). *Meaning-centered group psychotherapy for patients with advanced cancer: A treatment manual.* Oxford University Press.

Chochinov, H. M. (2012). *Dignity therapy: Final words for final days.* Oxford University Press.

Chochinov, H. M., Hack, T., Hassard, T., Kristjanson, L. J., McClement, S., & Harlos, M. (2005). Dignity Therapy: A novel psychotherapeutic intervention for patients near the end of life. *Journal of Clinical Oncology, 23,* 5520–5525. https://doi.org/10.1200/JCO.2005.08.391

Chochinov, H. M., Kristjanson, L. J., Breitbart, W., McClement, S., Hack, T. F., Hassard, T., & Harlos, M. (2011). Effect of Dignity Therapy on distress and end-of-life experience in terminally ill patients: A randomised controlled trial. *Lancet Oncology, 12,* 753–762. https://doi.org/10.1016/S1470-2045(11)70153-X

Dickinson, E. (1995). If I can stop one heart from breaking. In *Poems of Emily Dickinson: Collector's edition* (p. 16). Easton Press.

Eisma, M. C., Boelen, P. A., van den Bout, J., Stroebe, W., Schut, H. A., Lancee, J., & Stroebe, M. S. (2015). Internet-based exposure and behavioral activation for complicated grief and rumination: A randomized controlled trial. *Behavior Therapy, 46*(6), 729–748. https://doi.org/10.1016/j.beth.2015.05.007

Foa, E. B., Hembree, E. A., Rothbaum, B. O., & Rauch, S. A. M. (2019). *Prolonged exposure therapy for PTSD: Emotional processing of trauma experiences* (2nd ed.). Oxford University Press.

Frankl, V. (1959). *Man's search for meaning.* Beacon.

Gamino, L. A. (2012). Opening the family photo album. In R. A. Neimeyer (Ed.), *Techniques of grief therapy: Creative practices for counseling the bereaved* (pp. 231–233). Routledge.

Gamino, L. A., & Ritter, R. H., Jr. (2009). *Ethical practice in grief counseling.* Springer Publishing Company.

Gamino, L. A., Sewell, K. W., & Easterling, L. W. (1998). Scott & White grief study: An empirical test of predictors of intensified mourning. *Death Studies, 22*(4), 333–355. https://doi/abs/10.1080/074811898201524

Gamino, L. A., Sewell, K. W., & Easterling, L. W. (2000). Scott & White grief study—Phase II: Toward an adaptive model of grief. *Death Studies, 24*, 633–660. https://doi/abs/10.1080/07481180050132820

Gamino, L. A., Sewell, K. W., Hogan, N. S., & Mason, S. L. (2010). Who needs grief counseling? A report from the Scott & White grief study. *OMEGA-Journal of Death and Dying, 60*(3), 199–223. https://doi/abs/10.2190/om.60.3.a

Jordan, J. R. (2011). Principles of grief counseling with adult survivors. In J. R. Jordan & J. L. McIntosh (Eds.), *Grief after suicide: Understanding the consequences and caring for survivors* (pp. 179–223). Routledge.

Jordan, J. R. (2020). Lessons learned: Forty years of clinical work with suicide loss survivors. *Frontiers in Psychology, 11*, 766. https://doi.org/10.3389/fpsyg.2020.00766

Jordan, J. R., & McIntosh, J. L. (2011). Is suicide bereavement different? Perspectives from research and practice. In R. A. Neimeyer, H. Winokuer, D. Harris, & G. Thornton (Eds.), *Grief and bereavement in contemporary society: Bridging research and practice* (pp. 223–234). Routledge.

Klass, D., & Marwit, S. J. (1989). Toward a model of parental grief. *OMEGA—Journal of Death and Dying, 19*(1), 31–50. https://doi.org/10.2190/BVUR-67KR-F52F-VW35

Klerman, G. L., Weissman, M. M., Rounsaville, B. J., & Chevron, E. S. (2004). *Interpersonal psychotherapy of depression: A brief, focused, specific strategy*. Jason Aronson.

Kosminsky, P. S., & Jordan, J. R. (2024). *Attachment-informed grief therapy: The clinician's guide to foundations and applications* (2nd ed.). Routledge.

Lichtenthal, W. G., & Breitbart, W. (2015). The central role of meaning in adjustment to the loss of a child to cancer: Implications for the development of Meaning-Centered Grief Therapy. *Current Opinions in Supportive and Palliative Care, 9*(1), 46–51.

Lichtenthal, W. G., Catarozoli, C., Masterson, M., Slivjak, E., Schofield, E., Roberts, K. E., Neimeyer, R. A., Wiener, L., Prigerson, H. G., Kissane, D. W., Li, Y., & Breitbart, W. (2019). An open trial of Meaning-Centered Grief Therapy: Rationale and preliminary evaluation. *Palliative and Supportive Care, 17*(1), 2–12. https://doi.org/10.1017/S1478951518000925

Lichtenthal, W. G., Lacey, S., Roberts, K., Sweeney, C., & Slivjak, E. (2017). Meaning-Centered Grief Therapy: Using the concepts of choice in coping with loss. In W. Breitbart (Ed.), *Meaning-centered psychotherapy* (pp. 88–99). Oxford University Press.

Neimeyer, R. A., Pitcho-Prelorentzos, S., & Mahat-Shamir, M. (2021). "If only . . .": Counterfactual thinking in bereavement. *Death Studies, 45*(9), 692–701. https://doi.org/10.1080/07481187.2019.1679959

Norcross, J. C., & VandenBos, G. R. (2018). *Leaving it at the office: A guide to psychotherapist self-care* (2nd ed.). Guilford.

Norcross, J. C., & Wampold, B. E. (2011). What works for whom: Tailoring psychotherapy to the person. *Journal of Clinical Psychology, 67*(2), 127–132. https://doi.org/10.1002/jclp.20764

Parkes, C. M., & Weiss, R. S. (1983). *Recovery from bereavement*. Basic Books.

Resnick, P. A., Monson, C. M., & Chard, K. M. (2010). *Cognitive processing therapy: Veteran/military version*. Department of Veterans' Affairs.

Rheingold, A. A., Baddeley, J. L., Williams, J. L., Brown, C., Wallace, M. M., Correa, F., & Rynearson, E. K. (2015). Restorative retelling for violent death: An investigation of treatment effectiveness, influencing factors, and durability. *Journal of Loss and Trauma, 20*(6), 541–555. https://doi.org/10.1080/15325024.2014.957602

Rynearson, E. K. (2018). Disabling reenactment imagery after violent dying. *Death Studies, 42*(1), 4–8. https://doi.org/10.1080/07481187.2017.1370411

Rynearson, E. K., Correa, F., & Takacs, L. (2015). *Accommodation to violent dying: A guide to restorative retelling and support*. Virginia Mason Clinic. www.vmfh.org/content/dam/vmfhorg/pdf/legacy-vm/workfiles/Manual_Accommodation_Violent_Dying.pdf

Shear, M. K., Frank, E., Houck, P. R., & Reynolds, C. F. (2005). Treatment of complicated grief: A randomized controlled trial. *Journal of the American Medical Association, 293*, 2601–2608. https://doi.org/10.1001/jama.293.21.2601

Shear, M. K. (2015). *Complicated grief treatment*. Columbia Center for Complicated Grief.

Shear, M. K., Wang, Y., Skritskaya, N., Duan, N., Mauro, C., & Ghesquiere, A. (2014). Treatment of complicated grief in elderly persons: A randomized clinical trial. *JAMA Psychiatry, 71*, 1287–1295. https://doi.org/10.1001/jamapsychiatry.2014.1242

Stroebe, M. S., Hansson, R. O., Schut, H., & Stroebe, W. (2008). Bereavement research: 21st-century prospects. In M. S. Stroebe, R. O. Hansson, H. Schut, & W. Stroebe (Eds.), *Handbook of bereavement research and practices: Advances in theory and intervention* (pp. 577–603). American Psychological Association.

Stroebe, M. S., & Schut, H. (1999). The Dual Process Model of coping with bereavement: Rational and description. *Death Studies, 23*, 197–224. https://doi/abs/10.1080/074811899201046

Stroebe, M. S., & Schut, H. (2010). The Dual Process Model of coping with bereavement: A decade on. *OMEGA—Journal of Death and Dying, 61*, 273–289. https://doi/abs/10.2190/OM.61.4.b

Tedeschi, R. G., & Calhoun, L. G. (2004). *Helping bereaved parents: A clinician's guide*. Brunner-Routledge.

Worden, J. W. (2018). *Grief counseling & grief therapy: A handbook for the mental health practitioner* (5th ed.). Springer Publishing Company.

Part II

CHAPTER FIVE

Pregnancy Loss and Infant Death

Dead babies do not give us memories, they give us dreams.
—Thomas Lynch (1997)

Miscarriages, stillbirths, neonatal deaths, and sudden infant death syndrome cut short lives barely begun. Before making memories can even start, or after only a maddeningly brief time, a child dies and parents are left with only dreams of what might have been. As Thomas Lynch (1997) so pointedly reminds us in the previous quote, parents grieve the loss of their young child's life and the loss of enormous possibilities that died with them. This chapter explores these tragic losses, including special considerations for working with parents who elect termination of pregnancy following a diagnosis of fetal anomaly.

EARLY PREGNANCY LOSS AND MISCARRIAGE

CASE 5.A

Carrie and Mike already had a healthy 2-year-old daughter when they became pregnant a second time. Carrie's annual female exam coincidentally occurred about 6 weeks into the pregnancy, so the jubilant couple received ultrasound confirmation of the new baby's heartbeat. Around 8 weeks, Carrie started spotting and cramping—symptoms never experienced during her first pregnancy. Despite Carrie's alarm, the obstetrician did not seem particularly concerned. After several rounds of messaging, Carrie and Mike chose simply to carry on and hope for the best.

While on a beach vacation in the 11th week, Carrie's bleeding intensified, so the couple sought evaluation at a local emergency center. Another ultrasound was performed. With only a curtain separating their bay from adjacent patients, the emergency physician announced, "I wish I had better news." He told Carrie that no heartbeat was detected and there appeared to be no fetal development beyond about 6 weeks of gestation. The doctor told Carrie she was likely miscarrying. This news confirmed their worst fears. Medical intervention (dilation and curettage of the uterus) was offered, but Carrie declined. She was urged to seek medical follow-up with her regular obstetrician. On the trip home, Carrie passed a good deal of blood and tissue at a roadside restroom and did not know what else to do but flush. Later, they named their baby Samuel, after the Old Testament prophet given back to God at a young age by his mother (1 Samuel 1:9–28).

Returning to her obstetrician, Carrie was told she needed another ultrasound to determine "if the 'products of conception' are gone." Carrie found this language extremely off-putting because she viewed the miscarriage as the death of a baby son. Her obstetrician declared in a monotone that such events "are usually 'a chromosome issue' so you can try again." Carrie decided to switch doctors.

Carrie's new obstetrician provided good care and sympathized about the loss of their baby, commenting, "That must have been hard." The new doctor counseled them to wait one menstrual cycle before trying again. Carrie felt relief at the obstetrician's encouragement. At a practical level, she felt empowered to act, ". . . not that you can ever replace a child."

In memory of Samuel, they filled a special vase with seashells that Mike and their daughter had collected on the fateful beach trip and gave it a place of honor in their home. Neither member of the couple sought professional care but found self-help material comforting, along with sympathetic support from family and church friends. Later, Carrie and Mike had a third child—a healthy baby boy.

The terms *early pregnancy loss* and *miscarriage* apply to spontaneous loss of a pregnancy during the early months up to 20 weeks of gestation, exactly what happened to Carrie and Mike. Yet the terminology can be ambiguous or even misleading to parents because it blends two distinct physiologic events—intrauterine death and extremely preterm delivery—into one word or phrase (Bohn, 2023). Bohn argued for precision balanced with sensitivity when addressing such events.

Caregivers need to acknowledge and honor the intrauterine death that happened and minimize unwarranted, self-assigned guilt on the part of mothers that faulty delivery was the problem. Other medical language sometimes used, *spontaneous abortion*, for example, may be technically accurate but carries unfavorable connotations for parents who decry ever choosing to terminate their baby's life. *Early pregnancy loss* and *miscarriage* are used here as language more familiar and less technical but without abandoning a practitioner's obligation to recognize and acknowledge the sequential medical events they denote.

Many prospective parents do not realize the statistical chances of miscarrying a pregnancy. Based on a broad sample from Europe and North America, the miscarriage rate has been estimated at 15.3% (Quenby et al., 2021), although the true rate may be higher because some miscarriages happen so early they are unrecognized or may be managed at home without medical attention. This estimate means that one out of every six or seven pregnancies likely will end in miscarriage. Perhaps not wanting to dampen the enthusiasm of expecting couples or unduly frighten them, many physicians never mention the possibility of miscarriage, or they allude to it only indirectly by asking pregnant couples to take note of any unexpected bleeding or unusual cramping.

An array of risk factors has been associated with miscarriage. Demographic factors include younger (under 20) and older (over 35) maternal age, older paternal age (over 40), and Black ethnicity. Medical factors include very low or very high body mass index of the mother and history of previous miscarriages. Lifestyle and environmental risk factors include smoking, alcohol or drug use, stress, working night shifts, and exposure to air pollution or pesticides (Quenby et al., 2021). However, none of these factors imply direct causation, and practitioners should avoid any implication of shaming bereaved parents, especially for factors beyond their control such as age and ethnicity. Particularly for Black women, Evans et al. (2023) cautioned caregivers against "mother blame" for inequities that arise from social and cultural determinants of health, such as race-related stress, disadvantages in accessing prenatal care, biased medical care, and socioeconomic hardship.

Studies of post-miscarriage tissue samples suggest the majority of cases (60%) involve chromosomal abnormalities of some kind (Hardy et al., 2016). It is important to note that Carrie's original obstetrician was not inaccurate in telling her that most often a chromosomal abnormality is the reason for early pregnancy loss and miscarriage. However, it was the impersonal and cavalier tone of the message that ruptured the doctor-patient relationship. In failing to notice context clues indicating Carrie and Mike's belief that their pregnancy represented a baby (cf. Weiner, 2020), the obstetrician's "empathic failure" compounded their aggravation (cf. Neimeyer & Jordan, 2002). It is equally important to note how soothing were the words and ministrations of the second obstetrician who conveyed empathy and guided Carrie and Mike through the aftermath of their loss and toward the larger family they desired.

Parents bereaved by miscarriage desperately want to know what caused their child's demise. When there is no definite explanation, parents often feel guilty and question if they are to blame (Gamino & Cooney, 2002). Authentic reassurance can go a long way in debunking erroneous notions that they may have harmed the baby by doing things such as exercising too vigorously, riding a roller coaster at an amusement park, putting in long hours to finish work or school before the baby comes, or even having sexual relations. Such thoughts reflect a natural human desire to understand an outcome that otherwise cannot be explained or controlled. Sometimes parental guilt and second-guessing after miscarriage reflect ambivalence about the pregnancy itself—perhaps the timing was not preferred or the pregnancy was unexpected or unwanted—feelings they may be hesitant to disclose. Regardless, bereaved parents need to know that they did not cause the early pregnancy loss and that miscarriage does not mean the mother failed to properly carry or adequately protect the tiny baby.

Palmer and Murphy-Oikonen (2019) eloquently summarized several aspects of the psychology of women who experience early pregnancy loss and miscarriage. They emphasized how a unique bonding between mother and unborn baby begins at a very early stage of pregnancy as women begin to assume the role and identity of mother, even if news of the pregnancy was not initially welcomed. When women see themselves as carrying a baby, their grief over early pregnancy loss and miscarriage is similar to mothers who experience late-term pregnancy loss. The nebulous nature of many early pregnancy losses creates ambiguity—not knowing exactly what happened, or why, and losing something never fully possessed or realized. Those unanswered questions are particularly difficult for bereaved mothers to reconcile.

The case of Carrie and Mike certainly illustrates many of the points made by Palmer and Murphy-Oikonen (2019). They provided a list of helpful tips for practitioners who encounter parents bereaved by early pregnancy loss and miscarriage, either while the events occur or during the recovery period.

- Acknowledge the pregnancy loss and what it means for the parents. Listen for context clues to understand how parents think about the event (e.g., "baby" or "pregnancy") and mirror their language in your explanations. Avoid patronizing or dismissive responses that minimize the matter, such as, "Just try again" (cf. The Lancet, 2021).
- Reassure bereaved parents that they are not at fault for what happened and gently countermand erroneous assignment of guilt coming from themselves or others.
- Encourage parents who see their early pregnancy loss as the death of a child to name the baby as a way of conferring personhood and dignity. Gender-neutral names can minimize worry about whether the baby was a boy or a girl. Use the baby's name to validate their loss and show respect for the child.

PREGNANCY LOSS AND INFANT DEATH

- Allow parents who view their early pregnancy loss more clinically, that is, as an unfortunate medical event, to develop their own perspective without imposing moral or value judgments. Follow their lead.
- Urge grieving parents to seek support from trusted confidants. Likewise, empower them to ignore or correct hurtful comments made by others (e.g., "It's better it happened early," or "There must have been something wrong with the baby," or "God wanted an angel in heaven"). Straightforward declarative statements are usually enough, such as, "This loss makes us sad" or "That's not how we think about it."
- Recognize the parents' cultural context for how they react to and understand the loss. Keep in mind that some patriarchal cultures shame women who experience miscarriage by labeling them as defective or unfit. Demonstrate compassion for how those women may struggle.
- Respect bereaved parents' spirituality when applicable. When they introduce a faith framework, utilize their language. Seek consultation, if needed, to be better informed about their faith's traditions and practices.
- Suggest memorialization or rituals: retaining mementos such as ultrasound photos, creating keepsakes (such as Carrie and Mike's vase of seashells), holding a ceremony to honor the deceased child, planting a tree or flowers, journaling thoughts and feelings, writing a letter to the baby, burying or inurning the tissue remains, or other individualized ways of honoring the life that was lost.
- Educate bereaved parents about self-help resources available to them, such as Share Pregnancy & Infant Loss Support (www.nationalshare.org), testimonials (e.g., Saadi, 2020), and many print materials and books available on the subject.
- Remain cognizant of calendar dates likely to hold special meaning for bereaved parents because they signify the baby existed: when they first became aware of the pregnancy, the anticipated due date of the baby, and the anniversary of the baby's death. Parents will greatly appreciate such attentiveness to personal details.

STILLBIRTH AND NEONATAL DEATH

CASE 5.B

Carmen's abrupt loss of her second pregnancy came as a complete shock. The baby was growing as expected, and sonograms confirmed she was healthy. Then one morning in her 30th week, Carmen realized the baby had stopped moving. Medical evaluation revealed her baby had died in utero.

> The doctors recommended that labor be induced. After several hours, Carmen finally delivered her deceased daughter. Once her baby girl was born, the problem became clear. The umbilical cord was wrapped tightly around the baby's neck, a rare but fatal pregnancy complication beyond anyone's control. This "horrific tragedy" devastated Carmen. She felt totally helpless and experienced deep grief, rage, and inexplicable guilt.
>
> Aggravated and heartsick, Carmen felt betrayed by her body, which "does not recognize the baby is not here." Her milk let down at seemingly random times. After putting her son in his car seat, she would instinctively turn and reach for her absent daughter. Seeing other babies in public started her insides churning. For weeks afterward, there was no real change in her misery.
>
> Prior to the loss of her baby girl, Carmen's life had pretty much followed an ideal script. She came from a good home with supportive parents. She completed college and worked successfully in sales. She married a terrific man, and they purchased a home. The pregnancy and birth of her now 2-year-old son had gone smoothly and given her a sense of confidence about having another child. But the death of her baby girl exploded Carmen's dreams. Finally, she sought the help of a grief therapist to break out of her emotional tailspin and get her life restarted.

Like *miscarriage*, the term *stillbirth* is a misnomer. As Carmen's situation illustrates, her baby died while still in the uterus, and the subsequent delivery of her deceased infant was the natural consequence. In the United States, *stillbirth* is defined by the American College of Obstetricians and Gynecologists (ACOG; 2020) as the death of a fetus after 20 weeks' gestation, formally acknowledged with a certificate of fetal death or demise. Interestingly, ACOG reported the term preferred by bereaved parent groups is *stillbirth* rather than *fetal death* or *fetal demise*. The term *stillbirth* is used here due to this preference, as well as its familiarity. However, none of these terms are recommended when speaking with bereaved parents whose children die prior to birth, during labor, or shortly after birth. Simply saying, "I'm afraid your baby died, I'm so sorry" may be the most compassionate way to describe the outcome and express sympathy to bereaved parents.

In developed countries, problems leading to stillbirth are often detected during prenatal tests. Mothers like Carmen may face the unenviable prospect of laboring to deliver a child who is already dead. Unfortunately, there are a host of anatomical problems that can result in intrauterine death or stillbirth late in pregnancy. The top five causes of infant deaths in the United States in 2022 were congenital malformations, short gestation or low birthweight, SIDS, accidents, and maternal complications of pregnancy (Ely & Driscoll, 2023). Complications involving the placenta, cord, or membranes, such as happened with Carmen's daughter, was the sixth leading cause of infant death. Research has shown that mothers of stillborn babies are more likely to lack adequate social support at the time of delivery, making the presence and actions of professional caregivers even more crucial in addressing their acute grief (Gold et al., 2017).

In the United States, infant mortality is classified as infant deaths (birth up to 7 days of life), neonatal deaths (7 to 27 days of life), and post-neonatal deaths (28 days of life up to 1 year). Taken together, about 1% of children born each year in the United States die as babies, a rate that has generally declined since 1995, although it increased slightly in 2022 (Ely & Driscoll, 2023). With rates expressed as the number of infant deaths per 1,000 live births, according to maternal race and Hispanic origin, Asian women showed the lowest rates of infant mortality (3.50), while White (4.52) and Hispanic (4.88) mothers had lower infant death rates than Native Hawaiian and Pacific Islander (8.50) as well as American Indian and Alaska Native (9.06) mothers. The highest rate of infant mortality occurred among non-Hispanic Black mothers (10.86), more than double that of Asian, White, or Hispanic mothers.

Why are Black and Indigenous mothers more at risk for infant mortality? Social and cultural determinants of health affecting these mothers influence several clinical factors to create heightened risk for infant mortality (Henry et al., 2021). For example, less educational attainment by mothers typically corresponds with lower socioeconomic status, a hardship that may negatively affect diet, weight, and blood pressure. Social factors such as reduced access to prenatal care, lack of neighborhood safety, intimate partner violence, or an unstable relationship with the baby's father (Crear-Perry et al., 2021) can endanger pregnancy outcomes. Interpersonal and environmental stressors related to finances, incarceration (mother's partner or other key family members), a hospitalized family member, or partner conflict correlate with higher rates of stillbirth, and these stressors disproportionately affect Black women (Hogue et al., 2013). Awareness of these multifactorial risks for infant mortality that affect disadvantaged parents requires practitioners to advocate for just treatment in health-care settings.

Many of the recommendations for practitioners working with parents bereaved by early pregnancy loss and miscarriage apply to situations of stillbirth and neonatal death. Naming the baby is an important step in establishing their identity and claiming parental aegis over the child. Additionally, in cases of stillbirth and neonatal death, bereaved parents have the chance to view, hold, dress, groom, and cherish their deceased child—albeit for a preciously short period of time. Talking to the baby, reading aloud, singing songs, or performing religious rituals where appropriate, such as baptism or christening, are part of enacting a parent-child relationship before saying goodbye forever. These actions allow parents to capture some of those fleeting moments and turn them into memories they can hold, a tangible counterweight to mere dreams as described by Lynch in the quote at the beginning of this chapter. Most hospitals give bereaved parents latitude to decide how much time to spend with their deceased child before handing off the baby to staff or funeral personnel. While many bereaved parents will readily engage in these opportunities, some parents may hesitate, usually out of fear or uncertainty. Gentle encouragement in the moment can often convince hesitant parents to use these limited chances to create visual and kinesthetic memories—however brief—that may become important touchstones in their subsequent grief journey. At the same time, personal choice in these matters should be respected because some bereaved parents may forego the invitation to hold or address their deceased child.

Many hospitals have specific protocols for helping bereaved parents create tangible mementos of their deceased children following stillbirth or neonatal death. Memorial photos can be very important keepsakes when sensitivity is employed to produce images that comfort. Hospital personnel can assist with draping, angles, lighting, and grouping to help bereaved parents obtain artistic and tasteful poses that capture the love in the parent-child bond, rather than stark images of horror and grief. Other memento options include retaining locks of hair, making handprints and/or footprints of the baby (either paint or clay), or keeping the crib name card, the baby's cap, or the hospital bracelet. These items can be placed in a memory box at home that bereaved parents can open and revisit as desired.

Stillbirths and neonatal deaths raise questions about disposition and arrangements. Bereaved parents must decide what to do with their child's remains, either burial or cremation, and whether to hold any kind of ceremony or service. Newly bereaved parents will likely need considerable support to address such unthinkable questions. Experienced clergy, clinical staff, and funeral directors can provide invaluable assistance by explaining what is possible to bereaved parents who find themselves living a nightmare they never imagined.

The general advice is for bereaved parents to adhere to whatever customs and practices they find meaningful and consistent with their cultural, spiritual, and family traditions. As painful and difficult as it may be to plan a funeral for an infant, making those decisions and participating in the services give grieving mothers and fathers an opportunity to parent. Even though terribly sad, these functions legitimate parenthood and provide an outlet for expressing love that otherwise has no place to go. Actively planning funeral arrangements and formally saying goodbye to the baby helps bereaved parents in the aftermath of stillbirth or neonatal death (see Chapter 3, "Helpful Factors").

One compensatory activity chosen by some bereaved mothers after stillbirth is extracting and donating their milk for other babies whose mothers cannot supply the nourishment they need (Oreg, 2020). Pumping and donating became rituals that helped these mothers work out their grief. These activities provided meaning because their baby's legacy was associated with offering life-sustaining value to others. It also afforded these mothers a chance to regain control of their circumstances—and their grief—by weaning themselves on their own timetable. While this option may not appeal to everyone, it certainly may help some bereaved mothers. When amenable, discreetly informing bereaved mothers about this possibility and providing information about local milk banks is all practitioners need to do. Grieving mothers will decide for themselves whether to donate their milk.

CASE 5.B (Continued)

In Carmen's case, a funeral was held for her deceased daughter, whom they named Marianna, although it did little to bring her comfort. Her biggest challenge after the stillbirth was reconciling lost dreams of what would never come to be and realigning her life script with lived events. Those juxtapositions did not come easily. She did not want to reenvision her dreams; she wanted her daughter. Carmen's milk letting down presented especially anguishing moments awash with painful emotions, but she had no interest in donating milk. Mostly, Carmen preferred compartmentalizing the loss and not thinking about it as a way to limit her pain.

CASE 5.C

Amari, a young, bereaved mother, sought grief therapy following a stillbirth. She and the father were both college students, and the pregnancy had been unplanned. Nonetheless, in accord with their religious beliefs, they had accepted events as a gift of life not to be turned aside. However, problems were detected during routine ultrasounds. Ultimately, Amari was told that "the baby is not alive" due to placental abruption (separating from the uterine wall compromising oxygen and nutrient flow). Labor had to be induced. Amari and her partner put out a prayer request to their circle of friends.

> Amari's labor lasted 20 hours before she delivered a stillborn baby girl. Shortly after delivery, her hospital room was full of well-meaning supporters who distracted Amari in those initial moments and, in hindsight, limited her from attending to the baby in all the ways she might have otherwise. They named their baby Jasmine, like the delicate flower. Due to Jasmine's very small size, they had her cremated.
>
> Talking with her therapist, Amari expressed regret that she had not been more forceful in asking for privacy following Jasmine's birth and engaging in maternal actions such as cuddling and cooing. Because of exhaustion and the pain medicines, as well as fear and confusion, recollections of her hospital time with Jasmine were cloudy. Amari felt her emotions dangling. She never really had a chance to say goodbye. These regrets were heavy on her mind as Jasmine's original due date approached.
>
> With some gentle Socratic questioning, it became clear that Amari's friends would have hosted a baby shower for her about that time, either before or shortly after Jasmine's due date. The discussion sparked an idea. Amari resolved to hold a home memorial service for Jasmine instead. She asked a friend who was a seminary student to officiate. She sent out invitations and printed a program. The order of service included prayer, lighting a candle, scripture, songs, reflections by both parents, a balloon release, and, of course, jasmine flowers. They served light refreshments afterward. The same group of friends who had crowded their way into her hospital room came together to support Amari and the baby's father in honoring Jasmine and closing the circle of life. Empowering Amari to find a meaningful ritual to express her grief and say goodbye to Jasmine went a long way toward giving her a sense of peace and completion. That single action—accomplished beyond the walls of the consultation room—proved to be the single most healing thing Amari did on her path to personal recovery.

Practitioners need to remember fathers' grief also. Grappling with the unknowns and feelings of uncontrollability and helplessness that accompany stillbirth takes a toll on fathers as well as mothers. Bereaved fathers sometimes feel forgotten in the aftermath of stillbirth or neonatal death because so much attention from professional caregivers seems focused on the postpartum mother. Social expectations naturally fall on men to support their female partners at such a difficult time (e.g., "How's Chloe doing?" or "Jayla is so fortunate to have your strength"). In the process, fathers' grief may be overlooked or marginalized, or even deferred by fathers themselves when tasked with taking charge of the other children and the household while the mothers recover. Fulfilling these support roles can preclude fathers from addressing their own grief, thus interfering with their emotional recovery (Obst et al., 2020; 2021). Fathers who have attended prenatal appointments, viewed ultrasound images of their baby, and felt the baby's movements in their partner's abdomen develop their own version of bonding. They generally experience more grief than men less involved in these activities.

Astute practitioners can remedy a father being overlooked by directly asking how he is doing, perhaps using the third person to emphasize the point (e.g., "And how is *Kendrick* handling all this?"). The inquiry conveys the need for a bereaved father to take stock of himself. Additionally, it is important to find out who is available to support the father. Ask how he customarily relieves stress, and encourage healthy forms of release. Traditional men generally respond better to an approach that is more conversational and less clinical. In these situations, practitioners may temporarily adopt the stance of a social comrade relating on a horizontal level rather than maintaining the hierarchical position of educated expert.

SUDDEN INFANT DEATH SYNDROME

SIDS, formerly called crib death, presents a perplexing and profoundly tragic end to a baby's life. Parents who have successfully come through all the demands of pregnancy, the risks of miscarriage, the ardors of labor and delivery, and finally brought home a seemingly healthy infant are stunned beyond belief when their baby dies while sleeping. The devastation and grief can last for years. In a research sample including both non-White mothers with less education from lower socioeconomic strata and White mothers with more education and economic security, Goldstein et al. (2018) found approximately two-thirds of mothers bereaved by SIDS reported daily intrusive emotional pain and yearning for their dead infant up to four years after the death.

SIDS remains one of the leading causes of infant death worldwide (Park et al., 2022), including in the United States, where SIDS and other sleep-related or sudden unexplained infant deaths are the leading cause of mortality in the post-neonatal interval (ages 1 month to 1 year), especially between ages 1 to 4 months of life (Goldstein et al., 2018). As with miscarriage and stillbirth, racial and ethnic disparities also exist for SIDS rates in the United States (reported as number of cases per 100,000 live births; Centers for Disease Control and Prevention, 2023): American Indian or Alaska Native (213.5); Black (191.4); Native Hawaiian or Other Pacific Islander (164.5); White (83.6);

Hispanic (56.4); and Asian (22.6). Again, Indigenous and Black families show dramatically higher rates of SIDS.

The cause of SIDS is not completely understood and is thought to result from a combination of environmental factors such as unsafe sleep practices, exposure to secondhand smoke, and overheating. In addition, infant vulnerability due to immature cardiorespiratory systems or underdeveloped neurological arousal systems may interfere with an infant's response to airway obstruction (Moon et al., 2022).

Significant reductions in the number of SIDS deaths have resulted from widely disseminated public safety campaigns about the advisability of infants sleeping on their backs and the dangers of soft bedding, pillows, blankets, stuffed animals, and crib objects nearby (National Institute of Child Health and Human Development/National Institutes of Health, 2022). Hospital staff in labor and delivery units as well as pediatricians performing infant checkups routinely counsel new parents about these hazards. The American Academy of Pediatrics (Moon et al., 2022) issued updated recommendations that infants be placed on their backs, on a firm sleeping surface covered only with a fitted sheet and no other bedding, in the same room as parents ("room sharing") but not in the same bed or on the same sleep surface as parents ("bed sharing"). Breastfeeding and pacifier use were also encouraged to reduce the risk of SIDS.

The dominant psychological dynamic in cases of SIDS is the perception of preventability—a death that could have been avoided. Sometimes precautions about back sleeping and removal of soft crib bedding are not heeded, perhaps because the baby is seen as not comfortable or because cultural practices dictate otherwise. Sometimes parents fall asleep with their babies on sofas or in upholstered armchairs and babies die due to entrapment or overlaying. Sometimes co-sleeping arrangements in the parents' bed result in babies suffocating inadvertently. Issues of responsibility or culpability can tear apart couples or families when one party is singled out for blame. Even without such judgment from others, bereaved parents can suffer from enormous internal guilt when their baby dies from SIDS. In other cases, parents of the newborn may do everything according to recommended guidelines when it comes to sleeping and SIDS still happens. The unfathomable and inexplicable nature of SIDS can leave bereaved parents reeling in despair. Practitioners who work with parents (and grandparents) bereaved by SIDS need to be versed in how to manage such emotionally rending and potentially volatile situations.

Because there are so many unknowns in these situations, practitioners dealing with cases of SIDS should tread gingerly on the topic of causality. Allow bereaved parents to describe events of the death in their own words. Try phrasing questions in the first-person plural (e.g., "Do we know what happened to little Kalani?") to convey empathy and avoid implications of blame. In the aftermath of SIDS, emphasize parental love as the basis for grief. Statements such as, "With as much as you loved baby Destiny, her death must be quite a shock for you" can soften self-assigned recrimination or guilt. Leave official cause of death rulings to designated authorities: coroners, justices of the peace, or medical staff. Practitioners working with parents bereaved by SIDS should prioritize emotional and psychological healing, not assume a stance of judge or jury.

When bereaved parents acknowledge some degree of misjudgment or care errors contributing to SIDS, they often wrestle with self-blame and a sense of failure (Plews-Ogan et al., 2022). A helpful angle is to steer toward forgiveness as the most pragmatic outcome. Forgiveness needs to come from parents themselves as fallible human beings, from their partner and families (in cases where one parent was presumed at fault or held accountable by others), and from the deceased child whose life they intended to protect and preserve. These three forgiveness processes are interrelated.

Forgiveness of self can start by receiving a compassionate hearing from the practitioner in the safety of the professional consultation. Encourage bereaved parents who blame themselves for a SIDS death to speak with an understanding and sympathetic loved one or friend who may be able to reinforce a message of self-forgiveness. For bereaved parents who feel isolated in their guilt or remain unsure of how others might respond, the best source for receiving nonjudgmental compassion may come from designated organizations such as First Candle (www.firstcandle.org) that provide support to parents whose children die from SIDS. Peer validation from other parents bereaved by SIDS can be particularly affirming for someone seeking self-forgiveness. Additionally, for grieving parents actively affiliated with faith traditions that attribute death, and life, to a supreme being, reassurance from a minister or spiritual leader may facilitate self-forgiveness.

When reconciliation with the baby's other parent or the extended family is needed, practitioners can help the bereaved parent prepare for and rehearse critical conversations. Even so, balancing genuine remorse with a request for forgiveness can be a delicate proposition. Practitioners can offer to facilitate that conversation, if needed, to ensure objectivity and enhance the potential for rapprochement. That means keeping sessions from deteriorating into blame and defensiveness while at the same time promoting humility and graciousness by all parties. In these situations, restoration of the partnership or family unit is the immediate goal of any intervention, not delineation of who is at fault.

When it comes to obtaining forgiveness from the child who died, that process will necessarily be symbolic and unilateral. Sometimes bereaved parents who feel responsible for the infant's death will choose to express contrition through a letter or an imagined conversation with the deceased baby acknowledging the parent's shortcomings and regrets, similar to Shear's (2015) imaginal conversation technique or Rynearson et al.'s (2015) deconstruction and revision exercise (see Chapter 4, "Contemporary Treatment Approaches").

When parents speak from the heart this way, it often exorcises much of their guilt. The healing power of these actions comes from accentuating the parental love that brought their precious child into the world. An overriding theme of love can subsume negative emotions of self-blame and guilt.

When conducting interventions with grieving parents following SIDS or stillbirths, the protocol of Meaning-Centered Grief Therapy (Lichtenthal & Breitbart, 2015; Lichtenthal et al., 2019; Lichtenthal et al., 2017) can also be usefully adapted. For example, what did being a good parent mean *before* the SIDS death as far as meeting the baby's needs, keeping the baby safe, and demonstrating love and care? How did that change *after* the death, when the grief was most intense, parenting behavior disrupted, and self-blame ensued? In the *future*, how might the bereaved parent reclaim a parental role, keep the baby's memory alive, or foster a sense of legacy or continuity within the family and in the community? Plews-Ogan et al. (2022) reported that many parents bereaved by SIDS reenvision their parental role in a broader context, enacted in various ways: supporting SIDS research, sponsoring play areas that families can enjoy, helping other bereaved parents, or sometimes honoring their child's life by showing kindness or just being the best possible version of themselves. Such altruism can lead to salutary personal transformation (see Chapter 3, "Helpful Factors").

GRIEF FOLLOWING ELECTIVE ABORTION FOR FETAL ANOMALY

CASE 5.D

Ari and Sarah had postponed starting a family until their long professional training concluded. They were thrilled to get pregnant right away. Early prenatal checks went fine until routine imaging detected potential anatomical problems. Further tests revealed their baby had a severe neuromuscular disorder, with dire implications for the baby's health. Immediate surgery within hours of delivery would be required for the baby to have any chance for quality of life. A series of additional major surgeries would likely follow in the neonatal period, with no certainty as to outcome. Faced with the prospect of bringing into the world a child destined to suffer nearly nonstop medical procedures over the course of a lifetime, Ari and Sarah independently, and almost immediately, concluded that pregnancy termination was the most compassionate response.

Their decision was not made lightly or without ambivalence. Sarah already felt bonded with her baby boy and could feel him moving.

> Ari likewise looked forward to having a firstborn son. They called him Nathaniel, the name they had always planned for a son. In their minds and hearts, they were acting out of love for the son entrusted to them to spare him the lifelong pain and suffering his condition would entail. Sarah described "feeling him leave my body" during the abortion procedure, a stillbirth experience of sorts.
>
> Both members of the couple grieved. They initiated conjoint visits with a grief therapist. Sarah compiled a baby book containing their photos, ultrasound images of Nathaniel, some of her journal entries from the pregnancy, and a "letter of explanation" telling Nathaniel what they had done and why. She cried and reacted with jealous anger when other couples talked about or celebrated healthy babies. Ari read voluminously about the neuromuscular disorder, especially its causes and the likelihood of it happening with a subsequent pregnancy. He too experienced irritation with other new parents, especially a colleague proudly showing off his newborn son also named Nathaniel.
>
> The couple was extremely cautious about revealing their decision, out of concern for social or moral judgment. They told others, "We lost the pregnancy" and provided few details. Both Ari and Sarah hoped to get pregnant again as soon as medically advisable. They contextualized the loss of Nathaniel much like a stillbirth due to an unfortunate medical anomaly—a sad event they grieved but not a reason to forego having more children they hoped to raise and cherish. They would never forget their first son, Nathaniel, but acknowledged a full sense of resolution would likely come only after conceiving and delivering a healthy child.

Many similarities exist between the grief experienced by Ari and Sarah and the reactions of other parents bereaved through miscarriage, stillbirth, and SIDS. They dreamed of family life with their baby, dreams shattered by Nathaniel's overwhelming medical problems. They endured body blows of grief and rage. They experienced role disruption and feelings of helplessness. They questioned their assumptions about an orderly world and struggled to make sense of the injustice of it. They leaned on each other and turned to their families and trusted confidants for support. They consulted a therapist during their acute bereavement, realizing that, even with their hardiness in coping, additional help would be beneficial.

There were also distinct differences between the loss experienced by Ari and Sarah and the scenarios of other bereaved parents described earlier in this chapter. Whereas parents who lose a child to miscarriage, stillbirth, neonatal death, or SIDS often experience guilt, that guilt is less definite, vaguer, and even speculative—did they do something wrong to bring about the death of their child? In cases of elective abortion following a diagnosis of fetal anomaly, parental guilt hinges on the instrumental decision to end the pregnancy. An innovative study by Depoers-Béal et al. (2019) compared the perinatal grief of mothers who chose to continue pregnancy and provide comfort care for a baby diagnosed with a lethal condition and mothers who chose to terminate their pregnancy after a similar diagnosis. While much of their grief was similar, mothers electing termination more frequently endorsed feelings of guilt and self-blame.

McCoyd (2007) described how mothers who choose pregnancy termination for fetal anomaly ("chosen loss") face a dilemma exacerbated by implicit and contradictory societal messages: love and bond with an unborn baby but do not deliver a severely disabled child. One mother in McCoyd's study eloquently expressed her angst:

> My husband and I were faced with a moral dilemma no person should ever have to face. Do we sentence our son to death, or do we sentence him to a lifetime with a severe abnormality? These were our only options. Either choice would lead to tremendous suffering and regret. I have heard this situation described as choosing between having your left hand or your right hand cut off.
>
> (p. 44)

In short, the internalized guilt and second-guessing among parents who choose elective abortion, like Ari and Sarah, may never be completely silenced (Leon, 2017).

Leon (2017) emphasized the restorative power of genuine empathy by practitioners who acknowledge how profoundly difficult it must be to choose elective abortion for fetal anomaly. Parents in these situations face four sequential tasks: absorbing the impact of learning about the anomaly, defining what or who has been lost, deciding whether to continue or terminate the pregnancy, and deciding who to tell what. When parents view elective abortion for fetal anomaly as the death of a son or daughter, as did Ari and Sarah, efforts to memorialize the loss like a stillbirth will likely be beneficial. Dekkers et al. (2019) echoed the importance of recognizing the lost baby's existence when providing psychosocial care for these parents.

CASE 5.D (Continued)

Ari and Sarah wished to create significance for Nathaniel's life and memorialize him. Sarah's baby book was so thick she "put weights on it" to compress the bulging contents within its cover. The therapist utilized that metaphor to enhance her meaning making with co-constructed imagery (Clarke, 2014), observing that a) perhaps Nathaniel's life and significance were bigger than the book could contain and b) maybe Sarah's grief was not so easily compacted or stored either. Sarah found this extended metaphor inspiring and reassuring. She concluded, "It's okay to be 'not okay'."

Regarding Sarah's letter of explanation written to baby Nathaniel, the therapist suggested reading it not just to Nathaniel and Ari but also to a trusted friend who would then be able share the depth of her anguish and support her commensurately. The couple was cautioned about likely "Nathaniel moments" in the future when something might bring him to mind and grief emotions resurface. Even if disconcerting, such upsurges may eventually be more bittersweet and welcomed as a way of remembering.

SUMMARY

Helping parents bereaved by pregnancy loss or infant death requires sensitivity and compassion from practitioners. Understanding the physiology behind miscarriages, stillbirths, neonatal deaths, and SIDS is essential, along with a working knowledge of the psychological and emotional issues inherent in these tragic situations. The ability to suspend judgment, especially in cases of SIDS or pregnancy termination following a diagnosis of fetal anomaly, is a prerequisite for empathic accuracy. Evidence-based methods such as Lichtenthal's identity work speak to the heart of the matter for these grief-stricken parents. Cultural considerations and loss-specific findings from scholarly literature further refine the practitioner's approach, always respecting the uniqueness of each bereaved parent or grieving couple.

REFERENCES

American College of Obstetricians and Gynecologists. (2020). Obstetric care consensus: Management of stillbirth. *Obstetrics & Gynecology, 135*(3), e110–e132. https://doi.org/10.1097/AOG.0000000000003719

Bohn, J. A. (2023). When words fail: "Miscarriage," referential ambiguity, and psychological harm. *Journal of Medicine and Philosophy: A Forum for Bioethics and Philosophy of Medicine, 48*, 265–283. https://doi.org/10.1093/jmp/jhad013

Centers for Disease Control and Prevention. (2023, March 8). *Data and statistics for SIDS and sudden unexpected infant death*. Centers for Disease Control and Prevention. www.cdc.gov/sids/data.htm

Clarke, J. K. (2014). Utilization of clients' metaphors to punctuate solution-focused brief therapy interventions: A case illustration. *Contemporary Family Therapy, 36*, 426–441. https://doi.org/10.1007/s10591-013-9286-y

Crear-Perry, J., Correa-de-Araujo, R., Johnson, T. L., McLemore, M. R., Neilson, E., & Wallace, M. (2021). Social and structural determinants of health inequities in maternal health. *Journal of Women's Health, 30*, 230–235. https://doi.org/10.1089/jwh.2020.8882

Dekkers, F. H. W., Go, A. T. J. I., Stapersma, L., Eggink, A. J., & Utens, E. M. W. J. (2019). Termination of pregnancy for fetal anomalies: Parents' preferences for psychosocial care. *Prenatal Diagnosis, 39*, 575–587. https://doi.org/10.1002/pd.5464

Depoers-Béal, C., Le Baccon, F. A., Le Bauar, G., Prosiy, M., Arnaud, A., Legendre, G., Dayan, J., Bétrémieux, P., & Le Lous, M. (2019). Perinatal grief following neonatal comfort care for lethal fetal condition. *Journal of Neonatal-Perinatal Medicine, 12*, 457–464. https://doi.org/10.3233/NPM-180180

Ely, D. M., & Driscoll, A. K. (2023). *Infant mortality in the United States: Provisional data from the 2022 period linked birth/infant death file*. Vital Statistics Rapid Release; Report No. 33. National Center for Health Statistics. https://doi.org/10.15620/cdc:133699

Evans, N. M., Hsu, Y-L., Kabasele, C. M., Kirkland, C., Pantuso, D., & Hicks, S. (2023). A qualitative exploration of stressors: Voices of African American women who have experienced each type of fetal/infant loss: Miscarriage, stillbirth, and infant mortality. *Journal of Black Psychology, 49*, 236–263. https://doi.org/10.1177/00957984221127833

Gamino, L. A., & Cooney, A. T. (2002). *When you lose a child through miscarriage or stillbirth*. Augsburg Fortress.

Gold, K. J., Treadwell, M. C., Mieras, M. E., & Laventhal, N. T. (2017). Who tells a mother her baby has died? Communication and staff presence during stillbirth delivery and early infant death. *Journal of Perinatology, 37*, 1330–1334. https://doi.org/10.1038/jp.2017.125

Goldstein, R. D., Lederman, R. I., Lichtenthal, W. G., Morris, S. E., Human, M., Elliott, A. J., Tobacco, D., Angal, J., Odendaal, H., Kinney, H. C., & Prigerson, H. G. (2018). The grief of mothers after the sudden unexpected death of their infants. *Pediatrics, 141*(5), e20173651. https://doi.org/10.1542/peds.2017.3651

Hardy, K., Hardy, P. J., Jacobs, P. A., Lewallen, K., & Hassold, T. J. (2016). Temporal changes in chromosome abnormalities in human spontaneous abortions: Results of 40 years of analysis. *American Journal of Medial Genetics, Part A, 170A*, 2671–2680. https://doi.org/10.1002/ajmg.a.37795

Henry, C. J., Higgins, M., Carlson, N., & Song, M-K. (2021). Racial disparities in stillbirth risk factors among Non-Hispanic Black women and Non-Hispanic White women in the United States. *The American Journal of Maternal Child Nursing, 46*, 352–359. https://doi.org/10.1097/NMC.0000000000000772

Hogue, C. J. R., Parker, C. B., Willinger, M., Temple, J. R., Bann, C. M., Siver, R. M., Dudley, D. J., Koch, M. A., Coustan, D. R., Stoll, B. J., Reddy, U. M., Varner, M. W., Saade, G. R., Conway, D., & Goldenberg, R. L. (2013). A population-based case-control study of stillbirth: The relationship of significant life events to the racial disparity for African Americans. *American Journal of Epidemiology, 177*, 755–767. https://doi.org/10.1093/aje/kws381

The Lancet. (2021). Miscarriage: Worldwide reform of care is needed. *The Lancet, 397*, 1597. https://doi.org/10.1016/S0140-6736(21)00954-5

Leon, I. G. (2017). Empathic psychotherapy for pregnancy termination for fetal anomaly. *Psychotherapy, 54*(4), 394–399. https://doi.org/10.1037/pst0000124

Lichtenthal, W. G., & Breitbart, W. (2015). The central role of meaning in adjustment to the loss of a child to cancer: Implications for the development of Meaning-Centered Grief Therapy. *Current Opinions in Supportive and Palliative Care, 9*, 46–51. https://doi.org/10.1097/SPC.0000000000000117

Lichtenthal, W. G., Catarozoli, C., Masterson, M., Slivjak, E., Schofield, E., Roberts, K. E., Neimeyer, R. A., Wiener, L., Prigerson, H. G., Kissane, D. W., Li, Y., & Breitbart, W. (2019). An open trial of Meaning-Centered Grief Therapy: Rationale and preliminary evaluation. *Palliative & Supportive Care, 17*, 2–12. https://doi.org/10.1017/S1478951518000925

Lichtenthal, W. G., Lacey, S., Roberts, K., Sweeney, C., & Slivijak, E. (2017). Meaning-Centered Grief Therapy: Using the concepts of choice in coping with loss. In W. Breitbart (Ed.), *Meaning-centered psychotherapy* (pp. 88–99). Oxford University Press.

Lynch, T. (1997). *The undertaking: Life studies from the dismal trade* (p. 51). W. W. Norton.

McCoyd, J. L. M. (2007). Pregnancy interrupted: Loss of a desired pregnancy after diagnosis of fetal anomaly. *Journal of Psychosomatic Obstetrics & Gynecology, 28*(1), 37–48. https://doi.org/10.1080/01674820601096153

Moon, R. Y., Carlin, R. F., Hand, I., & American Academy of Pediatrics Task Force on Sudden Infant Death Syndrome and Committee on Fetus and Newborn. (2022). Evidence base for 2022 updated recommendations for a safe infant sleeping environment to reduce the risk of sleep-related infant deaths. *Pediatrics, 150*(1), e2022057991. httsp://doi.org/10.1542/peds.2022-057991

National Institute of Child Health and Human Development/National Institutes of Health. (2022). *Safe to sleep: Helping to reduce the risk of Sudden Infant Death Syndrome (SIDS) and other sleep-related causes of infant death.* https://safetosleep.nichd.nih.gov

Neimeyer, R. A., & Jordan, J. R. (2002). Disenfranchisement as empathic failure: Grief therapy and the co-construction of meaning. In K. Doka (Ed.), *Disenfranchised grief: New directions, challenges, and strategies for practice* (pp. 95–117). Research Press.

Obst, K. L., Due, C., Oxlad, M., & Middleton, P. (2020). Men's grief following pregnancy loss and neonatal loss: A systematic review and emerging theoretical model. *BMC Pregnancy and Childbirth, 20*, 11. https://doi.org/10.1186/s12884-019-2677-9

Obst, K. L., Oxlad, M., Due, C., & Middleton, P. (2021). Factors contributing to men's grief following pregnancy loss and neonatal death: Further development of an emerging model in an Australian sample. *BMC Pregnancy and Childbirth, 21*, 29. https://doi.org/10.1186/s12884-020-03514-6

Oreg, A. (2020). The grief ritual of extracting and donating human milk after perinatal loss. *Social Science & Medicine, 265*, 113312. https://doi.org/10.1016/j.socscimed.2020.113312

Palmer, A. D., & Murphy-Oikonen, J. (2019). Social work intervention for women experiencing early pregnancy loss in the emergency department. *Social Work in Health Care, 58*, 392–411. https://doi.org/10.1080/00981389.2019.1580237

Park, S., Han, J. H., Hwang, J., Yon, D. K., Lee, S. W., Kim, J. H., Koyanagi, A., Jacob, L., Oh, H., Kostev, K., Dragioti, E., Radua, J., Eun, H. S., Shin, J. I., & Smith, L. (2022). The global burden of sudden infant death syndrome from 1990 to 2019: A systematic analysis from the global burden of disease study 2019. *QJM: An International Journal of Medicine, 115*(11), 735–744. https://doi.org/10.1093/qjmed/hcac093

Plews-Ogan, E., Keywan, C., Morris, S. E., & Goldstein, R. D. (2022). The parental role before and after SIDS. *Death Studies, 46*(10), 2316–2326. https://doi.org/10.1080/07481187.2021.1936296

Quenby, S., Gallos, I. D., Dhillon-Smith, R. K., Podesek, M. Stephenson, M. D., Fisher, J. Brosens, J. J., Brewin, J., Ramhorst, R., Lucas, E. S., McCoy, R. C., Anderson, R., Daher, S., Regan, L. Al-Memar, M., Bourne, T., MacIntyre, D. A., Rai, R., Chrisiansen, O. B., Sugiura-Ogasawara, M., Odendaal, J., Devall, A. J., Bennett, P. R., Petrou, S., & Coomarasamy, A. (2021). Miscarriage 1—Miscarriage matters: The epidemiological, physical, psychological, and economic costs of early pregnancy loss. *The Lancet, 397*, 1658–1667. https://doi.org/10.1016/S0140-6736(21)00682-6

Rynearson, E. K., Correa, F., & Takacs, L. (2015). *Accommodation to violent dying: A guide to restorative retelling and support*. Virginia Mason Clinic. www.vmfh.org/content/dam/vmfhorg/pdf/legacy-vm/workfiles/Manual_Accommodation_Violent_Dying.pdf

Saadi, A. (2020). The silence and sorrow of miscarriage. *Journal of the American Medical Association, 324*(10), 941–942. https://doi.org/10.1001/jama.2020.15959

Shear, M. K. (2015). *Complicated grief treatment*. Columbia Center for Complicated Grief.

Weiner, S. J. (2020). *On becoming a healer: The journey from patient care to caring about your patients*. Johns Hopkins University Press.

CHAPTER SIX

Death of a Younger Child or Adolescent

> The death of a child forces you to re-evaluate all you believe and everything you do.
> —Donna L. Schuurman (personal communication, 2024)

CASE 6.A

Like many parents who conceive with the help of infertility treatments, Derrick and Annette gave birth to fraternal twins; they went by their nicknames, Sissy and Brother. Once the babies became toddlers, the couple arranged for licensed daycare services in a private home while both parents worked. The sickening phone message that the twins had both drowned in the backyard pool at the daycare tore their world apart. Approximately one year after this devastating loss, Derrick and Annette started conjoint grief therapy.

Previously, the proprietor of the daycare had been so attentive and conscientious that Derrick and Annette considered her almost one of the family. On the day in question, the twins had gone down for their afternoon naps, so the proprietor ran some errands, leaving the children in the care of her teenage assistant. The assistant, who was new to the job, dozed off while the twins slept and so was unaware when they later got up from their day beds. Apparently, the twins wandered out the back door and a faulty latch on the pool gate allowed them to

> push it open. Both twins were discovered dead, Brother on the bottom of the pool and Sissy floating face down on the surface. Authorities determined that Brother had been deceased longer. Derrick and Annette speculated that Brother, being more impulsive, had likely gone into the water first and Sissy, being more protective, had gone in after him to join or help.
>
> Although Annette had brought two older children into the marriage, the bereaved couple suddenly had no biological children from their union. The marriage strained under the emotional upheaval. They argued and blamed each other for not picking up the twins earlier that fateful day. Derrick turned to cannabis, and Annette started drinking. Annette's teenage daughter began looking after her out of concern, a sort of child-parent role reversal. The local district attorney opened an investigation into the proprietor's business and interrogated the assistant at length. The parents intended to file a civil lawsuit against the proprietor who was once their trusted caregiver, even though no amount of compensation could bring back the twins.

Several factors that complicate parental grief (see Chapter 2, "What Makes Parental Grief So Difficult?") applied to Derrick and Annette after the twins drowned. Their deaths were developmentally *off time* (Neugarten, 1979). The dynamic of *empty track* (Klass & Marwit, 1988–1989) left them empty-handed. Instead of enjoying lap time and play time, abundant hugs and rosy hopes, they experienced broken hearts and dashed dreams. Negative social comparisons with other parents who continued raising and enjoying their children were disheartening. The *future felt lost*, denying the bereaved parents an opportunity for legacy and continuation of their union. Even their *sense of themselves* was jeopardized—who am I or what am I now?

The tragic drowning of Derrick and Annette's twins involved additional complicating factors, such as the complete *unexpectedness* of what happened that day. The *traumatic* nature of the twins' drowning, replete with grotesque images—a toddler at the bottom of a swimming pool, another floating dead on the surface, and what may have been their final, futile flailing—seemed more than a parent's imagination could bear. The awful, inescapable realization that these horrific deaths were entirely *preventable* gnawed at the very marrow of their strength and incited unparalleled fury. Finally, underlying *tensions in the couple's relationship* intensified in the wake of the children's deaths, becoming a liability in their respective coping efforts.

HOW DO CHILDREN DIE?

In the United States, the National Center for Injury Prevention and Control, Centers for Disease Control and Prevention (2020a) reported that unintentional injuries are the leading cause of death for individuals 1 to 14 years of age (followed by congenital anomalies, cancers, homicides, and heart disease). For children ages 1 to 9, unintentional fatal injuries most frequently occur by drowning, as with Sissy and Brother, or motor vehicle collisions (National Center for Injury Prevention and Control, Centers for Disease Control and Prevention, 2020b). Admittedly, these national data reflect the realities of life in a developed, high-income country.

Globally, rates of child mortality are much higher in poorer countries, and the reasons children die are different. Data on leading causes of death for children and adolescents worldwide (aged 5 to 19 years) reveal road traffic injuries, cancers, malaria, drowning, diarrhea, and tuberculosis to be most prevalent (Liu et al., 2022). In developed countries, injuries and noncommunicable diseases like cancer account for most deaths in this age range. In less developed, lower-income countries, communicable diseases and nutritional deficiencies account for much of the mortality among children.

Liu et al. (2022) concluded that almost all global child deaths are preventable and called for social action to redress the causes. Because preventability is a key factor in parental grief, practitioners must be cognizant whether preventability stems from inadvertent accidents or negligence, such as in the United States and other developed countries, or from lack of basic necessities and sanitary conditions, especially wholesome food and clean water, contributing to child deaths in less developed countries.

Obviously, the setting in which practitioners work will determine regional considerations. Practitioners operating in global areas and communities where poverty conditions result in high rates of child death face a twofold challenge. First, they must address the grief of bereaved parents at a family and community level when a younger child or adolescent dies. Second, practitioners in these regions will almost certainly have to be involved in some form of social advocacy to have any credibility as a bereavement worker. Only with the stature that comes from efforts to rectify the conditions leading to tragically preventable child deaths—from causes such as nutritional deficits and communicable diseases—will bereaved parents likely allow a professional practitioner access to their personal grief.

In more developed countries, injury prevention efforts are one of the main forms of social advocacy to eliminate needless deaths of younger children and adolescents. In the United States, Mothers Against Drunk Driving (MADD; https://madd.org) started in 1980 when Candy Lightner, a bereaved mother whose 13-year-old daughter was killed by an intoxicated driver, sought to toughen laws pertaining to these offenders. Also, the American Academy of Pediatrics features The Injury Prevention Program (https://publications.aap.org/patiented/pages/c_tipp) providing educational materials for parents and caregivers on how to minimize risk to younger children and adolescents from a variety of potentially fatal causes such as drowning, firearms, poisoning, burns, wheeled-sports injuries, and unsafe driving practices. Practitioners versed in injury prevention efforts will be better able to empathize and communicate with bereaved parents when a child dies from an unintentional injury.

WHAT DO BEREAVED PARENTS NEED?

Based on a review of 15 bereavement intervention programs developed in medical centers throughout the United States, Europe, and Australia, Kochen et al. (2020) identified five principal interventions medical professionals use to assist bereaved parents. These methods were crafted from practice-based observations on what seemed to help parents whose younger children or adolescents died (compare with Chapter 3, "Helpful Factors"). Most parents attending these bereavement programs had lost children due to congenital anomalies or diseases like cancer rather than accidents or preventable injuries. These hospital-based protocols, many of which had documented empirical support for their efficacy, are broad enough to be implemented by health-care practitioners across a wide range of clinical settings where bereaved parents are seen. The five principal interventions can serve as general guidelines.

- *Acknowledge parenthood and the child's life*—Encourage parental ministrations with the child, such as holding, washing, and caring, both before and after death. Use the child's name. When applicable, promote the practice of religious or spiritual ceremonies that validate the child's life.
- *Establish (tangible) keepsakes*—Safeguard the child's memory by collecting items (such as locks of hair, blankets, caps, and toys) or making items (such as photographs, hand- or footprints, or poems) that can be retained in a memory box or a prominent place at home (see Chapter 5, "Pregnancy Loss and Infant Death," for similar ideas).
- *Follow-up contact*—Let bereaved parents know that they, and their child, are not forgotten (e.g., through follow-up phone calls, condolence letters, flowers, or future appointments). Note the parent's bereavement status in their record (along with the deceased child's name, birthday, and death date) to facilitate appropriate acknowledgment at follow-up visits (cf. Weaver et al., 2023). Condolences sent to bereaved parents can be enhanced with personal touches: hand writing the note, mentioning the child by name,

sharing a specific memory, conveying the impact of the child's legacy on one's work or life, and assuring bereaved parents their child will always be remembered (Weaver et al., 2019).

- *Education and information on coping and grief*—Provide practical information on child loss via print materials, videos, or websites of organizations that sponsor support groups or educational seminars on coping and grief (such as Bereaved Parents of the USA, www.bereavedparentsusa.org, and The Compassionate Friends, www.compassionatefriends.org); offer an opportunity to discuss autopsy results and answer parent questions.
- *Remembrance activities*—Promote parental participation and involvement in funerals, memorial services, legacy projects, and other activities to honor and remember the deceased child (see Chapter 3, "Helpful Factors"). Attend the child's funeral or memorial service.

> ### CASE 6.A (Continued)
>
> For Derrick and Annette, affirming their parenthood and speaking the twins' names meant a great deal, especially for Derrick, who had no other biological children. Though their lives were brief, Sissy and Brother showed distinct personalities, and those traits were interwoven into the memories their parents kept and the stories they told. For example, Derrick could chuckle over Brother's adventuresome nature and "terrible two's" stubbornness—traits they shared—while acknowledging those same traits likely contributed to his demise. The therapist emphasized how Derrick and Annette would always be the twins' parents, regardless of the children's deaths. Much of the treatment focused on psychoeducation about grief and coping, particularly suggestions for handling grief upsurges, dealing with their respective families, working with the two older children, returning to work, handling the death anniversary, and preparing for litigation (which concluded with a negotiated settlement).
>
> As far as remembrance and legacy, Annette developed a unique angle. She learned from a friend about a special swim program intended to help infants and toddlers learn how to roll onto their backs and float in water as a secondary protection against drowning (should adult supervision lapse). She became an instructor, and her dedication to teaching this skill helped assuage her grief. She concluded, "Something good out of something bad. That's how I flipped it." Annette took great satisfaction in teaching infants and toddlers to roll over and float successfully. While she could not save Sissy and Brother, each time she

taught a child how to survive in the water lessened some of the pain of their personal tragedy.

Unfortunately, Derrick and Annette's relationship eventually collapsed. Derrick fell further into chemical dependency and could not maintain employment, so they separated. The twins' deaths had frustrated Annette's parental longings but did not extinguish them. Some years after Sissy and Brother drowned, Annette retrieved their frozen embryos and got pregnant again. She was able to carry a baby to term and delivered an infant daughter! Having another child to raise made an enormous difference in Annette's grief trajectory. She experienced fullness, completion, and a sense of purpose in life by working as a health-care professional, raising her youngest daughter, and teaching water survival skills to infants and toddlers.

One question frequently asked after the death of a younger child or adolescent is what to do with the deceased child's room as well as their clothes and belongings. When is retaining treasured objects a healthy form of remembrance, and when is it problematic? Some bereaved parents choose to leave the child's things just the way they were at the time of death. The room and possessions become like a shrine or museum dedicated to the deceased child. This kind of preservation often leaves others uncomfortable, wondering if this response constitutes unhealthy denial or preoccupation.

CASE 6.B

One bereaved mother not only left her deceased son's room untouched, but she also closed the door and forbade anyone to enter. Recognizing that the response was part of the mother's reluctance to acknowledge the finality of her son's death, the practitioner counseled a gradual approach to modifying this off-limits policy. Entering the son's room and spending contemplative time there became part of the mother's situational revisiting (cf. Shear, 2015) as she learned to sit with the uncomfortable feelings and memories it evoked. In the process, she came to grips with the sad reality that he would not return. Slowly, the mother was able to convert the time in her son's room to a means of connection with him rather than a source of distress over his absence. Eventually, she was able to leave the door open and allow other members of the family to enter the room as well to remember the deceased son.

Knapp (1986) recommended that bereaved parents take their time making decisions about the deceased child's room and possessions rather than acting hastily when their emotions are raw and their executive thinking compromised. Usually, parents can keep significant mementos, personal possessions, or clothing items in special boxes or memorial spaces to honor the memory of the deceased child yet still permit living areas to be utilized. Often the child's clothing can be donated to persons in need or to special causes. (See Chapter 7, "Death of an Adult Child," for an example of creative disposition of a deceased son's clothing.)

PARENT IDENTITY

Lichtenthal's approach using Meaning-Centered Grief Therapy (Lichtenthal & Breitbart, 2015; Lichtenthal et al., 2019; Lichtenthal et al., 2017) is particularly applicable because her model evolved from treating parents whose children died from cancer (see Chapter 4, "Contemporary Treatment Approaches"). Parent identity work forms the heart of Lichtenthal's treatment: Who was I *before* my child died? Who am I *now*? Who do I want to be in the *future*? These questions address central concerns of bereaved parents struggling to find emotional and psychological equilibrium after the death of a younger child or adolescent.

Embedded in these provocative questions is a subtextual message that parenting is a longitudinal endeavor. Parenting constantly changes with the multifaceted demands made and innumerable adaptations required as children grow and develop. Parenting never really ends, even after the death of a child. Parents are parents permanently.

Yet the death of a child forces bereaved parents to reevaluate everything they thought they knew and believed, as eloquently stated by Donna Schuurman at the beginning of this chapter (D. L. Schuurman, personal communication, January 16, 2024). They must find their place in a new narrative understanding of themselves and their reality, what Attig (2010) calls relearning the world. Reworking and revising the parental narrative is a primary objective in Lichtenthal's Meaning-Centered Grief Therapy. Identity work is also a secondary goal in Shear's Prolonged Grief Treatment (Shear, 2015), Rynearson's Restorative Retelling (Rynearson et al., 2015), and Boelen's Cognitive Behavioral Therapy for Grief (Boelen et al., 2007).

How do bereaved parents address this compensatory identity work when all they really want is their child back, alive and well? Interestingly, none of the evidence-based treatment models start with identity work. Rather, efforts to reclaim self-worth, parental identity, and hope for the future are staged later in the treatment sequences. The prescient nature of clinical timing cannot be overstated: *Bereaved parents will be most receptive to identity work after some of the early emotional pain and trauma has subsided and a more reflective position can be assumed.*

Klass (2001) published a qualitative analysis of bereaved parents observed during their participation in a support group specifically designed for parents whose children had died. Klass's time-intensive immersion with the support group authenticated his findings and gave practitioners a fascinating account of how these parents adapted over time and moved toward a sense of resolution, or not, about their losses. Klass construed parental grief in phases, based on group members' self-descriptions of their journey: "newly bereaved," "into their grief," "well along in their grief," and "resolved as much as it will be" (p. 79). He described how bereaved parents develop and maintain inner representations of the deceased child in both their psychological and social worlds. These representations form the basis for revised parental identity in the aftermath of losing a child.

Newly bereaved parents found themselves in a nightmare world, a foreign country of grief (cf. Tedeschi & Calhoun, 2004), facing the awful truth that their child is gone. This loss was often so traumatic that they felt dissociated from daily reality and out of touch with the deceased child. They isolated from social networks when they perceived others either did not understand or could not tolerate their grief. Even though Klass (2001) did not assign specific time markers to the grief phases, newly bereaved parents generally described the first year post-loss in these terms.

Into their grief reflected the complexity bereaved parents faced in trying to assimilate the deaths of their children. Their interior psychological bond with the child required separating from the "living child," connecting with the child's pain (in dying), and wrestling with any ambivalence in the parent-child relationship. Socially, the support group performed a critical function by permitting parents to talk about their deceased child and allowing others in the group to get to know the deceased child. Such interactions created a social representation of who their child was and reinforced the idea that the bereaved parents were still parents. Group members also validated metaphysical or symbolic interactions with the deceased child, such as talking to the child, dreaming of the child, hearing the child's voice, finding objects emblematic of the child, or encountering natural phenomena interpreted as signals from the child, such as a cardinal or butterfly landing nearby or a special flower blooming. LaGrand (2006) described such occurrences as extraordinary experiences that can yield a rich sense of connection with the deceased.

Klass (2001) described a beautiful metaphoric example of one mother's efforts to express the complexity of her parental grief while others were celebrating seasonal holidays. She made a wreath for the front door with many colored ribbons, including a black one, declaring, "It is there. If they want to see it and mention it, they can. It is not me that didn't bring it up" (p. 86).

Well along in their grief meant bereaved parents had arrived at an emotional space where they could let go and hold on simultaneously. They identified more with the energy and love their living child had. They felt a positive bond with the deceased child and experienced a sense of healing within themselves. In sharing with the group, the inner representation of their deceased child became more accessible and more real. A sense of oneness with other bereaved parents helped consolidate that continuing bond, for example, at annual balloon releases or candle-lighting ceremonies.

Resolved as much as it will be exemplified learning to live with the sadness. As one parent in Klass's (2001) study observed, "You don't get over your grief, but it doesn't stay the same" (p. 89). The inner psychological representation of the deceased child transformed into a more *active* type of continuing bond. Often, bereaved parents felt their child accompanied them or even influenced them as an ongoing presence. Sometimes bereaved parents consciously assumed traits or virtues of the deceased child as part of that connection. Legacy projects took on greater significance. The support group was valued for helping them make the journey, with an acknowledgment that the trail never ends.

Annette's story seemed indicative of *resolved as much as it will be*. She reached a point where her energies were directed forward into life-giving activities—patient care, parenting, teaching—rather than stuck in a rear-view preoccupation with what had been taken from her. The twins and their lamentable deaths were never forgotten, but the pain of their loss diminished. Annette's legacy endeavor as a swim instructor brought its own rewards by ensuring that the children she taught might be spared a similar fate. She transformed her sense of helplessness and anger into empowered advocacy so that her personal tragedy might not be repeated with someone else. Such altruism is one hallmark of healthy adjustment (Vaillant, 1993).

SIBLING GRIEF

Many parents have other children at the time their younger child or adolescent dies, or they go on to have another child, or children, after the death. In Annette's case, it was both. In families with multiple children, bereaved parents grapple not only with their own grief but also with the grief of their other children. This dual responsibility of "grieving and parenting" can present significant challenges to bereaved parents who may already feel stretched beyond their limits (Buckle & Fleming, 2011). Practitioners attentive to this dilemma can help bereaved parents meet the needs of their other children who are grieving the loss of a sister or brother while at the same time managing their own subjective devastation.

Hogan and DeSantis (1992, 1996) posed a question to adolescents whose brother or sister had died: "If you could ask or tell your dead sibling something, what would it be?" Their qualitative analysis classified the thoughts and feelings of bereaved siblings into six broad categories: *regretting* what happened, *endeavoring to understand* the death, *"catching up"* with the deceased sibling about current events, *reaffirming* that the decedent is loved and missed, *seeking guidance* from the next world, and *anticipating reunion* in heaven. They detected an ongoing attachment between their respondents and the deceased sibling, reflecting a timeless quality to the sibling bond. Their categories form a conceptual roadmap of sibling grief. They help practitioners understand how adolescents will likely respond to the death of a brother or sister, enabling them to provide more incisive interventions. In addition, these findings can help bereaved parents better understand their surviving child(ren) and better support them in their grief.

Also, original work by Betty Davies (1999) and later collaboration with her colleagues (Kobler et al., in press) investigated the grief responses of adolescents whose sibling died from cancer in a pediatric hospital setting. She discovered four common themes in what siblings reported after losing a sister or brother, concerns their bereaved parents did not always recognize. The four themes could be succinctly expressed in first-person laments: *I hurt inside. I don't understand. I don't belong. I'm not enough.* Bereaved parents may need help recognizing these reactions among their surviving children and knowing how to respond appropriately.

Davies and colleagues theorized as follows. In sensitively supporting their surviving children following the death of a sister or brother, bereaved parents dispense a personal medicine only they can provide. Addressing these four sibling concerns reinforces the incontrovertible reality that they are still parents, still capable, and still needed, which can be a welcome balm for parents grieving the loss of a younger child or adolescent.

The first two concerns often expressed by bereaved siblings ("I hurt inside" and "I don't understand") may seem obvious. Most parents will naturally try to soothe the emotional pain of their children by comforting them. Also, most parents realize that difficult realities like death need to be explained to children in language and concepts matching their developmental and cognitive levels. For example, discussions about death with a 5-year-old are quite different from explanations to a 13-year-old (cf. Himelstein et al., 2004). Younger children understand better when parents use references to plants, pets, or grandparents who have died while older children require more detail about the physiology of their sibling's death.

The latter two sibling concerns ("I don't belong" and "I'm not enough") are more subtle. Sometimes, the enormous grief encompassing bereaved parents, often accentuated by solicitous concern from friends and family, can leave surviving children feeling unincluded or pushed to the periphery because they are not the principal grievers ("I don't belong"). Annette's two older children from a previous marriage acknowledged feeling left out by the grief storm that struck their family. Reassuring bereaved siblings about their place in the family and in the hearts of their grieving parents means helping them feel included. Examples might be finding ways for them to participate in caregiving for a dying sibling or finding meaningful roles for them in funeral or memorial services.

When witnessing the amount of emotional attention accorded to the dying or deceased child, siblings sometimes feel less significant by comparison ("I'm not enough"). Validation of surviving siblings requires affirmation of their personal uniqueness (e.g., "You'll always be our little scientist" or "No one cares for animals like you do") and confirmation of the parent-child bond (e.g., "You're my fishing buddy" or "Who else can I bake with?"), things more important than ever in the aftermath of their sister's or brother's death. Once bereaved parents understand the need for validation, they can usually think of ways to make a surviving sibling feel special.

Survivor guilt can also be a major concern for bereaved siblings (Weaver et al., 2023). Siblings sometimes feel guilty just for being alive when their sister or brother is dead. Children aged 12 and under who still engage in "magical thinking" may erroneously believe they somehow caused their sibling's death or did not do enough to save them. Siblings may feel less worthy than their deceased sister or brother when post-death idealization of the deceased child occurs. They may even harbor feelings that they should have died instead. Sometimes siblings feel guilty because they find ways to deal with the loss and adapt better or faster than their parents. They may hesitate to mention or talk about the deceased sibling for fear of "hurting" or "triggering" their grieving parents. Siblings born after the loss of a child can bring great joy to bereaved parents, but sometimes those later-born siblings feel a burden to measure up, or sometimes they carry ambivalence about assuming their own identity apart from the deceased sibling.

Another variation with sibling grief occurs when the surviving sister or brother becomes "parentified" because the bereaved parent is not coping well. In the case of the drowned twins, Annette was initially so shattered and despondent that she resorted to self-medicating with alcohol. Out of concern, her older daughter became a solicitous caretaker. Obviously, practitioners who become aware of problem patterns like the parentified child need to work toward restoring family structure and roles along more salutary lines. Given all these possible permutations of sibling grief, practitioners can help bereaved parents respond in restorative and healing ways as they juggle the twin challenges of handling their own grief while continuing to parent their surviving children.

FAMILY THERAPY

Family therapy models provide additional strategies when working conjointly with bereaved parents and siblings after the death of a younger children or adolescent. For example, Family Focused Grief Therapy (FFGT), developed in

Australia by David Kissane and colleagues (Kissane & Bloch, 2002; Kissane et al., 2008; Kissane et al., 2006), was designed to help families cope when a loved one is in palliative care. They rated how adaptively families functioned as their loved one neared death, then focused their interventions on families displaying high conflict levels, low cohesion, and poor expressiveness. Thus, the target population for FFGT—families struggling with the impending death of a loved one—resembles the grieving parents and siblings that practitioners may encounter when a child is dying or has died. Admittedly, FFGT was validated on a sample of older patients and their younger family members. However, for practitioners trained in family work or those inclined to conceptualize cases with a systems framework, FFGT may be usefully adapted with families grieving the death of a younger child or adolescent.

Kissane and Bloch's (2002) interventions are intended to promote communication, strengthen family cohesion, and facilitate conflict resolution. Their repertoire of thematically guided questions can be utilized in strategic ways when serving bereaved parents and family members together. Consider how artfully they address their three therapeutic objectives in the following sample questions from their treatment protocol (pp. 56–58). Notice how some queries are direct while others are "circular" and devised to generate discussion among the family members about the topic.

- *Communication*—"Who does most of the talking in this family?" "Who does the least?" "Do you talk much as a family about [name's] death?" "What's it like when you try to tell the family about important things?"
- *Cohesion*—"How well do you team together as a family?" "Has [name's] death led you as a family to become closer or more distant?" "Do you tend to be open or closed in expressing your feelings?"
- *Conflict*—"Can we examine the usual way your family handles disagreements?" "Who is the crucial decision-maker in this family?" "Are you a family that forgives?" "Does the family regard the way you [argue/avoid/overtalk] as a problem?"

FFGT also helps families clarify role expectations and explore deeply held values. It uses session summaries to promote consensus and maintain therapeutic focus. Practitioners wanting to refine or expand their skills to include family therapy approaches will find evidence-based FFGT a rich source for ideas and options.

Employing circular questions with bereaved families to encourage potential meaning making is a hallmark of Nadeau's (1998) approach. For example, Nadeau coined the term *coincidancing* to describe how some families *collectively* come to see significance in dreams, events, or natural phenomena as a way of coping with grief, such as interpreting a rainbow that appeared on the day of the loved one's funeral as an indication they are safely in the afterlife, or when families together assign meaning to important dimensions of the deceased's life to help explain the timing or nature of death. Such mutual meaning making was evident in Derrick and Annette's shared conclusion that Sissy, who was protective, probably died trying to save Brother, who undoubtedly ventured into the pool first because of his impulsivity. Addressing the complexity of families in grief demands a holistic view of bereavement where the family is seen as the unit of care, not just the bereaved parents (Breen et al., 2019).

CHILD BEREAVEMENT RESOURCES

Bereaved parents do not have to act alone to help their surviving children grieve the loss of a sibling. Across the United States, there are many independent child bereavement centers offering support to grieving children and families, including programs for bereaved siblings. These centers generally provide exceptional programming carried out by dedicated staff and volunteers. Examples of these facilities are listed here (alphabetically): Amelia Center in Birmingham, Alabama (www.childrensal.org/services/amelia-center); Children's Bereavement Center of South Texas in San Antonio (https://cbcst.org); Dougy Center in Portland, Oregon (www.dougy.org); Highmark Caring Place in Pittsburgh, Pennsylvania (www.highmarkcaringplace.com); Judi's House in Denver, Colorado (https://judishouse.org). In the United Kingdom, the Child Bereavement Network (https://childhoodbereavementnetwork.org.uk) offers similar programming. Practitioners in North America with a special interest in helping bereaved parents address sibling grief can also refer to the National Alliance for Children's Grief (https://nacg.org) in the United States or the Canadian Alliance for Children's Grief (www.grievingchildrencanada.org).

Besides traditional counseling and educational activities, some of these centers and organizations sponsor bereavement camps for siblings, typically during the summer months, as an alternate way to promote healthy grieving. Camps use developmentally calibrated psychoeducation about loss and feature hands-on, multimodal ways for children and adolescents to express grief, perform leave-taking, give and receive support, and engage in remembrance or legacy projects. Parents are usually involved at the conclusion of camp so siblings can share what they have learned and experienced to promote mutual understanding and family healing.

SUMMARY

Fathers and mothers of younger children or adolescents have already progressed on the road of parenthood when the tragedy of child loss strikes.

Mid-stride in building a family life, they encounter unintended injury deaths or unforeseen fatal diseases that cut short their visions of a future with their child. The empty track pulsates with pain, and the cruelty of fate seems unbearable. Distilled clinical wisdom on what bereaved parents need, together with translatable research findings on how grieving parents (and bereaved siblings) struggle with their losses, provide practitioners with a wide range of therapeutic tools. Family therapy approaches may be useful as well. Numerous psychoeducational resources, support organizations, and treatment centers are available to supplement the efforts of professional caregivers who work with bereaved parents whose younger children or adolescents have died, as well as bereaved siblings.

REFERENCES

Attig, T. (2010). *How we grieve: Relearning the world*. Oxford University Press.

Boelen, P. A., de Keijser, J., van den Hout, M. A., & van den Bout, J. (2007). Treatment of complicated grief: A comparison between cognitive-behavioral therapy and supportive counseling. *Journal of Consulting and Clinical Psychology, 75*(2), 277–284. https://doi.org/10.1037/0022-006X.75.2.277

Breen, L. J., Szylit, R., Gilbert, K. R., Macpherson, C., Murphy, I., Nadeau, J. W., Reis, E., Silva, D., Wiegand, D. L., & International Work Group on Death, Dying, and Bereavement. (2019). Invitation to grief in the family context. *Death Studies, 43*(3), 173–182. https://doi.org/10.1080/07481187.2018.1442375

Buckle, J. L., & Fleming, S. J. (2011). *Parenting after the death of a child: A Practitioner's Guide*. Routledge.

Davies, B. (1999). *Shadows in the sun: Experiences of sibling bereavement in childhood*. Brunner/Mazel.

Himelstein, B. P., Hilden, J. M., Boldt, A. M., & Weissman, D. (2004). Pediatric palliative care. *The New England Journal of Medicine, 350*(17), 1752–1762. https://doi.org/10.1056/NEJMra030334

Hogan, N., & DeSantis, L. (1992). Adolescent sibling bereavement: An ongoing attachment. *Qualitative Health Research, 2*(2), 159–177. https://doi.org/10.1177/104973239200200204

Hogan, N., & DeSantis, L. (1996). Adolescent sibling bereavement: Toward a new theory. In C. A. Corr & D. E. Balk (Eds.), *Handbook of adolescent death and bereavement* (pp. 173–195). Springer Publishing Company.

Kissane, D. W., & Bloch, S. (2002). *Family Focused Grief Therapy: A model of family-centred care during palliative care and bereavement*. Open University Press.

Kissane, D. W., Lichtenthal, W. G., & Zaider, T. (2008). Family care before and after bereavement. *OMEGA—Journal of Death and Dying, 56*(1), 21–32. https://doi.org/10.2190/om.56.1.c

Kissane, D. W., McKenzie, M., Bloch, S., Moskowitz, C., McKenzie, D. P., & O'Neill, I. (2006). Family Focused Grief Therapy: A randomized, controlled trial in palliative care and bereavement. *The American Journal of Psychiatry, 163*(7), 1208–1218. https://doi.org/10.1176/ajp.2006.163.7.1208

Klass, D. (2001). The inner representation of the dead child in the psychic and social narratives of bereaved parents. In R. A. Neimeyer (Ed.), *Meaning *reconstruction and the experience of loss* (pp. 77–94). American Psychological Association.

Klass, D., & Marwit, S. J. (1988–1989). Toward a model of parental grief. *OMEGA—Journal of Death and Dying, 19,* 31–50. https://doi.org/10.2190/BVUR-67KR-F52F-VW35

Kobler, K., Limbo, R., & Davies, B. (in press). Grief and bereavement in perinatal and pediatric palliative care. In B. R. Ferrell, V. Battista, & J. A. Paice (Eds.), *Oxford textbook of palliative nursing* (6th ed.). Oxford University Press.

Kochen, E. M., Jenken, F., Boelen, P. A., Deben, L. M. A., Fahner, J. C., van den Hoogen, A., Teunissen, S. C. C. M., Geleijns, K., & Kars, M. C. (2020). When a child dies: A systematic review of well-defined parent-focused bereavement interventions and their alignment with grief- and loss theories. *BMC Palliative Care, 19,* 28. https://doi.org/10.1186/s12904-020-0529-z

Knapp, R. J. (1986). *Beyond endurance: When a child dies.* Schocken.

LaGrand, L. E. (2006). *Love lives on: Learning from the extraordinary experiences of the bereaved.* Berkley.

Lichtenthal, W. G., & Breitbart, W. (2015). The central role of meaning in adjustment to the loss of a child to cancer: Implications for the development of Meaning-Centered Grief Therapy. *Current Opinions in Supportive and Palliative Care, 9,* 46–51. https://doi.org/10.1097/SPC.0000000000000117

Lichtenthal, W. G., Catarozoli, C., Masterson, M., Slivjak, E., Schofield, E., Roberts, K. E., Neimeyer, R. A., Wiener, L., Prigerson, H. G., Kissane, D. W., Li, Y., & Breitbart, W. (2019). An open trial of Meaning-Centered Grief Therapy: Rationale and preliminary evaluation. *Palliative & Supportive Care, 17,* 2–12. https://doi.org/10.1017/S1478951518000925

Lichtenthal, W. G., Lacey, S., Roberts, K., Sweeney, C., & Slivijak, E. (2017). Meaning-Centered Grief Therapy: Using the concepts of choice in coping with loss. In W. Breitbart (Ed.), *Meaning-centered psychotherapy* (pp. 88–99). Oxford University Press.

Liu, L., Villavicencio, F., Yeung, D., Perin, J., Lopez, G., Strong, K. L., & Black, R. E. (2022). National, regional, and global causes of mortality in 5–19-year-olds from 2000 to 2019: A systematic analysis. *Lancet Global Health, 10,* e337–e347. https://doi.org/10.1016/s2214-109x(21)00566-0

Nadeau, J. W. (1998). *Families making sense of death.* Sage.

National Center for Injury Prevention and Control, Centers for Disease Control and Prevention. (2020a). *10 leading causes of death, United States, 2020, both sexes, all ages, all races.* WISQARS Data Visualization. (n.d.). Retrieved November 13, 2024, from https://stacks.cdc.gov/view/cdc/136409

National Center for Injury Prevention and Control, Centers for Disease Control and Prevention. (2020b). *10 leading causes of injury deaths by age group, 2020, both sexes, all ages, all races.* WISQARS Data Visualization. (n.d.). Retrieved November 13, 2024, from https://stacks.cdc.gov/view/cdc/136409

Neugarten, B. (1979). Time, age, and the life cycle. *The American Journal of Psychiatry, 136,* 887–894. https://doi.org/10.1176/ajp.136.7.887

Rynearson, E. K., Correa, F., & Takacs, L. (2015). *Accommodation to violent dying: A guide to restorative retelling and support.* Virginia Mason Clinic. www.vmfh.org/content/dam/vmfhorg/pdf/legacy-vm/workfiles/Manual_Accommodation_Violent_Dying.pdf

Shear, M. K. (2015). *Complicated grief treatment.* Columbia Center for Complicated Grief.

Tedeschi, R. G., & Calhoun, L. G. (2004). *Helping bereaved parents: A clinician's guide*. Brunner-Routledge.

Vaillant, G. E. (1993). *The wisdom of the ego*. Harvard University Press.

Weaver, M. S., Lichtenthal, W. G., Larson, K., & Wiener, L. (2019). How I approach expressing condolences and longitudinal remembering to a family after the death of a child. *Pediatric Blood Cancer, 66*, e27489. https://doi.org/10.1002/pbc.27489

Weaver, M. S., Nasir, A., Lord, B. T., Starin, A., Linebarger, J. S., Committee on Psychosocial Aspects of Child and Family Health, & Section on Hospice and Palliative Medicine. (2023). Supporting the family after the death of a child or adolescent. *Pediatrics, 152*(6), e2023064426. https://doi.org/10.1542/peds.2023-064426

CHAPTER SEVEN

Death of an Adult Child

> Somewhere out there is a new order that will come out of this chaotic experience.
> —Rabbi Daniel A. Roberts (2022)

Everyone is someone's child. Greater longevity rates mean more parents will outlive their adult children. When and how an adult child dies, as well as the nature of the relationship at the time of death, strongly affects parental grief. As Roberts (2022) indicates, finding a new order after losing an adult son or daughter entails special hardships for bereaved parents.

CASE 7.A

Eddie and Beverly's middle son Mark died from COVID-19. Mark had been a difficult teenager and, even in his 20s, would not readily accept influence from his parents. Mark was exceptionally obese and did not practice conscientious health habits. He lived out of state, alone, in a rented house where he worked virtually and knew almost no one in the local community.

Despite the pandemic, Mark had agreed to join his parents and two siblings for a family weekend at a resort destination. After everyone returned home, various members of the family started feeling ill and tested positive for COVID-19. Eddie and Beverly reached out to Mark to make him aware of the situation and encouraged him to get tested. Characteristically a spotty communicator, Mark did not answer their initial text messages and phone calls. He finally responded, acknowledging that he also was not feeling well and was having trouble breathing. At an emergency department, he tested positive for COVID-19 but was not sick enough to be admitted to a hospital. Instead, he was scheduled for a pulmonary function test later that same day and sent home. They never heard from Mark again.

Eddie and Beverly continued reaching out to Mark but without success. They feared for his well-being but also did not know whether he was sleeping to recover or just not answering his phone. They had never visited where he lived and did not know anyone there to call. Finally, after 48 hours without any word, they contacted local authorities to perform a welfare check. Mark was found dead in his bed. His body was transported to a local mortuary, already distended and discolored.

Paralyzed with grief, Eddie and Beverly had no idea what to do next. Local authorities where Mark lived asked for the family to identify his body before releasing it. In desperation, Eddie and Beverly contacted a funeral home in their locality, and the staff suggested sending a photograph of Mark to verify his identity. Because of COVID-19 contamination concerns, funeral staff recommended immediate cremation rather than transporting Mark's body home. Not really seeing any other options, Eddie and Beverly reluctantly agreed. Mark's body was cremated by a funeral home in the town where he died, and his cremains were shipped home. They never saw Mark's body after he died.

Not being religious in any way, Eddie and Beverly could not see the point in a funeral or memorial service. They did not think their respective families, who lived in distant states and with whom they were not especially close, would come to a service anyway. They were unsure of their ultimate retirement location and so did not want to bury Mark's cremains where they would not be living. Eddie and Beverly consulted a mental health clinician, who opined that Mark's death was a result of his poor choices about health matters. Feeling affronted, they never went back. They experienced indescribable emotional pain and persistent disbelief that Mark had actually died. On advice from their primary care physician, Eddie and Beverly scheduled an appointment with a practitioner specializing in grief-related problems.

HOW ADULT CHILDREN DIE

In the United States, the majority of individuals aged 25 to 64 who die succumb to natural causes such as cancer, heart disease, or infectious diseases, although a significant number die from unintentional injuries (National Center for Injury Prevention and Control, 2020; see Chapter 8, "Accidental Death"). Regardless of the cause, from a life-cycle perspective, these deaths would be considered premature and off time (Neugarten, 1979) in a society where lifespans average 80.2 years for women and 74.8 years for men (Arias et al., 2023). Prior to the COVID-19 pandemic, average lifespans worldwide were 75.9 years for women and 70.8 years for men. Yet rates varied dramatically between richer and poorer countries (averaging 83.3 years versus 67.2 years for women and 78.4 years versus 63 years for men, respectively; World Health Statistics, 2019). These realities often lead to implicit expectations about lifespan and certainly reinforce the generational expectation that children will outlive their parents.

The tragic death of Eddie and Beverly's adult son illustrates the interplay of several risk factors for complications in grieving. His death was completely unforeseen and unanticipated. Expectations for Mark to thrive independently, even as his parents approached retirement, were turned upside down by his death. Eddie and Beverly's hopes for legacy took a severe blow from the death of one of their three children. Their sense of self was battered, particularly from feelings of failure and a perception of not doing enough to save Mark from a deadly virus. Moreover, his abrupt death was entirely preventable in their minds, especially if Mark had been more proactive on his own behalf. Living away from their families, Eddie and Beverly felt a dearth of social support. They had never put stock in religion or faith-based views of life. They admitted having no idea how to think about death as a concept and felt completely at a loss for perspective on Mark's death. It all seemed so unreal and meaningless.

The conflictual relationship Eddie and Beverly had with Mark really intensified their grief. Mark had not been an easy child to raise. During high school, he was a marginal student and began using drugs. Later, he dropped out of college and returned home to live but would not find work. Mark maintained a covert social life, so Eddie and Beverly rarely knew who his companions were or what he was doing. They frequently found themselves angry with Mark over his lack of industry as well as his poor health habits. Eventually, the tense situation came to a head when they issued an ultimatum—get a job or get out. So, Mark left to move in with an out-of-state friend enlisted in the military. That friend subsequently deployed, leaving Mark alone in the house.

Eddie and Beverly repeatedly second-guessed how they had handled the situation with Mark, leading to an endless stream of "what if" questions about how things may have turned out differently had they made other choices, an example of *counterfactual* thinking (Neimeyer et al., 2021; Shear, 2015). What if they had been more accommodating? More understanding? More patient? What if they had been less judgmental? Less harsh? Less demanding? Speculating about those alternate possibilities left them with inordinate feelings of guilt.

Also contributing to Eddie and Beverly's grief was the striking absence of helpful factors that can aid coping and ameliorate distress (see Chapter 3, "Helpful Factors"). Despite being reasonably capable people who held responsible jobs, they did not demonstrate the robust features of personal hardiness. They tended to be somewhat passive in their approach to life and death. They sought advice from professionals but, in the middle of the crisis, lacked the presence of mind to fully evaluate the soundness of the counsel they received. Guilt and shame prevented them from consulting with friends or family who may have helped them think things through more carefully and provide needed support. They did not endorse intrinsic spirituality. In fact, Eddie and Beverly exhibited few of the adaptive behaviors listed in Chapter 3 that can lower the distress of bereaved parents. They never said goodbye. They experienced an acute sense of meaninglessness. Overwhelmed by the tragedy, they could recall few positive memories about Mark. They had limited social support.

VIEWING THE BODY

When an adult child dies from natural causes in a hospital or even at home, parents and families are often there, so seeing the body after death is taken for granted. However, when adult children live in other locations or die away from home, as with Mark, the situation can be quite different. Depending on the death circumstances, law enforcement personnel or a coroner may require a family member to make a positive identification of the body before a death certificate can be issued.

For many bereaved parents, viewing the body helps them grasp the painful reality of the child's death, an outcome they do not want to believe is true and one they may even find themselves doubting, much like Eddie and Beverly. Seeing the body of a deceased son or daughter, and even touching the body, makes the death undeniably real. Viewing can also provide an important opportunity for leave-taking and saying goodbye. Mowll et al. (2016) studied individuals whose loved ones died suddenly and found that electively choosing to view the body of the deceased was important for absorbing the reality of the death. Some grievers took advantage of the opportunity to physically express love and care for the body of the deceased (e.g., stroking, caressing, dressing) before relinquishing it.

However, a decision to view the deceased child's body should not be forced. Some bereaved parents may be reluctant, perhaps unsure of what they will see or how they will react, especially if the child's body has been damaged or disfigured. They may be concerned that a last look could be traumatizing or produce horrific, indelible images. Or they may fear losing control of their emotions by "breaking down" in a manner not conducive to their coping or upsetting to others who are also grieving the loss. (For special considerations about viewing a child's body following homicide, see Chapter 10, "Homicide"). With appropriate guidance and support, some parents who are initially hesitant will make the decision to view the body and confirm the death for themselves. However, when a bereaved parent ultimately declines viewing, their choice should be respected. For some bereaved parents, choosing not to view the deceased child's body may serve a protective function against trauma (Mowll et al., 2017). Phrases such as, "That's not how I want to remember [child's name]" generally mean the individual has concluded that viewing would be too much to bear or be otherwise unhelpful.

> ### CASE 7.A (Continued)
>
> With Eddie and Beverly, the advice they received about how they could identify Mark's body, and whether to view his remains, appeared to be based on pragmatism and cost containment rather than consideration for their mental and emotional health. Never seeing Mark's body after his death left lingering questions about whether he had really died. They actively wondered if perhaps they were the victims of a cruel joke. No one suggested they could drive or fly the 500 miles to Mark's home to handle these sad duties in person or see where Mark was living and retrieve his belongings. They admitted to the second therapist that lack of viewing made it more difficult to accept the reality of Mark's death. In addition, contamination fears on the part of both law enforcement and funeral home personnel seemed to dominate deliberations about disposition and transfer of Mark's remains. Most likely, Eddie and Beverly would have chosen cremation anyway, but immediate cremation by the out-of-state funeral home eliminated any chance to view Mark's body.

The sad truth is that death poses many inconveniences. Yet when mourners are forced to grapple with these inconvenient circumstances, those efforts reinforce the reality and finality of the death. Mourners mobilize potentially adaptive coping behaviors, such as engagement and problem-solving, that facilitate a healthy grief response.

RITUALS OF REMEMBRANCE

Bereaved parents who belong to a particular faith tradition can rely on and incorporate the rubrics of that tradition during funerals, memorial services, and burial or disposition of remains—practices imbued with deep spiritual and personal meaning that can bring comfort and support to the bereft (Hoy, 2025; Irion, 1999). However, not all bereaved parents have a faith affiliation to fall back on when a child dies. Furthermore, family conflict can erupt when deceased adult children are married or have families of their own who either do not share the same faith beliefs as the parents or practice no faith at all. Spouses of deceased adult children are the primary decision-makers, and their preferences in these matters can differ sharply from the sensibilities of bereaved parents. Hurt feelings as well as foreshortened or precluded leave-taking can result from such differences, adding complications to an already devastating loss. Family conflict at funerals or memorial services detracts from the comfort mourners can gain (Gamino et al., 2000).

CASE 7.A (Continued)

Eddie and Beverly were not affiliated with any faith or religious tradition and had never given much thought to how they might handle the death of a family member for whom they were responsible. Because they viewed religious practices as meaningless, they did not see the potential psychological and social benefits associated with ritualized or ceremonial leave-taking. Geographic and emotional distance from their respective families of origin further reinforced their subjective isolation on a metaphoric island of grief with little access to support.

Gradually and gently, their practitioner began to introduce the idea of saying goodbye to Mark in a more intentional manner as a part of their grief work. Despite initial objections that no one in their families would bother to participate, further exploration revealed that Eddie's sisters had reached out shortly after Mark's death to express condolences. When Eddie informed them that no services were planned and nothing was really needed from them, his sisters afforded the couple the privacy they requested. Once Eddie reestablished communication, it surprised him that his sisters were still sympathetic to his grief. They welcomed an opportunity to say goodbye to Mark and support the couple in their loss. Eddie and Beverly began to reconsider the notion of a family gathering to honor Mark that would include their other two adult children and Eddie's sisters.

Mitima-Verloop et al. (2019) studied personal rituals of remembrance reported by a diverse group of Dutch grievers (see Chapter 3, "Helpful Factors"). Study participants utilized several different individualized practices, none of which were specifically linked to a particular faith tradition or denominational practice. Beyond a religious context, the possibilities for memorializing are limitless. Lester and Frye (2020) wrote a detailed account of a memorial service crafted for the first author's deceased mother, who was not affiliated with conventional religion. The ceremony occurred at the seaside and was attended by family members and close friends. Deliberate but informal, it incorporated elements such as carrying colorful pennants along a course laid out on the beach, singing her mother's favorite songs, reciting poetry, writing goodbye messages in the sand, releasing flower petals in the water, and partaking in refreshments afterward at a beachfront establishment. It was a proverbial celebration of life.

CASE 7.A (Continued)

Ultimately, Eddie and Beverly chose to return to the resort as a favorite spot for the entire family and coordinated the trip to include Eddie's sisters and nieces. They took along a photo album containing pictures of Mark at various ages to stimulate conversation and memory sharing. They cooked some of Mark's favorite foods. They planned an evening bonfire where they gave tributes and toasts to Mark. The trip ended with a family photo and resolutions to stay in closer touch. The weekend brought Eddie and Beverly considerable comfort and the solace of knowing their family supported them in their grief over Mark's death.

LIFE REARRANGED

Settling the estate of an adult child who dies sometimes requires participation from the bereaved parents. Such activities can be a positive form of advocacy after death as well as a way of honoring and remembering (see Chapter 3, "Helpful Factors"). Following Mark's death, Eddie and Beverly received what few personal possessions he had. They took responsibility for closing his bank account and stopping his phone service. Their surviving children helped them deactivate Mark's social media accounts. Some social media platforms permit a deceased person's account to be "memorialized," thus retaining that individual's digital presence in perpetuity. This option allows friends and family to continue posting condolences and remembrances on the deceased person's page, a feature many bereaved parents treasure as an indication their deceased son or daughter is not forgotten.

Unfortunately, settling estate matters can sometimes become problematic, adding further misery to bereaved parents' grief. Just as funeral or memorial services and body disposition can become controversial when bereaved parents have a strained relationship with a son-in-law, a daughter-in-law, or grown grandchildren, estate matters can result in fierce acrimony. Practitioners working with bereaved parents whose adult child has died are likely to encounter such socially explosive situations and may be asked for guidance regarding the distribution of personal effects or clothing and the allocation of valued heirlooms or tangible assets. Delineating a clear boundary between what can be controlled and what is beyond the parents' purview is generally a good starting point. Avoiding cutoffs and maintaining the best possible relationship with the deceased child's family is usually in the best interest of all concerned. However, such outcomes are not always attainable. Seemingly simple requests for items such as a deceased son's ballcap or briefcase, or a deceased daughter's necklace (perhaps one given to her by the bereaved parents) or one of her vases, may be denied. Sometimes bereaved parents must live with such secondary losses as a regrettable consequence of family conflict after the death of an adult son or daughter.

Another example of post-death consequences bereaved parents may face is generational shifts in life responsibilities. Consider the following case example.

CASE 7.B

Latrice's daughter, Shalonda, had been impulsive and irresponsible in her 20s and 30s. After divorcing, she came home to live with her widowed mother, along with her three young children. They managed to forge a rapprochement, and Latrice lovingly doted on her three grandchildren who craved her nurturing and stability. Shalonda's health was not good. Extremely obese, she suffered from asthma and high blood pressure. When mother and daughter both caught COVID-19, Shalonda's comorbidities made her case severe. She subsequently died from respiratory complications. For Latrice, Shalonda's death seemed like a particularly cruel twist of fate, given that they had finally achieved the loving relationship she always wanted. To make matters worse, the former son-in-law, who had remarried, claimed his parental rights to the three grandchildren and moved them to his home more than 100 miles away. Latrice found herself facing the double grief of losing both a middle-aged daughter and access to her precious grandchildren.

Grandparents parenting again after the death of an adult child presents both challenges and rewards. Keeping up with active young grandchildren may be physically taxing for an older grandparent. Dealing with adolescent grandchildren may be even more daunting at an emotional level. If a retirement lifestyle has already been adopted—whether the more sedate version of a slower pace at home or the more active version of traveling and socializing—raising grandchildren can necessitate a sharp course correction. Some grandparents may experience, in addition to grief over their adult child's death, a sense of resentment. They may feel angry or burdened with a responsibility they do not welcome, especially if the deceased child displayed a cavalier attitude toward their own health that contributed to their demise or if the grandchildren are difficult to handle. Practitioners need to approach such situations carefully, suspending any preconceived assumptions. Hearing out bereaved parents who are raising grandchildren and ensuring a safe space where they can freely express disappointments or joys is essential to good care.

For other bereaved parents who find themselves raising grandchildren left behind by their deceased son or daughter, nothing compares to the healing this role provides. They relish the chance to parent again and find innumerable reminders of their deceased child in the appearance and antics of the grandchildren. Wonderful reciprocity can occur when each party represents a living link to the deceased person, yielding an immeasurable source of compensatory comfort. Grandparents serve as a familial proxy for the deceased parent. Grandchildren personify, in uncanny ways, many of the traits and attributes of the deceased son or daughter. Through sharing a common loss, bereaved grandparents and grandchildren help each other.

CASE 7.B (Continued)

Latrice very much wanted to raise the grandchildren, both as a way of honoring Shalonda's legacy and as a way of staying connected to her deceased daughter. She saw many similarities between the grandchildren and their mother. Being a grandmother gave Latrice something constructive that quelled her grief. Their moving away meant additional sadness, not relief. Latrice stayed in touch via phone calls, text messages, and in-person visits during school holidays, lavishing them with maternal love and attention. Nothing helped her grief more than being around those grandchildren, who returned such vitality to her existence. In turn, the grandchildren flocked to her like a mother hen. Their mutual comfort in each other assuaged Latrice's grief. Loving the grandchildren also brought Latrice her strongest sense of a continuing bond with her deceased daughter.

However, these emotional benefits came at a financial price. Latrice's fixed budget in retirement had little leeway for accommodating the extra expenses generated by the grandchildren's visits. Those limitations caused Latrice considerable worry and stirred resentment toward her former son-in-law, who provided only nominal assistance during their extended summer visits. She managed with some extra help from her adult son, the grandchildren's uncle. Given how the grandchildren seemed to thrive under her care, Latrice deemed the rewards worth the sacrifices.

CONVERTING ABSENCE INTO PRESENCE

Holidays and anniversaries can be a painful time for bereaved parents who often feel the absence of their deceased son or daughter more acutely on those occasions due to the "empty seat" at the table. Engaging rituals of remembrance that invoke the spirit of the deceased child can forge a pathway to continuing connection. Practitioners can sometimes jumpstart bereaved parents' own creativity in this regard, thus promoting a sense of presence rather than absence, as the following case exemplified (cf. Gamino, 2020).

CASE 7.C

Harriet was in her 80s and widowed when her adult daughter Janice died from natural causes. Janice was born with Down syndrome, an intellectual disability. She had always lived at home. Following the death of her husband and the departure of the two older children (now married with families of their own), Harriet's life mission focused singularly on Janice. They served as the primary companions for one another. Janice's death meant stark emptiness for Harriet. With her precious daughter gone, Harriet struggled to get through each day, as if there was not enough air in the room to breathe.

As the Christmas holiday approached, Harriet felt completely out of step with the seasonal celebrations. All she could see ahead was sadness. Historically, no one loved Christmas more than Janice. In fact, Harriet helped turn that enthusiasm into a yearlong project for the two of them. They kept a large paper bag for each member of the family and collected gift items over the months in preparation for a big Christmas blowout. Harriet's grandchildren—Janice's nieces and nephews—always eagerly anticipated their aunt's gifts during their traditional Christmas afternoon gathering.

In discussions with her grief therapist, Harriet conceded that the customary distribution of gifts already collected that year needed to go on even though her heart was not in it. Harriet's biggest quandary was Janice's stocking: "I would hate not to put it up on the mantle, but I don't want an empty stocking hanging there. That would be just too sad." Her therapist suggested, "Why not fill it?"

That idea prompted an animated discussion about how magical it would be for everyone to find Harriet's stocking filled—not with gifts *for* her, but with gifts *from* her, for every member of the family! That surprise would be so characteristic of Janice's over-the-top Christmas enthusiasm. An expression of joy replaced Harriet's dour look as she envisioned how the gifts in Janice's stocking could be tree ornaments, followed by a new ritual of each family member telling a favorite story about Janice as they hung their ornament on the tree. "Then she really would be there," Harriet concluded, not as a static memory but as a vibrant, dynamic spirit.

This case shows how absence can be converted into presence through the use of meaningful ritual. Such innovations exemplify one of the ten key therapeutic elements listed in Chapter 4, "Contemporary Treatment Approaches": finding ways to honor and remember the deceased child and affirming their legacy. Based on getting to know Janice through Harriet's eyes (cf. Tedeschi & Calhoun, 2004), the therapist generated the initial suggestion about filling Janice's stocking with items for the rest of the family. Harriet's elaboration of that idea beautifully captured Janice's Christmas spirit. In the process, Harriet and her therapist collaborated in co-constructing a new ritual involving everyone in the family (Angus et al., 1999, Neimeyer, 2019), a result neither one might have envisioned alone. Lichtenthal's Meaning-Centered Grief Therapy emphasizes such living legacy interventions to bring solace and comfort to bereaved parents by enabling them to experience their deceased child living on through personalized rituals that carry so much meaning and significance (Lichtenthal & Breitbart, 2015; Lichtenthal et al., 2019; Lichtenthal et al., 2017).

FOCUSED TECHNIQUES

> **CASE 7.D**
>
> Liam's son, Judd, suffered a fatal heart attack in the middle of the night, a few days after the placement of a stent for coronary artery disease. In his 40s and overweight, Judd's recent hospital stay had been concerning enough that Liam traveled several hundred miles to be there when he was discharged from the hospital. When his daughter-in-law frantically woke him, Liam immediately tried to position Judd on the bedroom floor, where he attempted resuscitation while emergency medical services was called. When paramedics arrived, they requested Liam leave the room. Judd was transported back to the hospital in an uncertain status and later pronounced dead in the emergency department. Judd left behind a widow and a teenage son, Caleb. The final, chaotic moments of Liam's struggle to save Judd haunted his memories.
>
> Liam was a recovering drug addict with decades of sobriety. He had managed to build a successful business. However, when Judd was young and Liam still in the throes of his addiction, he was often "not there" for the family and eventually divorced Judd's mother. When Judd became an adult, they had a stormy father-son relationship. Judd caused lots of family problems by having an affair with his stepbrother's wife (the son of Liam's current wife). Additionally, they worked together in the family business, but Liam acknowledged, "I fired him," over differences in handling employees. Resentments on both sides led to a love-hate relationship, which Liam deeply regretted because now there was no way to fix it. Approximately six months after Judd's death, Liam consulted a grief therapist to address his misgivings and emotional anguish.

The therapist's initial treatment plan involved supportive listening, rapport building, history taking, and psychoeducation on parental grief. The turmoil within the stepfamily resulting from Judd's affair was convoluted and required careful management to enable both sides of the family to gather at holidays. Also, Liam felt considerable responsibility for helping his daughter-in-law and providing a grandfatherly presence for Caleb. Liam's requests for practical advice on these matters occupied the first several sessions. In the process, therapeutic trust and a strong working alliance developed, a foundation necessary for the difficult grief work ahead.

The longer-term treatment plan for Liam included a) the imaginal conversation technique from Shear's Prolonged Grief Treatment (2015) to address Liam's ambivalence toward Judd and b) the deconstruction and revision technique from Rynearson et al.'s Restorative Retelling (2015) to defuse Liam's reenactment imagery associated with trying to resuscitate Judd. Despite his stoic veneer, Liam appeared to be an intuitive griever (Doka & Martin, 2010) who needed to talk out his intense distress as part of coping with the tragedy of Judd's death.

Once Liam found ways to neutralize family conflict, he could turn his full attention to grief over Judd. The therapist adapted the imaginal conversation via an empty chair exercise (see Chapter 12, "Non-Death Loss," for a detailed description of the rationale and procedures for chair work). The goal was to afford Liam an opportunity to express love and care for Judd as well as convey regret and remorse about his own shortcomings as a father. In doing so, he hoped to reduce the ambivalence he carried and settle their "unfinished business."

CASE 7.D (Continued)

During chair work, the therapist facilitated the action much like a psychodrama director (cf. Dayton, 2005). Liam came into the session knowing he would speak to Judd in a simulated manner (first scene). In articulating what he felt and why, Liam's message to Judd was one of unconditional affection regardless of their differences. What Liam did not know ahead of time was that, after his initial soliloquy, he would switch chairs and assume the role of Judd speaking back to him (second scene). Responding as Judd, he verbalized not only reciprocal love and affirmation but also consternation that Liam had been "checked out" as a father, that is, physically and emotionally absent due to his addiction. Then, Liam moved back to his original seat (third scene) to speak for himself again. Liam apologized in a deep and more profound way for his shortcomings as a parent. He asked for forgiveness. He reiterated deep love. Shifting once more to Judd's chair (fourth scene), forgiveness came from Judd, paired with a request to take special care of Caleb. During the final (fifth) scene back in his seat, Liam pledged that he would indeed look out for Caleb, assuring Judd that he would represent him as a father. To close the exercise, the therapist gently suggested, "It's time to say goodbye." Liam wailed aloud in protest, "I don't want to say goodbye." But after gathering himself, he sputtered out a tearful parting amid effusive expressions of love and care. By the end of the exercise, Liam was emotionally drained. He agreed to do something self-soothing later that day in deference to the intensity of his grief work. However, a thorough debriefing was postponed to the following session by mutual agreement.

Ultimately, the outcome of the imaginal conversation via the empty chair technique was extremely positive. Liam felt much emotional catharsis from expressing deep emotion during the simulation and from a sense of being forgiven. He felt "peace." He gained clarity on the bilateral nature of the blame and resentment between Judd and himself and could objectively see how they had disappointed each other. Emboldened by Judd's request, Liam's commitment to being a surrogate father for Caleb surged with new energy. He was determined to make sure Caleb knew Judd as a person by sharing stories and memories of Judd as well as engaging in activities all three of them enjoyed, such as hunting and fishing. Overall, the air-clearing conversation and emotional goodbye left Liam much stronger and more confident he could move forward. The therapist requested Liam share his experience of the empty chair exercise with at least one other person to consolidate its benefits and ensure a key support person knew what he had been through.

Due to subsequent health problems and his travel schedule, it was a few months before Liam's reenactment imagery could be addressed. He was motivated to do something beyond compartmentalizing this aspect of his grief, even without knowing all that the deconstruction and revision technique would involve.

CASE 7.D (Continued)

Because of a tremor that would have made drawing difficult, the therapist suggested the movie screen method for Liam's retelling of Judd's fatal heart attack. The therapist sat next to Liam rather than facing him, as if looking at the screen together. In vivid detail, Liam recounted the chaotic scene when his daughter-in-law screamed that Judd was having a heart attack. He found Judd wedged in a tight space between the bed and the wall, making efforts at rescue and resuscitation even more harrowing. They called Liam's wife to coach the chest compressions while they waited for emergency responders. He prayed in desperation. As the paramedics loaded Judd into the ambulance, Liam asked, "Is he alive?" but received no answer.

Then the recounting shifted to earlier that afternoon when Liam "had a great day" with Judd. In view of his son's heart condition, Liam had talked frankly with Judd about the need for a will, an advance directive, and a decision about earth burial or cremation to spare his family the burden of uncertainty if he became medically unresponsive or died suddenly. Instead of his usual bullheadedness, Judd listened and heeded the advice. He immediately made an appointment with his attorney, then called the funeral home and expressed a preference for cremation. Because Liam and his daughter-in-law both heard Judd's conversation, there was no question later about what to do with his body. Liam was so grateful for that directive.

Recounting continued with the hospital. Judd could not breathe without mechanical support. Finally, Liam and his daughter-in-law together concluded, "Turn it off, and let him go." After Judd's compassionate extubation, Liam was given the option to go back into Judd's room to view his body and say goodbye. He declined. That concluded the retelling phase.

Reprocessing commenced with a granular review of the first two segments. The physical difficulties maneuvering Judd's body in the tight space at home resulted in an *impossible situation*. Liam related, "[It was] the most helpless I've ever felt in my entire life. A father should protect [his son]. I couldn't protect Judd." In hindsight, expectations of being able to save Judd could be seen as unrealistic: "Even a heart surgeon laying [sic] next to him would not have been able to keep him alive." Toward the medical team, Liam expressed rage for discharging Judd only two days earlier: "I hold you responsible for Judd's death. How can you send somebody home [like that]? Why? Why? Why?" His anger mounted. On the other hand, Liam took great satisfaction from having provided wise counsel to Judd that afternoon. He told Judd he was proud of him. He acted as a *good and benevolent father*.

The third focal point during reprocessing concerned Liam's decision not to view Judd's body or say goodbye at the hospital. The therapist took Liam into a private hallway outside the consultation room, as if to replay the choice—Liam could go back into the room and *address his deceased son* or leave the premises. (While Liam pondered his choice, the therapist positioned chairs and blankets in the room to represent Judd's body). Given the chance to reconsider, Liam elected to reenter the room. At the makeshift bedside, Liam cried softly:

> I love you. I never said it enough. I'll try to be there for Caleb. I don't know why it had to happen. I don't know that I'll ever get over this. I'd give anything to trade places with you. [*Touching the 'body'*] I know you're in a better place.

Liam left the room and departed the clinic, just as he would have walked out of the hospital after saying goodbye. He declined the therapist's offer to accompany him to his vehicle or further debrief at that time.

Reviewing the deconstruction-revision exercise at the next session, Liam acknowledged it took him a few days to recover. However, he realized significant progress and could even anticipate termination of treatment in the foreseeable future, commenting, "I'm close to getting there." The three themes of *impossible situation*, *good and benevolent father*, and *addressing his deceased son* were reiterated as anchor points of the reprocessing. He now felt a sense of closure about the goodbye, commenting, "I think he knows I love him and miss him." Liam even speculated what Judd's rejoinder might have been: "Thanks, Dad."

SUMMARY

When adult children predecease their older parents, explicit and implicit life-cycle expectations go topsy-turvy. Options for viewing the body present opportunities and challenges. The rearranged life order for bereaved parents can have serious consequences: aging without the adult child, wondering about sources of support in the future (emotional, physical, financial), or dealing with bereaved grandchildren. Disposition of the body, funeral planning, and estate matters can become complicated with two families involved—the bereaved parents and siblings of the deceased adult and the spouse and children of the decedent. Several case studies illustrated how rituals of remembrance can be creatively deployed and absence converted into a sense of continuing presence. A clinical example adapting focused techniques from two different evidence-based treatment protocols showed how practitioners can customize their interventions to meet the needs of a particular bereaved parent.

REFERENCES

Angus, L., Levitt, H., & Hardtke, K. (1999). The narrative processes coding system: Research applications and implications for clinical practice. *Journal of Clinical Psychology, 55,* 1255–1270. https://doi.org/10.1002/(SICI)1097-4679(199910)55:10<1255::AID-JCLP7>3.0.CO;2-F

Arias, E., Kochanek, K. D., Xu, J. Q., & Tejada-Vera, B. (2023, November). *Provisional life expectancy estimates for 2022.* Vital Statistics Rapid Release; No. 31. Hyattsville, MD: National Center for Health Statistics. https://dx.doi.org/10.15620/cdc:133703

Dayton, T. (2005). *The living stage: A step-by-step guide to psychodrama, sociometry and experiential group therapy.* Health Communications.

Doka, K. J., & Martin, T. (2010). *Grieving beyond gender: Understanding the ways men and women mourn.* Routledge.

Gamino, L. A. (2020, December). Honoring the faithful departed during our holiday celebrations. *Catholic Spirit, 38*(11), 15.

Gamino, L. A., Sewell, K. W., Easterling, L. W., & Stirman, L. (2000). Grief adjustment as influenced by funeral participation and occurrence of adverse funeral events. *OMEGA—Journal of Death and Dying*, *41*(2), 79–92. https://doi.org/10.2190/QMV2-3NT5-BKD5-6AAV

Hoy, W. G. (2025). *Creating meaning in funerals: How families and communities make sense of death*. Routledge.

Irion, P. E. (1999). Ritual responses to death. In J. D. Davidson & K. J. Doka (Eds.), *Living with grief at work, at school, at worship* (pp. 157–165). Routledge.

Lester, A. J., & Frye, M. A. (Illustrator). (2020). *Absolutely delicious: A chronicle of extraordinary dying*. Bench Press.

Lichtenthal, W. G., & Breitbart, W. (2015). The central role of meaning in adjustment to the loss of a child to cancer: Implications for the development of Meaning-Centered Grief Therapy. *Current Opinions in Supportive and Palliative Care*, *9*(1), 46–51.

Lichtenthal, W. G., Catarozoli, C., Masterson, M., Slivjak, E., Schofield, E., Roberts, K. E., Neimeyer, R. A., Wiener, L., Prigerson, H. G., Kissane, D. W., Li, Y., & Breitbart, W. (2019). An open trial of Meaning-Centered Grief Therapy: Rationale and preliminary evaluation. *Palliative and Supportive Care*, *17*(1), 2–12. https://doi.org/10.1017/S1478951518000925

Lichtenthal, W. G., Lacey, S., Roberts, K., Sweeney, C., & Slivijak, E. (2017). Meaning centered grief therapy: Using the concepts of choice in coping with loss. In W. Breitbart (Ed.), *Meaning-centered psychotherapy* (pp. 88–99). Oxford University Press.

Mitima-Verloop, H. B., Mooren, T. T. M., & Boelen, P. A. (2019). Facilitating grief: An exploration of the function of funerals and rituals in relation to grief reactions. *Death Studies*, *45*, 1–11. https://doi/full/10.1080/07481187.2019.1686090

Mowll, J., Adams, G., & Darling, J. (2017). Facilitating access to scene photographs and CCTV footage for relatives bereaved after violent death. *Bereavement Care*, *36*, 11–18. https://doi.org/10.1080/02682621.2017.1305042

Mowll, J., Lobb, E. A., & Wearing, M. (2016). The transformative meanings of viewing or not viewing the body after sudden death. *Death Studies*, *40*, 46–53. https://doi.org/10.1080/07481187.2015.1059385

National Center for Injury Prevention and Control. (2020). *10 leading causes of injury deaths by age group, both sexes, all ages, all races*. Centers for Disease Control and Prevention. www.cdc.gov/injury/wisqars/LeadingCauses.html

Neimeyer, R. A. (2019). Meaning reconstruction in bereavement: Development of a research program. *Death Studies*, *43*(2), 79–91. https://doi.org/10.1080/07481187.2018.1456620

Neimeyer, R. A., Pitcho-Prelorentzos, S., & Mahat-Shamir, M. (2021). "If only . . .": Counterfactual thinking in bereavement. *Death Studies*, *45*(9), 692–701. https://doi.org/10.1080/07481187.2019.1679959

Neugarten, B. (1979). Time, age, and the life cycle. *The American Journal of Psychiatry*, *136*, 887–894. https://doi.org/10.1176/ajp.136.7.887

Roberts, D. A. (2022). A journey to . . . reconciliation? Words of wisdom from a Rabbi. In M. Moore & D. A. Roberts (Eds.), *After the suicide funeral: Wisdom on the path to post-traumatic growth* (p. 112). Resource.

Rynearson, E. K., Correa, F., & Takacs, L. (2015). *Accommodation to violent dying: A guide to restorative retelling and support*. Virginia Mason Clinic. www.

vmfh.org/content/dam/vmfhorg/pdf/legacy-vm/workfiles/Manual_Accommodation_Violent_Dying.pdf

Shear, M. K. (2015). *Complicated grief treatment*. Columbia Center for Complicated Grief.

Tedeschi, R. G., & Calhoun, L. G. (2004). *Helping bereaved parents: A clinician's guide*. Brunner-Routledge.

World Health Statistics. (2019). *Life expectancy and healthy life expectancy data by World Bank income group*. Retrieved March 1, 2024, from https://apps.who.int/gho/data/view.searo.SDG2020LEXWBv?lang=en

CHAPTER EIGHT

Accidental Death

> It's so wrong, so profoundly wrong, for a child to die before [the] parents.
> —Nicholas Wolterstorff (1987)

Accidental deaths are unforeseen and unintended. Their sudden, abrupt nature and the fact that younger people are often the victims make them especially difficult to bear. In the chapter epigraph, Wolterstorff's (1987) lament for his son, who died from a fall while mountain climbing, echoes the grief of many bereaved parents.

CASE 8.A

Jason's sudden death came as an absolute shock to his mother, Wallis. The call came on a stormy summer afternoon informing her that Jason had died on the construction site where he worked. His crew was building a shopping center with facades nearly three stories tall. Gale-force winds brought work to a halt. Coworkers trying to bring down a very tall ladder struggled with the crosswinds, so Jason rushed over to help. He grabbed the unwieldy ladder just before it fell into nearby power lines. He was killed instantly.

Wallis was devastated. Jason was her pride and joy. A strong, vigorous young man, Jason was kind and generous to a fault, as his untimely death illustrated so poignantly. An eyewitness confided that, when the ladder began to tilt toward the electrical lines, the other men let go, leaving Jason alone contending with its momentum. Wallis could not find it in her heart to blame the other men or Jason. Doing good turns for others was his nature. Regardless of the circumstances, Jason was gone, and Wallis was crushed.

Wallis had experienced previous hardships in life, including a difficult divorce and the deaths of her parents, but nothing compared with losing a son. She was "in a fog" for weeks thereafter. Wallis had two other adult sons and she also worried about how their brother's death affected them. Wallis relied on support from her second husband and a sister.

Wallis sought grief therapy shortly before the first anniversary of Jason's death. She dreaded that milestone and felt uncertain how she would fare. So, she planted a little garden in Jason's memory, reasoning, "If I did not do something, the day would get me." When an upsurge of grief hit, Wallis set an alarm clock to limit how long she permitted the sadness to linger. Her family planted a time capsule including photos and mementos of Jason. Wallis carried a "survival bag" in her purse containing various comfort objects: a white cloth dove, a heart-shaped stone, a special broach from her mother, and Jason's favorite ring. Stroking those objects soothed her.

But there was no escaping the emotional exhaustion and loss of passion Wallis felt. Many days, she just went through the motions as an elementary educator. She avoided dealing with Jason's possessions until her oldest son suggested they sort Jason's clothing and personal effects to find something for each of the cousins. They gift-wrapped those items and distributed them at Christmas. She felt good about reinforcing Jason's memory this way. Wallis attended the December candle-lighting vigil held by The Compassionate Friends chapter and found it "very healing." The arrival of grandchildren helped. Her youngest son named his firstborn child Jason in memory of his deceased brother.

Adapting proved to be a rocky road for Wallis. At the wedding of a friend's son who was the same age as Jason, overwhelming grief struck when she realized, "[Jason] will never have this." Crying as hard as she did at his funeral, Wallis tried to leave the celebration. Her sons intercepted her and insisted on taking a family photo before she left. She recounted, "They have never held me that tight." As Mother's Day approached in early May, Wallis wrote love letters to all her sons, affirming them and thanking them for making her a mother. At the cemetery on Memorial Day (late May), Wallis tried to "release" her grief by attaching Jason's letter to a balloon. However, the note was "too heavy" and the balloon stuck in a tree—a telling metaphor about her grief (cf. Clarke, 2014).

The second summer after Jason's death, Wallis volunteered to work at a camp for bereaved children to honor Justin's memory. That activity helped. She began to feel more engaged in family life and recovered some of her passion for teaching. She stopped therapy.

Wallis returned to treatment the third summer after Jason's death, concerned she was regressing by "hibernating" again. She wanted to do something to memorialize Jason on the anniversary of his death. From a list of suggestions provided by the therapist, Wallis decided to distribute flowers at the local senior center with a small card attached, "In loving memory of someone special, like you. Enjoy today! Jason's Mom."

In session, the therapist wanted to use the imaginal conversation technique from Prolonged Grief Therapy (cf. Shear, 2015). The goal was to simulate a dialogue, allowing Wallis to speak to Jason and consider his potential responses. Wallis tried but found the exercise too upsetting. She lost her words, especially when invited to verbalize from Jason's perspective. The therapist stopped the exercise and switched approaches. Borrowing from Meaning-Centered Grief Therapy (Lichtenthal et al., 2017), the therapist suggested that Wallis write out the conversation at home. Later, when Wallis sat down to write, she chose a different color pen. To her surprise, out "flowed" a letter from Jason to her!

> Hey Mama, whatz up? My flowers are great. I gathered everyone around and cheered you on as you carried that bucket of flowers into the Senior Center. I told everyone, "That's my Mom! Look what she did for me." Thank you for always believing in me. I could always count on you. You listened, offered your advice, and stepped back so I could follow my heart. You were the best mom. You loved me unconditionally. Mama—know that I am better than OK. Time here is meaningless. We will be reunited soon enough. You use your time to love. Don't get lost in your pain—I know it hurts but I'm in God's hands now. You have to keep making memories. Keep moving. Slow and steady—just keep on growing and loving. Love ya! Your son, Jason.

NATURE OF ACCIDENTAL DEATHS

Accidental deaths, termed *unintentional injury deaths* by statisticians, constituted the fourth leading cause of death in the United States in 2022 (Kochanek et al., 2023). For individuals between ages 1 and 44 years, unintentional injuries were the leading cause of death (National Center for Injury Prevention and Control, 2020a). Many of those minor children and young adults who died by accident left behind bereaved parents. Analyzing these data further, for children between ages 1 and 4 years, drowning was most frequent. Between ages 5 and 24 years, motor vehicle deaths were most common. Between ages of 25 and 44, unintentional poisoning (including unintended overdose) was the leading cause of death. (By comparison, among elderly individuals aged 65 and older, falls were the most frequent fatal accident; National Center for Injury Prevention and Control, 2020b). These statistical findings may be summarized with the following formula: for toddlers—drowning; for minors and younger adults—motor vehicle collisions; for middle-aged adults—unintended poisoning; for the elderly—falls.

Accidental death of a child can involve almost every known risk factor complicating parental grief (see Chapter 2, "What Makes Parental Grief So Difficult?"). In the case example, Wallis had no inkling Jason would die that day, so his death came as a total shock. She could scarcely believe what she heard on the phone. Miraculously, the electricity left no visible burn marks on Jason's face or hands, so they were able to have a full viewing at his funeral, which helped neutralize the impact of his traumatic death. Wallis drew a modicum of consolation from the fact that Jason died instantly and did not suffer. While his selfless attempt to assist coworkers gave his death nobility, Wallis still reeled from the senselessness of it. Yet how does one prevent a freak accident? Ultimately, there was no one to blame, and nothing could reverse what happened. Wallis would live the rest of her life without her precious son.

What may be most instructive for practitioners is the many active things Wallis did to cope: planting a garden, carrying a survival bag of keepsakes, working at a children's summer camp, focusing on her surviving sons and grandchildren, accepting social support, distributing Jason's belongings as gifts, observing his death date by distributing flowers to elderly people, and seeking grief therapy.

The simulated letter from Jason to Wallis gave her a sense of peace about his untimely death. Although never the same, Wallis reached the point described by many bereaved parents, "Resolved as much as it will be" (Klass, 2001), with the memory of her deceased son internalized as a psychological reality. Wallis returned to therapy a couple of years later after her second husband died suddenly from a heart attack. His death left Wallis unmoored and directionless. She began re-grieving Jason. Eventually, Wallis found semblances of a new rhythm, albeit one she embraced reluctantly and only with continued longing for her son and husband.

Wallis's treatment shows how practitioners must be flexible when introducing specific interventions. Just because a simulated conversation is part of an evidence-based therapy protocol does not mean it will work with every bereaved parent. The practitioner can thoroughly explain its rationale and purpose, yet some bereaved parents may not be receptive. Timing is critical. Techniques such as imaginal conversation typically work best when a therapeutic moment presents itself, instead of being programmed to occur in a particular sequence. If the exercise commences but resistance is too great, improvising an alternative is advisable. Wallis clearly understood the mechanism involved—simulated dialogue—but she was not willing or able to enact it. Ultimately, Wallis did the exercise her own way, at a moment of her own choosing, in the privacy of her home. The outcome speaks for itself.

MOTOR VEHICLE CRASHES

As noted earlier, for children between the ages of 5 and 24, motor vehicle wrecks account for the majority of accidental deaths in the United States. Consider the following examples.

CASE 8.B

It was a beautiful California day for vacationing as a mother drove her teenage son on a remote highway, but when she lost control of the vehicle, her unbelted son was ejected through the open sunroof. He died on impact. No other cars were involved. Suffering a concussion herself, the mother had no recollection of the events preceding the crash or during it. She wondered if insects or a bird had flown into the car and distracted her. The sad reality that her son was gone forever was compounded by the realization that there would never be answers to the question, "What happened?" The mother was burdened with overwhelming guilt and regret because she was the driver.

> **CASE 8.C**
>
> A bereaved father mourned the death of his young adult daughter in a car-train crash not long after she graduated from college. She was the passenger in a vehicle driven by a female friend. They collided with a freight train at a grade-level crossing, apparently oblivious to its approach. The contents of the wrecked car showed evidence of alcohol consumption. In the CD player, investigators discovered music from a popular group who incorporated train whistles and track sounds into their songs. The father speculated that perhaps the music was playing so loudly that they did not hear the oncoming train. He not only grieved her death but also the loss of "what might have been" had his daughter been able to start her career, marry, and have children of her own.

> **CASE 8.D**
>
> A divorced mother's young adult son was struck and killed by a car late at night while walking home from a bar. Intoxicated and belligerent, he had called his father for a ride (they resided together). The father was disgusted with the son's irresponsible drinking and mistakenly thought he was at a friend's house. He angrily told him to sleep it off where he was. The son set out on foot and was only a short distance from the bar when he was struck by a motorist who reported "hitting something in the road." The pattern of his injuries suggested that he may have already been down in the roadway at the time of impact. His bereaved mother wondered whether he had passed out, whether someone from the bar had knocked him unconscious and left him in the road, or whether he had weaved into the path of the car.

These sad situations show how heartbreaking fatal road accidents can be. Parents often wonder whether their child perished instantly, as Jason did, or whether they suffered before dying. Sometimes injuries are so extensive they prevent a complete viewing of the child's body, adding to the parents' distress. The perception of preventability figured prominently in how these bereaved parents reacted. In case 8.B, the mother who was driving wondered whether her son would still be alive if he had been wearing his seat belt. In Case 8.C, the bereaved father focused on faulty driving by the friend who put his daughter in harm's way. In Case 8.D, the divorced mother kept replaying the fatal events in hindsight, wishing the father had just picked up their son. Clearly, each of these deaths was preventable in the eyes of the bereaved parents.

Questions of culpability were complex and multifaceted in these cases. The bereaved mother who was driving (Case 8.B) blamed herself for not insisting that her son be belted and for whatever unknown event caused her to lose control of the car. She did not blame him. The bereaved father (Case 8.C) blamed the driver, whom he believed was alcohol impaired at the time of the crash. In a secondary way, he blamed his own daughter for putting herself in that situation and not exercising better judgment about consuming alcohol in a moving vehicle. The divorced mother (Case 8.D) blamed her ex-husband for being a bad influence and for not responding to the son's call. She blamed her son for drinking too much and being difficult. She blamed herself for agreeing to let the son live with his alcoholic father after their divorce.

Each of the victims in these three cases appeared to contribute indirectly to their own deaths. However, practitioners should permit bereaved parents to reach their own conclusions about assigning culpability to their deceased children (see Chapter 2, "What Makes Parental Grief So Difficult?," and Chapter 10, "Homicide").

Assertions of wrongful death in cases of fatal road accidents come from concluding that another party was negligent, reckless, or somehow endangered the victim. All three cases described here involved considerable ambiguity, and none led to legal action against any party. However, in accidental deaths with more clear-cut attributions of blame, some bereaved parents pursue litigation to seek justice for their deceased child and hold responsible parties accountable. Such advocacy is an important dimension of grief recovery, as noted in Chapter 3, "Helpful Factors."

Also, in these three cases, the bereaved parents sought grief therapy. Selected moments from their treatment sessions illustrate the importance of meaning-making efforts in the aftermath of these accidental deaths.

CASE 8.B (Continued)

The mother driving the car when her son was ejected and killed took years to come to grips with his loss. During treatment, a major turning point came when her therapist asked her to bring photos of her son to the session (cf. Gamino, 2012). Included were two enigmatic photos taken by her son shortly before his death that she had discovered while cleaning out a drawer. From her extensive collection of angel statues, her

> son had photographed one angel figurine blowing a kiss. He had taken the photo in front of a mirror, and the flash from the camera appeared perfectly positioned in the profile as the kiss itself! Based on a suggestion from the therapist, she reinterpreted the photo as a signal of love from the world beyond where her wonderful son now resided as an "angel." The second photo displayed her son's hand showing a simple "thumbs up" sign. Visible in the background was the stairway to the second floor of their home. Again, with the therapist's participation, the mother chose to see not only the obvious implication that her son was okay but also a metaphoric implication that he had relocated to another realm of existence "upstairs," or, consistent with her Judeo-Christian worldview, in heaven. She broke down during this discussion, crying tears of grief mixed with joy.

The therapist's intervention showed how it is possible to work together with grieving parents in co-constructing a meaning framework for the loss that resonates with their beliefs and values (cf. Angus et al., 1999; Neimeyer, 2019). Such takeaway meanings can help enormously as bereaved parents attempt to build a durable narrative of their child's death and learn to live with the loss over their remaining lifetimes (Hoy, 2025; Walter, 1999).

> ### CASE 8.C (Continued)
>
> With the bereaved father whose daughter died in a train-car collision, the therapist employed psychoeducation about the empty track concept (Klass & Marwit, 1988–1989) to help the bereaved father better understand the extent of his grief response. His daughter's death was not just a tragic event in the past. It also meant ongoing and progressive losses for the father, including having no grandchildren from her. That reality left him bitter. However, grasping this dynamic enabled him to recognize upsurges of grief when other young people his daughter's age achieved such milestones or when he encountered other grandparents simply enjoying their grandchildren. Finding out about the CD in the car enabled him to modify his explanatory narrative away from a sole focus on drinking and driving. Instead, he allowed for an unintended error of mistaking the actual train's whistle for the CD's soundtrack. The therapist encouraged this view of what may have happened because it incorporated human fallibility and helped the bereaved father be more

forgiving. The father also found the therapist's explanation of "loving in absence" (Attig, 2010) particularly useful for developing a sense of continuing connection after his daughter's death. Because he did not see her very often, he mostly loved her from afar even before she died. When he would think of her or miss her now, the bereaved father tried recalling sweet, positive memories, such as when he was roofing their home and his daughter (preteen then) brought him a "picnic" to share on the roof where he was working. The tender feelings associated with their special bond were bittersweet—both emotionally aching and yet strangely consoling at the same time.

CASE 8.D (Continued)

The divorced mother whose son left the bar and was hit by a car went to therapy during the immediate aftermath of his tragic death. She was wracked with guilt over not being there, thinking perhaps her presence could have prevented his death. Early interventions emphasized "being his parent" in death the way she wanted to during his life had he not shunned her influence and chosen to live with his father. Resolving to reclaim her position as mother, she traveled to the out-of-state location where the accident happened to see the site for herself. While there, she spoke with local law enforcement personnel about their investigation.

That same weekend, local friends of her son organized a memorial service at a rodeo arena. The mother attended the event and identified herself as his mother when greeting sympathizers. During the program, she delivered an extemporaneous tribute to her son. When they released a riderless bull into the arena as a cowboy's goodbye gesture, she allowed herself to weep.

Prior to her trip, the therapist had encouraged the bereaved mother's ideas about the visit (seeing the accident site) and suggested some actions she might take to make the experience more impactful (meeting with local authorities). The discussion empowered the bereaved mother to step into these various roles rather than holding back out of hesitation or fears related to her ex-husband. These compensatory steps produced psychological and social benefits from post-death advocacy on her son's behalf and from active participation in the memorial service (cf. Gamino et al., 2000), where she honored her son's memory and received much-needed condolences (see Chapter 3, "Helpful Factors").

UNINTENTIONAL OVERDOSES

CASE 8.E

Sidney knew his son, Junior, struggled with addiction. Sidney himself grew up in an impoverished neighborhood and knew the telltale signs of drug problems. During the last month before his accidental overdose, Junior's hygiene declined and his body smelled of the drugs he ingested. Sidney allowed Junior to live at home, but his fatherly efforts to talk through the troubles his son faced were ignored. On the night of his fatal overdose, Junior was in the company of known drug dealers. Emergency medical services was called and naloxone administered, but Junior could not be revived. After Sidney arrived on the scene, law enforcement officers asked him to identify Junior. He recalled, "I saw my son in the body bag—it still hurts." The coroner ruled the death accidental. No criminal charges were levied against any individuals present when Junior died.

Sidney bore his grief silently for several years. In his African American community, mental health treatment was taboo. He relied on stoic self-preservation, saying, "I don't let too many people into my world. I'm not that open with [my] family." Sidney's wife did not want "their business" broadcast to others and was more inclined to cope through containment strategies. She rarely mentioned Junior but was an attentive grandmother to Junior's four children. However, Sidney wanted to keep Junior's memory alive, insisting, "I don't want my son to 'die twice,' the point where no one talks about him."

As a teenager, Sidney's uncles had groomed him for drug trafficking. Seeking a different life, he extricated himself from the drug-based economy around him and went to work as a roofer. He was proud of making an honest living and avoiding the drug world. Now, decades later, Sidney again broke ranks with family and friends by consulting a grief therapist.

In the safety of the consultant's office, Sidney explained his reasoning: "I wanted to try it. I know this is something Black folks are not supposed to do, but I feel free talking to you, no judgment." Sidney shared photos of Junior's body at the time of death, images he revisited periodically to remember his son and desensitize himself to what happened. He expressed his grief in words and tears, even to the point of wailing. Sidney struggled to assimilate Junior's death. While Sidney had freed himself from the drug environment into which he was born, tragically Junior did not

> make it out. Sidney's participation in grief therapy was itself a statement of personal autonomy, not defining himself according to prevailing mores but rather seeking experiences consistent with his drive toward personal growth and resilience. He was deeply appreciative of the therapist's efforts to help him rediscover meaning in life after Junior's death and maintain a continuing bond with his son, stating, "His soul is still here."

Unfortunately, unintentional overdose deaths such as Junior's are far too common. In the United States in 2021, more than 100,000 drug overdose deaths occurred, with 92% deemed unintentional (National Center for Health Statistics, 2022). On a global scale, the World Health Organization determined that about 600,000 people worldwide died from drug use in 2019 (World Health Organization, 2023). Close to 80% of those deaths, or nearly half a million, involved opioid misuse. Wide availability of these drugs, together with increased use of highly potent synthetic opioids such as fentanyl, have accelerated the problem. The clandestine nature of street drugs, which may be laced with synthetic opioids, presents great risk of unintended overdose among unsuspecting users (Gamino et al., 2021).

Fractured family relationships prior to an overdose death can strongly influence parental bereavement. Valentine et al. (2016) characterized overdose deaths as "double deaths" because many parents feel they had already lost their child to addiction even before their physical death (cf. Chapter 12, "Non-Death Loss"). Parents feel helpless as they observe their addicted child on a collision course with fate, a phenomenon described as a "death spiral" by some bereaved parents (Feigelman et al., 2020). Certainly, Sydney watched Junior gradually succumb without being able to stop it. Because of such relationship struggles, the overdose death of a child addicted to drugs may bring a macabre mixture of both grief and relief.

Recent data on the intensity of grief symptoms as measured by the PG-13-Revised (PG-13-R) scale (Prigerson et al., 2021) showed parents grieving the drug overdose deaths of their children exhibiting the highest rates of Prolonged Grief Disorder when compared with individuals grieving the deaths of spouses, parents, or siblings (Thieleman et al., 2023). Their distress was even higher than levels reported by survivors grieving violent deaths such as homicide or suicide. Yet this same data also revealed that a clear majority of bereaved parents (68%)—already reeling from the unintentional overdose deaths of their children—indicated a diagnosis of Prolonged Grief Disorder would not be welcomed.

Indeed, Sterling et al. (2022) identified stigma as a prominent problem among parents bereaved by the opioid-overdose deaths of their children. *Internalized* stigmatization—self-assigned guilt, shame, and blame—arises from bereaved parents' own feelings of subjective responsibility for their children's deaths. They question themselves, "What did I do wrong? What could I have done differently? What did I miss?" Internalized stigma can lead bereaved parents to avoid disclosure about the true nature of their child's death. Instead, many parents regularly misrepresent the cause of the child's death to friends, coworkers, and even close family members (Feigelman et al., 2020). They fear implications of blame on themselves, or their parenting, should others learn that unintentional overdose caused their child's death.

Sterling et al. (2022) also described *external* stigmatization—negative judgment by others directed toward the bereaved parent, the deceased child, or both—which can have a deleterious effect on parental grief following unintentional overdose. Derogatory attributions may be verbalized directly or implied by tone, gesture, or facial expression. Bereaved parents worry that the deceased child's reputation will be permanently tarnished. Criticism leveled at the deceased child feels like an emotional assault on the surviving parents. External judgments can compound internal stigmatization and reinforce self-accusations of ineffectiveness bereaved parents already harbor, such as, "What kind of parent am I that my child died by overdose?"

Bereaved parents also fear social discounting of the child who died by overdose. When others avoid mentioning the child's death, it minimizes their grief and deprives them of much-needed solace and support.

Understanding how stigmatization degrades people helps practitioners maintain a compassionate and affirming stance when working with bereaved parents such as Sidney. The first caveat for practitioners is to carefully *avoid language or designations that carry stigma* while striving to build a shared lexicon for talking about the death (Sterling et al., 2022). For example, Sidney seemed to have no doubt that drug addiction led to Junior's overdose death. Talking about addiction objectively as an impersonal factor that influenced Junior's decisions meant using neutral language, such as, "How long had Junior struggled with addiction?" By contrast, referring to Junior as "an addict" could be potentially dismissive and stigmatizing—an ad hominem designation characterizing Junior himself as the problem and connoting several possible unfavorable attributes: defective, unworthy, or criminal.

Another helpful strategy in reducing stigma is to *humanize and individualize the deceased child* as a person with intrinsic value (Sterling et al., 2022). Talking with bereaved parents about their child's unique identity and personal history both limits stigmatization associated with overdose deaths and enables practitioners to grasp the full extent of their loss (cf. Tedeschi & Calhoun, 2004). Knowing who the deceased child was and how significant they were—along with understanding their flaws and challenges—makes for a more nuanced, clinically sensitive discourse. It conveys empathy and precludes judgment. Junior was Sidney's firstborn, a son for whom he had many hopes and dreams. Junior's death shattered the possibility of those precious dreams being fully realized.

Finally, parents whose children die from unintentional overdoses often find their *best support comes from groups of similarly bereaved parents*. Because these parents sometimes find that even their closest loved ones may fall short in offering the support they expected, or they encounter social condemnation from family or friends, the role of support groups is keenly important. Grief Recovery After Substance Passing—GRASP (http://grasphelp.org)—is one such support network. Titlestad et al. (2020) found that giving and receiving support was a key dimension strengthening bereaved parents' ability to adjust. At the same time, caution is warranted as empathic failure (cf. Neimeyer & Jordan, 2002) can occur when parents feel marginalized in support groups not tailored to unintentional overdose deaths, such as those geared to individuals grieving other relational losses (e.g., death of spouses or parents) or even bereaved parents whose children died from illnesses (Sterling et al., 2022).

CASE 8.E (Continued)

Sidney's did not receive the level of emotional support from his wife that he desired, perhaps because of her own struggles grieving Junior's death. She did not exhibit a similar need to talk about Junior. Rather, his wife seemed to prefer concealment strategies to limit her pain and not burden other family members (see Chapter 10, "Homicide"). Sidney's other children rarely spoke of their deceased brother without prompting—the "dying twice" Sidney sought to counteract. Because the family's collective grief response was one of containment, Sidney turned to professional consultation to find a forum where he could express his grief openly.

Prompted by the benefits he gained during treatment, Sidney resolved to do certain things differently at home. At the next holiday celebration, Sidney gathered his wife, surviving children, and grandchildren before the meal. Through the vehicle of prayer, Sidney modeled how to acknowledge Junior—missing him yet still recognizing him as a valued member of the family. He then invited others to follow his lead. Sidney was especially pleased to hear his grandson—Junior's youngest child—mention how his father (Junior) would be proud of him. Even Sidney's wife prayed aloud about Junior. That circle prayer opened the door to more candid conversation about Junior within the context of the family's faith beliefs. Sidney found this development positive and reassuring. It gave him a stronger sense of Junior's legacy. It helped him and his family progress beyond a sterile silence of shame about Junior.

SUMMARY

Accidental deaths do not have to happen, and many would be completely preventable if the parties involved exercised more prudence and caution. These sad realities plague the adaptation process for bereaved parents whose children die accidental deaths. Bereaved parents lament the misfortune of freak accidents such as Jason's. They contend with the maddening knowledge that many motor vehicle crashes could have been avoided. They speculate endlessly how unintentional overdoses such as Junior's could have been averted. Anger and a sense of injustice haunt these parents. Several case examples illustrated how practical techniques can be applied when working with parents whose sons or daughters died accidentally. Interventions bringing comfort are those that promote meaning in the child's life and death, encourage continuing connection, develop legacy, reduce stigma (especially in situations of unintended overdose), and respect the positive attributes of the child, even if their own behavior contributed to their demise.

REFERENCES

Angus, L., Levitt, H., & Hardtke, K. (1999). The narrative processes coding system: Research applications and implications for clinical practice. *Journal of Clinical Psychology, 55*, 1255–1270. https://doi.org/10.1002/(SICI)1097-4679(199910)55:10<1255::AID-JCLP7>3.0.CO;2-F

Attig, T. (2010). *How we grieve: Relearning the world.* Oxford University Press.

Clarke, J. K. (2014). Utilization of clients' metaphors to punctuate solution-focused brief therapy interventions: A case illustration. *Contemporary Family Therapy, 36*, 426–441. https://doi.org/10.1007/s10591-013-9286-y

Feigelman, W., Feigelman, B., & Range, L. M. (2020). Grief and healing trajectories of drug-death bereaved parents. *OMEGA—Journal of Death and Dying, 80*, 629–647. https://doi.org/10.1177/0030222818754669

Gamino, L. A. (2012). Opening the family photo album. In R. A. Neimeyer (Ed.), *Techniques of grief therapy: Creative practices for counseling the bereaved* (pp. 231–233). Routledge.

Gamino, L. A., Mowll, J., & Hogan, N. S. (2021). Grief following sudden non-volitional death. In H. L. Servaty-Seib & H. S. Chapple (Eds.), *Handbook of thanatology: The essential body of knowledge for the study of death, dying, and bereavement* (3rd ed., pp. 336–361). Association for Death Education and Counseling.

Gamino, L. A., Sewell, K. W., Easterling, L. W., & Stirman, L. (2000). Grief adjustment as influenced by funeral participation and occurrence of adverse funeral events. *OMEGA—Journal of Death and Dying, 41*(2), 79–92. https://doi/abs/10.2190/qmv2-3nt5-bkd5-6aav

Hoy, W. G. (2025). *Creating meaning in funerals: How families and communities make sense of death.* Routledge.

Klass, D. (2001). The inner representation of the dead child in the psychic and social narratives of bereaved parents. In R. A. Neimeyer (Ed.), *Meaning reconstruction and the experience of loss* (pp. 77–94). American Psychological Association.

Klass, D., & Marwit, S. J. (1988–1989). Toward a model of parental grief. *OMEGA—Journal of Death and Dying*, *19*, 31–50. https://doi.org/10.2190/BVUR-67KR-F52F-VW35

Kochanek, K. D., Murphy, S. L., Xu, J. Q., & Arias, E. (2023). Deaths: Final data for 2020. *National Vital Statistics Reports*, *72*(10). National Center for Health Statistics. https://dx.doi.org/10.15620/cdc:131355

Lichtenthal, W. G., Lacey, S., Roberts, K., Sweeney, C., & Slivijak, E. (2017). Meaning-Centered Grief Therapy: Using the concepts of choice in coping with loss. In W. Breitbart (Ed.), *Meaning-centered psychotherapy* (pp. 88–99). Oxford University Press.

National Center for Health Statistics. (2022). *Drug overdose deaths in the United States, 2001–2021*. Centers for Disease Control and Prevention, U.S. Department of Health and Human Services. www.cdc.gov/nchs/products/index.htm

National Center for Injury Prevention and Control. (2020a). *10 leading causes of death, United States, both sexes, all ages, all races*. Centers for Disease Control and Prevention. www.cdc.gov/injury/wisqars/LeadingCauses.html

National Center for Injury Prevention and Control. (2020b). *10 leading causes of injury deaths by age group, both sexes, all ages, all races*. Centers for Disease Control and Prevention. www.cdc.gov/injury/wisqars/LeadingCauses.html

Neimeyer, R. A. (2019). Meaning reconstruction in bereavement: Development of a research program. *Death Studies*, *43*(2), 79–91. https://doi.org/10.1080/07481187.2018.1456620

Neimeyer, R. A., & Jordan, J. R. (2002). Disenfranchisement as empathic failure: Grief therapy and the co-construction of meaning. In K. Doka (Ed.), *Disenfranchised grief: New directions, challenges, and strategies for practice* (pp. 95–117). Research Press.

Prigerson, H. G., Boelen, P. A., Xu, J., Smith, K. V., & Maciejewski, P. K. (2021). Validation of the new DSM-5-TR criteria for prolonged grief disorder and the PG-13-Revised (PG-13-R) scale. *World Psychiatry*, *20*, 96–106. https://doi.org/10.1002/wps.20823

Shear, M. K. (2015). *Complicated grief treatment*. Columbia Center for Complicated Grief.

Sterling, P. B., Muruthi, B. A., Allmendinger, A., Thompson-Cañas, R., Romero, L., & Tung, J. (2022). The grieving process of opioid overdose bereaved parents in Maryland. *OMEGA—Journal of Death and Dying*. https://doi.org/10.1177/00302228221124521

Tedeschi, R. G., & Calhoun, L. G. (2004). *Helping bereaved parents: A clinician's guide*. Brunner-Routledge.

Thieleman, K., Cacciatore, J., & Frances, A. (2023). Rates of prolonged grief disorder: Considering relationship to the person who died and cause of death. *Journal of Affective Disorders*, *339*, 832–837. https://doi.org/10.1016/j.jad.2023.07.094

Titlestad, K. B., Stroebe, M., & Dyregrov, K. (2020). How do drug-death-bereaved parents adjust to life without the deceased? A qualitative study. *OMEGA—Journal of Death and Dying, 82*, 141–164. https://doi.org/10.1177/0030222820923168

Valentine, C., Bauld, L., & Walter, T. (2016). Bereavement following substance misuse: A disenfranchised grief. *OMEGA—Journal of Death and Dying, 72*, 283–301. https://doi.org/10.1177/0030222815625174

Walter, T. (1999). *On bereavement: The culture of grief.* Open University Press.

Wolterstorff, N. (1987). *Lament for a son* (p. 16). William R. Eerdmans.

World Health Organization. (2023, August). *Opioid overdose.* https://www.int/news-room/fact-sheets/detail/opioid-overdose

CHAPTER NINE

Suicide

> After a child dies by suicide, bereaved parents ask why? The question without an answer.
> —Janet McCord (personal communication, 2024)

CASE 9.A

Harmony did not want to believe police reports that her daughter Evangeline had died by suicide. A friend of Evangeline called the police to conduct a welfare check after not hearing from her for several days. Police found Evangeline's apartment unlocked and discovered her dead from a gunshot wound to the head. A handgun was located near her body. On Evangeline's computer was a copy of her living will stipulating she did not want resuscitation but wished to be an organ donor. There were no indications of struggle, forced entry, or foul play. The coroner ruled her death a suicide. No autopsy was ordered. The police removed some personal items from the apartment, such as Evangeline's computer and notebooks, in the event a criminal investigation might open in the future.

Harmony was devastated. She had raised her three children as a single mother after her divorce, when Evangeline was only a toddler. Later, Evangeline's father moved overseas to work and maintained only occasional contact. Typically, mother and daughter would call or text daily, but things ran hot and cold in their relationship. Prior to the suicide, Harmony had not spoken to Evangeline for a week after they quarreled over the unexpected return of Evangeline's father after almost 20 years. Evangeline wanted nothing to do with her father, while Harmony counseled respect and engagement. Their conflict became so intense that Harmony deleted the last text from Evangeline without ever reading it. According to Evangeline's calendar, she most likely died the next day.

Harmony felt enormous guilt for not checking on her daughter earlier. She regretted that Evangeline's last wish to be an organ donor could not be honored because of body decomposition. She viewed Evangeline's body at the funeral home prior to burial and left with terrible images. Harmony was dismayed that an autopsy was not performed. She suspected the county was concerned only with saving money and decided to forego the expense of an autopsy because Evangeline was Black.

Several signs pointed to Evangeline's mental health problems. She had always been a willful child and subject to periods of depression. As a senior in high school, Evangeline started dating a soldier who was older. He never came to the door but would honk for Evangeline from the driveway. He drove a minivan, so Harmony suspected he was probably married with a family. Evangeline became pregnant by him at one point but told Harmony she miscarried. Harmony believed her daughter obtained an abortion.

Evangeline became erratic in the months preceding her death. She was secretive and evasive. She may have been dating more than one person. She had been to the emergency department several times for suicidal ideation and once even hospitalized after an attempted overdose. She took medicine for depression. Shortly before she died, Evangeline gave away her treasured dog. Her financial records showed, on the probable day of her death, that Evangeline paid her next semester's college tuition. She had also purchased a car seat that was found in her apartment. Harmony suspected that Evangeline was pregnant again, a possibility never investigated medically because there was no autopsy.

Harmony first sought help through her Employee Assistance Program and then from a social worker employed by the psychiatric hospital where Evangeline had been previously admitted. Neither therapist seemed prepared to address parental grief, perhaps lacking the death competence needed (Gamino & Ritter, 2009, 2012). Harmony also tried a grief support group, but she felt overwhelmed by hearing the loss experiences of other attendees. To make matters worse, her other two children faced struggles in their own lives that kept them from being emotionally available. Harmony's father, who had always been the nurturing parent, had died several years earlier, leaving only her mother, who was critical and overbearing. Finally, about a year after Evangeline's death, Harmony consulted a grief therapist.

Harmony's treatment extended over a four-year interval with sessions planned monthly. Sometimes Harmony went several months between appointments due to moves or finances. At a deeper level, Harmony's own attachment style seemed inconsistent and mixed (Kosminsky & Jordan, 2024), perhaps a reflection of growing up with one supportive parent (father) and one critical parent (mother). The resulting ambivalence was reflected in the on-and-off character of her relationship with Evangeline and her in-and-out schedule with therapy.

The treatment plan devised to help Harmony featured two primary objectives: reversing the avoidance pattern that maintained Harmony's depression and hampered her coping, and second, helping Harmony craft a retrospective narrative of Evangeline's death. That narrative needed to evaluate as objectively as possible what was known or surmised about Evangeline's suicide as well as consider how Harmony understood her daughter as a person.

For Harmony, Evangeline's suicide triggered the effects of all seven general risk factors for complicated grief described in Chapter 2, "What Makes Parental Grief So Difficult?" Her death was unexpected, traumatic in nature, and potentially preventable. The sharp conflict between mother and daughter, about not only the reemergence of Evangeline's birth father but also her dating choices and secretive lifestyle, left much unresolved between them. Harmony's social support network was sparse: deceased father, critical mother, two other children preoccupied with their own troubles, and lack of friends. Harmony herself had suffered intermittently from depression since high school. Thus, her own mental health problems, general life stresses, and pressures from her surviving adult children (who often requested financial assistance or childcare for the grandchildren) depleted Harmony's coping ability. Finally, neither faith nor spirituality afforded Harmony any comfort following Evangeline's death.

Making matters even worse, Harmony showed little evidence of the protective factors described in Chapter 3, "Helpful Factors." Though she managed to survive from one day to the next, Harmony did not demonstrate personal hardiness. Any spiritual inclinations were dormant. Harmony never really said goodbye to Evangeline. She focused mostly on negative memories about their conflicts and did little to memorialize her daughter or cultivate a continuing connection. It never occurred to Harmony how she could have pressed for an autopsy at the time of Evangeline's death, demanded a fuller investigation of the circumstances, or retrieved her daughter's personal items from the police. She felt powerless to advocate. She could not formulate a coherent account of Evangeline's death. Harmony saw no positive outcomes from the tragedy, and the concept of personal growth was beyond consideration.

Demographically, Evangeline was a young adult African American female who left behind a single mother and two siblings. Suicide rates for young Black and Hispanic women ages 15 to 24 have historically been among the lowest in the United States, well below rates for American Indian or Alaska Natives and Whites (Ramchand et al., 2021). Yet, suicide rates among younger Black and Hispanic women have increased significantly over the past two decades (Curtin & Hedegaard, 2019). Suicide rates among young Black and Hispanic males are increasing as well. Cultural attunement requires questioning why these trends are happening. Although definitive data on this complex question are elusive, increasing rates of suicide among Black and Hispanic youth have been linked to unrecognized or untreated mental health problems (such as depression, social anxiety, and substance misuse), living in poverty, witnessing violence, and exposure to both overt racism and microaggressions (Meza & Bath, 2021). Protective factors that mitigate depression and suicidal ideation in these groups include better social support from families and peers as well as more cohesive community connectedness (Matlin et al., 2011), higher levels of hope (Davidson et al., 2010), and stronger religiosity (Meza & Bath, 2021; O'Donnell et al., 2004).

The remainder of this chapter details how the grief therapist incorporated major aspects of suicide bereavement while working with Harmony on the two identified treatment objectives. Additional case examples are included where appropriate to augment explanations of specific concepts and methods. (Please note the problem of suicide deaths among members of the armed forces is addressed in Chapter 11—Military or Combat Death.)

DIFFERENCES IN SUICIDE BEREAVEMENT

Death by suicide is one of the cruelest forms of child loss. Jordan and McIntosh (2011a) identified several aspects of suicide bereavement that distinguish it from grieving other losses. Feelings of abandonment and rejection are common. How could a beloved child choose to end their life altogether rather than reach out for help or continue to live another day in hopes their troubles might improve? The child's unilateral decision to withdraw from the parent-child relationship—to forego life altogether—bewilders bereaved parents (Bolton & Mitchell, 1983). After all, they brought the child into this world. They nurtured and protected their child. To have that child respond by taking their life does not make any sense at all. Parents who have sacrificed so much to preserve the viability of their offspring are overwhelmingly dismayed when a child does not exercise that same level of care in preserving their own life.

Parental feelings of abandonment and rejection following suicide reflect the bereaved parents' attachment to their deceased child. Practitioners can use psychoeducation to normalize these emotions. Supportive listening, affirmation of what is felt, and empathic responding are needed. Feelings of abandonment and rejection typically begin to subside as bereaved parents develop a more contextualized understanding of what happened to their deceased son or daughter. In coming to understand the suicide scenario differently, bereaved parents begin to see the events resulting from forces other than a direct repudiation of the parent-child relationship.

CASE 9.B

One bereaved father, whose young adult son poisoned himself following several apparent life failures, moved from abandonment and rejection to feelings of compassion as he reflected, "He sold himself a 'bill of goods' [that life could not improve]." The father came to understand his son's suicide as a consequence of pernicious, fatalistic thinking, not a rejection of his parents and their love for him.

Suicide deaths often carry stigma and shame (see Chapter 8, "Accidental Death"). Parents may be reluctant to acknowledge the truth for fear of being judged. They believe a suicide death reflects badly on the child and on them. They dread uncomfortable questions for which there are no ready answers. What happened? Was he depressed? Did she leave a note? Did you know there was a problem? How did you try to help? The inescapable thought that something must have been terribly wrong for the child to resort to suicide weighs heavily and saddles survivors with enormous guilt. Bereaved parents fear others may find fault with their parenting. Because of stigma, some parents do not disclose suicide as the cause of death, fabricate a false death story, or avoid the subject altogether.

Ironically, any benefits realized from self-protective nondisclosure are usually short-lived. In the long run, this tactic amplifies the distress of bereaved parents and accentuates their social isolation. Inevitably, rumors circulate, suspicions grow, and questions about the cause of death become the proverbial elephant in the room no one will acknowledge. Clergy can play a helpful role with this dilemma at the time of the funeral or memorial service if they are prepared to address the matter sensitively (Roberts, 2017). Parents who choose to acknowledge the truth during the funeral are often surprised by the compassionate support they receive. Should parents prefer to keep specific details of the death private, they can politely sidestep further probing with statements such as, "We don't really know all that happened. We just know he's gone, and we miss him terribly. It's hard losing a child. You never expect to go through that."

Sometimes professional therapy—with its codified confidentiality—is the only forum where bereaved parents will allow themselves to openly discuss the suicide death of a son or daughter. In those instances, practitioners have a dual responsibility—honoring the confidence of parents who share such sensitive information and encouraging parents to cultivate a broader network of social support. As with parents who lose children to unintentional overdose (see Chapter 8, "Accidental Death"), parents bereaved by the suicide deaths of their children are best directed to support groups specific to suicide, ideally including other parents. Jordan and McIntosh's (2011b) book contains several chapters describing suicide survivor support groups and postvention programs (in person and online) available in the United States and around the world.

Stigma and shame certainly played a major role in Harmony's response to Evangeline's suicide. She did not want anyone at work to know how Evangeline died. She kept a photo of Evangeline at her cubicle but otherwise never spoke about her death. Harmony blamed herself for the suicide, feeling that she had failed as a parent. She expected herself to know what was really going on in her daughter's life, coax Evangeline into confiding in her, or intervene somehow when Evangeline's depression and desperation manifested. Harmony felt guilty about not reading Evangeline's final text message the night they quarreled. Harmony wanted to believe that, had she read the text message, she could have accurately decoded its disguised meaning and gone to rescue Evangeline. One of Jordan's (2011) patients referred to such counterfactual thinking as the "tyranny of hindsight" (p. 199).

The guilt that Harmony and many other bereaved parents carry from such counterfactual thinking can be difficult to resolve (see Chapter 10, "Homicide"). Embedded in their guilt is a fantasy that they could have controlled the situation had they been there or done something differently. Even though unrealistic, that fantasy of control is preferable to its abhorrent alternative—utter powerlessness. Unpacking the embedded control fantasy sustaining protracted guilt requires careful tact and timing by practitioners.

The therapist's approach to Harmony's shame and stigma started with acknowledging the professional privilege of hearing her story. Allowing Harmony to relate what she knew about Evangeline's death at a deliberate pace meant unfolding the story in its entirety over the span of three sessions. Hearing how Harmony viewed her daughter's death—including her concern it may have been a homicide committed by the shadowy boyfriend (a possibility dismissed by the police who never investigated that angle)—enabled the therapist to grasp the narrative elements in her account. The therapist suspended judgment while gathering that information, taking it as the starting point from which a fuller, revised narrative may eventually emerge.

Harmony's behavioral avoidance also required a paced approach. The therapist lobbied to include Harmony's surviving daughter, the emotionally safest person in Harmony's circle, in one of the sessions as a step toward opening a dialogue between them about Evangeline's death. It was envisioned Harmony would start mentioning Evangeline at holiday celebrations or family gatherings, rather than remaining conspicuously silent about her absence. Harmony's trips to the cemetery had consisted mostly of brief stops that intensified her agitation until she could only find relief by leaving. That counterproductive pattern was modified by employing distress-reduction techniques that enabled Harmony to calm herself, stay longer at the graveside, engage in more reflective processing, and come away with a different emotional experience.

VICTIM-PERPETRATOR PARADOX

The intentional nature of a suicide death presents one of the biggest stumbling blocks for survivors, including bereaved parents. One reason Harmony preferred to entertain a theory of possible homicide is that, while still a horrible outcome, it would shift responsibility for Evangeline's death to a third party—one more easily vilified and blamed. The emotional calculus for homicide survivors can be reduced to a simple formula: focus negative feelings and reprisal urges on the perpetrator, and reserve positive feelings of sympathy, love, and compassion for the deceased victim (see Chapter 10, "Homicide"). Inconsistent details or implicit feelings to the contrary can be swept under these stronger emotional currents.

The haunting paradox of suicide is that the deceased child was, at the same time, both victim and perpetrator of the killing (Jordan & McIntosh, 2011c). Bereaved parents find this juxtaposition unfathomable. How could a beloved child do such a thing to herself? What could he possibly have been thinking when he pulled the trigger, jumped from the bridge, or tied the noose? Even while mourning their deceased son or daughter as a tragic victim, bereaved parents also contend with inevitable feelings of anger toward that same son or daughter for perpetrating their own death with volitional and aggressive action. Practitioners can see why it is often easier for bereaved parents to blame themselves, or someone else, than it is for them to come to grips with the hard reality that their own child killed someone they dearly loved. Self-blame may manifest as lament over not recognizing the problem, failing to intervene in a timely way, or even precipitating the lethal act via conflict or mistreatment.

Handling the victim-perpetrator paradox requires sensitivity. Identifying the complementary roles involved often occurs during psychoeducation early in treatment. Even then, the discussion cannot be hurried because this paradox is too unwieldly to absorb all at once. While bereaved parents may grasp the notion intellectually, it usually takes much longer to sort through the contradictory feelings generated. Identifying their various emotions and clarifying the attributions driving them can be healing for bereaved parents who juggle a plethora of reactions to suicide by a son or daughter.

Psychodynamic theory can be useful during discussions of the victim-perpetrator paradox (Maltsberger, 2004; Maltsberger & Buie, 1980). Identifying suicide as a form of murder and acknowledging that murder entails a high degree of aggressive anger serves as a starting point. In retrospect, many suicides appear to be homicides "turned inward," that is, the murderous rage that resulted in killing oneself was really pointed toward someone or something else. Instead of lashing out at another person, the unfortunate victim turns the aggression onto self as an alternative. Systematic review of what was happening prior to the suicide frequently identifies a personal nemesis in the child's life or an impossible situation with which the child was struggling. In these instances, the child's aggression can be understood in reference to that nemesis or vexing situation rather than seen as an unqualified attack on self. Bereaved parents may then be able to shift their focus away from potentially malevolent attributions about the deceased child as culpable in their own death. They move toward more acceptable attributions of the child wrestling with unassailable demons yet ultimately striking at self.

Sometimes evidence points in the direction of bankrupt self-esteem, such as the child viewing themselves as toxic, defective, or disposable. Sometimes it is a fragmented part of the self that is viewed as objectionable and therefore attacked, as if the child is at war with some alien, loathsome part of the self (Fowler et al., 2012). With these internal dynamics operating, suicide can be rationalized as the only way of eliminating a problem or saving others from the trouble of dealing with such liabilities.

In other instances, overwhelming and inescapable emotional pain becomes unbearable, and suicide represents a last-ditch effort to turn off or escape such mental pain. Highly respected suicidologist Edwin Shneidman (1993) described such extreme mental pain as "psychache" (p. 147), a highly noxious form of psychological suffering that drives desperate individuals to end their own lives as the only solution to unrelenting anguish and misery. Maltsberger (2004) observed how some suicidal individuals rationalize "body jettison" (p. 654) as a survival scheme accompanied by grandiose thoughts of somehow going on to life somewhere else, possibly where they may be better understood and more loved or free of the pain that plagues them.

INQUEST INTO THE DEATH

A helpful part of Jordan's (2011) paradigm is the process of conducting an inquest following a suicide death. Practitioners invite bereaved parents to conduct their own investigation, examining as honestly as possible what is known about their child's death while considering all factors that may have contributed to it. The practitioner functions as a referee, tasked with ensuring that the inquest remains even-handed and objective, neither overly superficial nor overly punitive where the parents are concerned. Nagging questions about parental accountability can be safely explored without a predetermined judgment. Jordan assumes suicide survivors will engage in such self-questioning anyway. The logic is opening the process to make it transparent and capitalizing on the participation of the practitioner to keep the inquest unbiased and fair.

The quote from Janet McCord (personal communication, June 28, 2024) at the beginning of this chapter sums up the unwelcome reality that must be posited at the outset of any inquest—bereaved parents will never know for sure what was going on in the mind of their child who died by suicide, regardless of whether they left a note or otherwise attempted to explain their actions. Suicide notes often raise more questions than they answer.

> ### CASE 9.C
>
> One bereaved father's athletically gifted teenage son shot himself in the head. He left a brief note declaring, "The reason I killed myself is that I couldn't take the pressure." This sentence left the father wondering exactly what his son meant by that statement. What pressure? Did the father push too hard? Did the coaches push too hard trying to develop his son's prodigious talent? Were there other pressures going on in his son's life he did not know about? The sinking realization that a conversation to clarify the ambiguity could never happen left the bereaved father holding enormous guilt and regret.

Nonetheless, a thorough investigation of the available evidence usually leads to some reasonable inferences about the deceased child's state of mind. Sometimes an inquest requires bereaved parents to seek additional information from law enforcement authorities, family members, friends, and associates. Also revealing may be the deceased child's journals, essays, artwork, poetry, songs, favorite music, photo galleries, text messages, social media posts, computer search histories, online affiliations, and so forth. However, no postmortem inquest of a child's death by suicide can ever reveal all the answers or lead to incontrovertible conclusions. Bereaved parents must learn to live with the uncomfortable truth that there will always be missing parts in the narrative and blank spaces in the storyline because suicide deaths almost always leave unanswered questions.

CASE 9.D

A middle-aged son completed suicide by shooting himself in the front seat of his vehicle. He had suffered from bone cancer and became addicted to opiate-based pain medicine. Unwittingly, he had married a woman who turned out to be addicted to heroin. He began diverting some of his medicine to her. Later, they became embroiled in a drug distribution ring. On the night in question, the son and his wife were fleeing police pursuit. He pulled off the roadway and shot himself while his wife sat in the passenger seat. The bereaved parents were beside themselves and frantic to question their daughter-in-law. What transpired prior to that moment? What did she witness? What did their son communicate in his final moments? Why did she not intervene? However, shortly after the incident, the daughter-in-law disappeared completely, eluding all further attempts to contact her. The bereaved parents felt they could not obtain any peace of mind about their son's death until they heard her story. They were torn between settling for an incomplete account of events or holding out for more information from someone intent on remaining undiscovered and whose veracity was questionable anyway. Circumstances forced them to live with the former option, an unsatisfying partial narrative that gnawed at their hearts.

Similarly, Evangeline's suicide left Harmony with many unanswered questions. Did Evangeline shoot herself, or was she murdered in a manner arranged to look like suicide? Did she intend to die, as some of the evidence suggested, such as leaving instructions about no resuscitation and organ donation? Or did she want to keep living, as other evidence hinted, such as purchasing a baby's car seat and paying her college tuition the same day she died? Was Evangeline pregnant, and, if so, did she refuse an abortion and make her boyfriend angry? Or was she scared and confused and so chose to take her baby's life along with her own? If Evangeline did kill herself, what drove her to such a point of desperation? Why did she not reach out for help if her mental state was so impaired? Should Harmony have been able to recognize the signs leading up to the suicide, such as Evangeline giving away her treasured dog, purchasing firearms and ammunition, and isolating herself? Difficult as it may be to live without all the answers, the alternative is a never-ending inquest relegating bereaved parents to a nonstop treadmill of searching.

One of the therapeutic challenges in Harmony's case was her reluctance to go through Evangeline's personal possessions and papers. They stayed untouched in storage boxes. Harmony's initial attempt to examine those materials triggered severe emotional flooding. Harmony first had to learn distress-reduction techniques so she could better modulate her emotions and not end up retraumatized. The concept of dosing was also employed to empower Harmony. She could break down the task into manageable steps by going through one box at a time, or part of a box, rather than opening all of them at once. She was encouraged to have someone else present for moral support. The therapist even offered to examine a box with her during the session. Looking through Evangeline's personal effects for clues about her state of mind and her intentions was a major thrust of the inquest because it could help Harmony develop a retrospective narrative of Evangeline's death.

RETROSPECTIVE NARRATIVE

Jordan (2011) described the process of developing a retrospective narrative following suicide—sometimes called a retrospective profile (Schwartz, 2011)—as an exercise in meaning reconstruction, one of the compensatory strategies described in Chapter 3, "Helpful Factors." The goal is finding some level of coherency in the emerging narrative, but not absolute truth which is nearly impossible after a suicide death. He emphasized formulating "a 'believable enough' story of the death that the survivor is relieved from the need to compulsively search for an answer to the question 'Why?'" (p. 199).

In addition, Jordan (2011, 2020) stressed the concept of relational repair. Relational repair may be needed between the survivors and the deceased, especially given survivors' prominent feelings of abandonment, rejection, and anger. Relational repair is sometimes needed among survivors as they evaluate their own culpability and the accountability of others who may have been able to influence the outcome. Sometimes repair is needed between the two parents, such as when one blames the other for the death or when different grieving styles lead to perceptions that the other parent is under-grieving or over-grieving or perhaps loved the child too much or not enough.

It is proposed here that retrospective narratives of suicide deaths need to include three specific dimensions to be effective. First, the narrative needs to be *plausible* enough to explain and account for what is known about the death and its circumstances. Second, the narrative needs to be *comprehensive* enough to accommodate the unknowns present in every suicide scenario. Third, the narrative must be *compelling* enough to resonate emotionally with the bereaved parents, capturing essentials of the story in a manner consistent with the character of their deceased son or daughter. A good retrospective narrative will combine a durable biography of the deceased's life (Walter, 1999) with a believable enough account of the child's suicide death (Jordan, 2011, 2020). Developing such a postmortem narrative with all these features is a tall order but one that carries promise for eventual comfort.

Thomas Joiner (2005) and his collaborators (Joiner et al., 2009) formulated an interpersonal-psychological theory of suicide that may also help bereaved parents develop a narrative account of their son or daughter's death. Joiner proposed that three distinct conditions are necessary before a person's suicidal inclinations can overcome powerful, innate survival instincts. Those conditions include *perceived burdensomeness*, *thwarted belongingness*, and the *capacity to act on a desire for death*. Perceived burdensomeness is the view that one's existence poses a significant burden to family, friends, or society—a fatal misperception justifying the conclusion that everyone would be better off without having to contend with the difficulties that individual's life presents. Thwarted belongingness refers to a sense of alienation from others: not being a valued part of a natural group (family, friends, coworkers), being excluded from a group to which one aspires to belong, or being denied a coveted friendship or a romantic partnership. The capacity to act on a desire for death means developing a tolerance for painful or fear-inducing experiences, typically acquired through serial attempts with self-harm behaviors or repeated exposure to others' efforts at self-harm (in person or virtually). Joiner's theory posited that perceived burdensomeness and thwarted belongingness produce a desire to die but that this desire translates into lethal or near-lethal behavior only in the presence of an acquired capacity to act on it. Recognizing these three conditions enables practitioners to highlight their importance for understanding how a deceased child could take their own life.

One of Harmony's early discoveries pointing toward suicide came from Evangeline's bedroom closet. Harmony found a photo shrine dedicated to a young man Evangeline had dated briefly in high school. About a year before Evangeline's death, the young man killed himself. No one knew about Evangeline's romantic preoccupation, not even her sister. Once Harmony finally brought herself to search Evangeline's computer files (three years after her death), she found an electronic journal containing extensive entries about the deceased young man. Evangeline clearly felt a strong connection with him and loved him. She expressed admiration for his courage in completing suicide. That fascination potentially contributed to Evangeline's capacity to act on a desire for death, as did her prior overdose attempt that led to her hospitalization.

Investigating Evangeline's personal papers proved to be a significant turning point in Harmony's recovery. What she found led her to conclude, finally, that Evangeline had intended to take her life and made significant preparations toward that end. Repugnant as it was to contemplate Evangeline killing herself, Harmony belatedly conceded that deduction given the evidence at hand. Evangeline had drafted a living will document listing all her computer passwords, bank account numbers, and cell phone account information to facilitate closing out her affairs. She gave detailed instructions and contact information for individuals she wanted to be notified "that I passed away." She asked that her Facebook account be memorialized. She requested to be an organ and tissue donor. She suggested that anyone who wanted to remember her could get a tattoo like hers, and she posted photos of it on her Facebook page.

Evangeline also wrote several essays about depression, containing vivid depictions of her long-standing struggle with mood disorder. Although she did not leave a note directly explaining her decision to die by suicide, Evangeline's essays spoke volumes about her mental suffering—the *psychache* referenced by Shneidman (1993). Excerpts from Evangeline's essays are included here as a firsthand account of her struggle with depression.

> Depression is a menacing monster that you're always fighting up against. Some days you try and face it head on but most days you run and hide but no matter how well you hide or how fast you run, it is still there breathing its breath down the nape of your neck. Still breathing its horrid breath into your soul.
>
> Depression is feeling like everything that goes bad is your fault. Like you're everyone's disappointment.
>
> Depression is like standing on the edge of a window. On the inside of the house there is a burning fire and it is getting closer and closer to you. It is debating on waiting to get help or just deciding to jump before the fire gets worse and reaches you.
>
> Depression is the loneliest thing you will ever experience. No longer do you want to hang out with your friends or even family. Everyone becomes a distant memory. Eventually everyone fades out and you're left alone with nothing but your loud, sad, and angry thoughts.
>
> Everyone tells you to open your eyes but you can't. They are glued shut. You only see the darkness both behind and in front of you. No matter how much people speak of light you just do not believe that it exists. Eventually

you get to a point to [sic] where you could no longer even fake smile. The poker face becomes permanent. You no longer feel sadness, anger, or even fake happiness. You just feel numb.

Maintaining this retrospective narrative did not come easily to Harmony. At the next session after sharing the information she had discovered, Harmony returned to her earlier preoccupation with the shadowy boyfriend and the possibility he murdered Evangeline. Misgivings about no autopsy and no pregnancy test resurfaced. She even mentioned exhuming her daughter's body to run tests. The therapist listened patiently to Harmony but also gently summarized the bulk of evidence indicating suicide. The ensuing discussion zigzagged in this manner over several sessions. Harmony's cognitive vacillation about Evangeline's death seemed to mirror their relational ambivalence.

The prolonged nature of Harmony's bereavement struggle and the complexity of her case exemplifies the need for practitioners to *stick with it* as long as it takes (Tedeschi & Calhoun, 2004). Harmony did make progress with her visits to the cemetery, staying longer and speaking out loud to Evangeline while she was there, her own versions of situational revisiting and imaginal conversation. On the other hand, Harmony repeatedly declined the invitation to enact a simulated conversation with Evangeline in session, declaring, "I'm not ready for that."

Four years after Evangeline's death, Harmony seemed to fully accept that her daughter's death had been suicide. She could now use that term in conversation. She began to focus on memorializing and legacy. On Evangeline's birthday, she posted memories on Facebook and solicited comments from others. The response was overwhelming. She received many humorous anecdotes that made her laugh and touching stories that indicated how much her daughter was loved. Evangeline liked bead work, so Harmony crafted some bead bracelets for family and friends and wore one herself that she vowed never to take off—a symbol of her perpetual connection with her deceased daughter. From time to time, unanswered questions regarding the boyfriend, the possibility that Evangeline was pregnant, and the contradiction of having paid her college tuition the same day she died still hovered on the periphery of her mind. The concept of ambivalence proved useful—simultaneously holding mixed or conflicting emotions toward a person or thing.

Escaping intolerable depression became the central construct explaining Evangeline's suicide (cf. Maltsberger, 2004). That explanation in Harmony's retrospective narrative met the criteria of being plausible, comprehensive, and compelling enough to account for what happened to Evangeline. Therapy ended with a sense of completion. Harmony felt freer to embrace the positive aspects of her mother-daughter history with Evangeline. She expressed heartfelt gratitude and respect for the help received from the practitioner.

SPIRITUAL CONSIDERATIONS

Not everyone endorses a spiritual or faith viewpoint, including on the topic of suicide. But for bereaved parents who demonstrate intrinsic spirituality or affiliate with a formal religion, spiritual considerations can be important in the aftermath of a son or daughter's suicide. Among the world's major religions—Buddhism, Hinduism, Judaism, Christianity, and Islam—life is considered precious and suicide is opposed (Gearing & Alonzo, 2018; Norko et al., 2017). Buddhism holds that human life has great value. Hinduism strongly condemns suicide as the destruction of a sacred life and a truncation of that life's special purpose. (There are cultural variations such as the ancient Hindu practice of suttee where a widow self-immolates on the funeral pyre of her dead husband.) Judaism places great value on the preservation of life, and suicide violates that principle. Christianity has traditionally taught that suicide is a violation of the Decalogue, or Ten Commandments ("Thou shalt not kill," Exodus 20:13 and Deuteronomy 5:17). Correspondingly, one who completes suicide is thought to be condemned to hell with no hope of redemption. Islam's Qu'ran expressly forbids suicide ("do not kill or destroy yourself" in Surah 4, verses 29 and 30) with the prohibition based on considering the suicidal act to be self-murder.

All three monotheistic faiths (Judaism, Christianity, and Islam) allow for some mitigation of responsibility in cases of suicide where the individual suffered from mental illness or severe psychological disturbances (Gearing & Alonzo, 2018). Historically, mental disorder has been the factor most strongly associated with completing suicide (Cavanagh et al., 2003), although at least one review has disputed that conclusion (Hjelmeland et al., 2012). Mental disorder, such as the depression that hounded Evangeline, can skew a person's thinking, thereby reducing the culpability of the individual who completes suicide. The *Catechism of the Catholic Church* (United States Catholic Conference, 1994) posited the following rationale:

> Grave psychological disturbances, anguish, or grave fear of hardship, suffering, or torture can diminish the responsibility of the one committing suicide. We should not despair of the eternal salvation of persons who have taken their own lives. By ways known to him alone, God can provide the opportunity for salutary repentance.
>
> (p. 550)

Of course, religious affiliation alone does not always explain the views of an individual believer, who may or may not endorse all the teachings of a particular tradition. Cultural influences sometimes supersede faith doctrines or moderate how suicide is viewed in a specific context. For example, Chow and Yip (2011) explained how Chinese culture, despite the prevalence of Confucianism and

Buddhism, which both condemn suicide, maintains a certain level of tolerance toward suicide, depending on the apparent motivation of the person. Such tolerance might extend toward suicides meant to teach or make a point, show one's loyalty or love, or pay a debt for one's misdeeds in this lifetime. In Japan, where atheism is prevalent, "suicides of resolve" may be seen as culturally acceptable when the intention is honorable, such as ending one's life to provide insurance money to the family (Kitanaka, 2008). Japanese models of honorable self-execution practiced by ancient Samurai warriors—seppuku or self-evisceration—may contribute to a permissive view of suicide (Russell et al., 2017).

Gearing and Alonzo (2018) encouraged practitioners to take a person-centered approach to understanding how religious beliefs may influence a survivor's reaction to the suicide death of a loved one. They recommended that practitioners show interest in and respect for the survivor's beliefs and values regarding suicide within a particular religious or spiritual frame of reference. For bereaved parents already reeling from the suicide death of their son or daughter, additional pain presented by the prospect that their deceased child may be condemned for eternity or unable to enter heaven (as they understand it) is almost unbearable. Cultural attunement is necessary in guiding these conversations. Where appropriate, introducing contemporary viewpoints on mitigating conditions such as psychological distress can be comforting, as well as identifying cultural contexts wherein suicide may be viewed in a less malevolent, perhaps even honorable, manner.

> ### CASE 9.E
>
> A bereaved mother and her husband found their adult son hanging from the ceiling fan in his bedroom, an apparent suicide. Panicked, they managed to extricate him and call emergency medical services, but his body was already "so cold." Their son suffered from schizophrenia, including active hallucinations and delusions. As a means of self-medicating, he was also addicted to alcohol and drugs. To some extent, the mother could allow for the possibility her son was trying to escape "inner demons." Yet, even after years of professional therapy with three different clinicians, she still worried that her son's salvation was in jeopardy because of his suicide.
>
> As a child, the mother had attended a Catholic parochial school where the idea was instilled in her that suicide leads to eternal damnation, with no hope of reprieve. As an adult, her Christian practice became more moderate, but those internalized childhood teachings proved

> difficult to dismiss. A different practitioner gently informed her how updated teachings were more compassionate on how mental illness can reduce culpability for suicide and allow for divine forgiveness. Only then did the bereaved mother begin to release her concerns about God's judgment and her son's destiny in the afterlife.

SUMMARY

This chapter chronicled in detail the struggles of one mother to assimilate her daughter's suicide death. Together with additional case examples, her story illustrated how suicide bereavement differs from other forms of child loss, presenting unique challenges for the emotional state of the bereaved parent. Exploration of the victim-perpetrator paradox showed how ambiguity and blame can plague bereaved parents whose children die by suicide. Conducting a therapeutic inquest into the death can help parents evolve a retrospective narrative of what caused the suicide—a "believable enough" account that is plausible, comprehensive, and compelling—even in the face of inevitable unanswered questions. Embracing the memory of the deceased child by recalling the totality of their life, not just what happened in the last few moments as they died, can shift the internal narrative in more positive directions.

REFERENCES

Bolton, I., & Mitchell, C. (1983). *My son . . . my son . . .: A guide to healing after death, loss or suicide*. Bolton Press.

Cavanagh, J. T., Carson, A. J., Sharpe, M., & Lawrie, S. M. (2003). Psychological autopsy studies of suicide: A systematic review. *Psychological Medicine, 33*(3), 395–405. https://doi.org/10.1017/s0033291702006943

Chow, A., & Yip, P. (2011). Grief after suicide: A Hong Kong Chinese perspective. In J. R. Jordan & J. L. McIntosh (Eds.), *Grief after suicide: Understanding the consequences and caring for survivors* (pp. 427–437). Routledge.

Curtin, S. C., & Hedegaard, H. (2019, June). *Suicide rates for females and males by race and ethnicity: United States, 1999 and 2017*. National Center for Health Statistics, Health E-Stats. www.cde.gov/nchs/products/index.htm

Davidson, C. L., Wingate, L. R., Slish, M. L., & Rasmussen, K. A. (2010). The great Black hope: Hope and its relation to suicide risk among African Americans. *Suicide and Life-Threatening Behavior, 40*(2), 170–180. https://doi.org/10.1521/suli.2010.40.2.170

Fowler, J. C., Hilsenroth, M. J., Groat, M., Biel, S., Biedermann, C., & Ackerman, S. (2012). Risk factors for medically serious suicide attempts: Evidence for a psychodynamic formulation of suicidal crisis. *Journal of the*

American Psychoanalytic Association, 60(3), 555–576. https://doi.org/10.1177/0003065112442240

Gamino, L. A., & Ritter, R. H., Jr. (2009). *Ethical practice in grief counseling*. Springer Publishing Company.

Gamino, L. A., & Ritter, R. H., Jr. (2012). Death competence: An ethical imperative. *Death Studies, 36*, 23–40. https://doi.org/10.1080/07481187.2011.553503

Gearing, R. E., & Alonzo, D. (2018). Religion and suicide: New findings. *Journal of Religion and Health, 57*(6), 2478–2499. https://doi.org/10.1007/s10943-018-0629-8

Hjelmeland, H., Dieserud, G., Dyregrov, K., Knizek, B. L., & Leenaars, A. A. (2012). Psychological autopsy studies as diagnostic tools: Are they methodologically flawed? *Death Studies, 36*, 605–626. https://doi.org/10.1080/07481187.2011.584015

Joiner, T. E., Jr. (2005). *Why people die by suicide*. Harvard University Press.

Joiner, T. E., Jr., Van Orden, K. A., Witte, T. K., Selby, E. A., Ribeiro, J. D., Lewis, R., & Rudd, M. D. (2009). Main predictions of the interpersonal-psychological theory of suicidal behavior: Empirical tests in two samples of young adults. *Journal of Abnormal Psychology, 118*(3), 634–646. https://doi.org/10.1037/a0016500

Jordan, J. R. (2011). Principles of grief counseling with adult survivors. In J. R. Jordan & J. L. McIntosh (Eds.), *Grief after suicide: Understanding the consequences and caring for survivors* (pp. 179–223). Routledge.

Jordan, J. R. (2020). Lessons learned: Forty years of clinical work with suicide loss survivors. *Frontiers in Psychology, 11*, 530993. https://doi.org/10.3389/fpsyg.2020.00766

Jordan, J. R., & McIntosh, J. L. (2011a). Is suicide bereavement different? Perspectives from research and practice. In R. A. Neimeyer, H. Winokuer, D. Harris, & G. Thornton (Eds.), *Grief and bereavement in contemporary society: Bridging research and practice* (pp. 223–234). Routledge.

Jordan, J. R., & McIntosh, J. L. (Eds.). (2011b). *Grief after suicide: Understanding the consequences and caring for survivors*. Routledge.

Jordan, J. R., & McIntosh, J. L. (2011c). Is suicide bereavement different? A framework for rethinking the question. In J. R. Jordan & J. L. McIntosh (Eds.), *Grief after suicide: Understanding the consequences and caring for survivors* (pp. 19–42). Routledge.

Kitanaka, J. (2008). Diagnosing suicides of resolve: Psychiatric practice in contemporary Japan. *Culture, Medicine, and Psychiatry, 32*, 152–176. https://doi.org/10.1007/s11013-008-9087-1

Kosminsky, P. S., & Jordan, J. R. (2024). *Attachment-informed grief therapy: The clinician's guide to foundations and applications* (2nd ed.). Routledge.

Maltsberger, J. T. (2004). The descent into suicide. *The International Journal of Psychoanalysis, 85*(3), 653–668. https://doi.org/10.1516/3C96-URET-TLWX-6LWU

Maltsberger, J. T., & Buie, D. H. (1980). The devices of suicide: Revenge, riddance, and rebirth. *International Review of Psycho-Analysis, 7*(1), 61–72.

Matlin, S. L., Molock, S. D., & Tebes, J. K. (2011). Suicidality and depression among African American adolescents: The role of family and peer support and community connectedness. *The American Journal of Orthopsychiatry, 81*(1), 108–117. https://doi.org/10.1111/j.1939-0025.2010.01078.x

Meza, J. I., & Bath, E. (2021). One size does not fit all: Making suicide prevention and interventions equitable for our increasingly diverse communities. *Journal of the American Academy of Child and Adolescent Psychiatry, 60*(2), 209–212. https://doi.org/10.1016/j.jaac.2020.09.019

Norko, M. A., Freeman, D., Phillips, J., Hunter, W., Lewis, R., & Viswanathan, R. (2017). Can religion protect against suicide? *The Journal of Nervous and Mental Disease, 205*(1), 9–14. https://doi.org/10.1097/NMD.0000000000000615

O'Donnell, L., O'Donnell, C., Wardlaw, D. M., & Stueve, A. (2004). Risk and resiliency factors influencing suicidality among urban African American and Latino youth. *American Journal of Community Psychology, 33*(1–2), 37–49. https://doi/abs/10.1023/B:AJCP.0000014317.20704.0b

Ramchand, R., Gordon, J. A., & Pearson, J. L. (2021). Trends in suicide rates by race and ethnicity in the United States. *JAMA Network Open, 4*(5), e2111563. https://doi.org/10.1001/jamanetworkopen.2021.11563

Roberts, D. A. (2017). Preparing a eulogy or memorial service for one who died by suicide. In M. Moore & D. A. Roberts (Eds.), *The suicide funeral (or memorial service): Honoring their memory, comforting their survivors* (pp. 12–18). Resource Publications.

Russell, R., Metraux, D., & Tohen, M. (2017). Cultural influences on suicide in Japan. *Psychiatry and Clinical Neurosciences, 71*(1), 2–5. https://doi.org/10.1111/pcn.12428

Schwartz, M. (2011). The retrospective profile and the facilitated family retreat. In J. R. Jordan & J. L. McIntosh (Eds.), *Grief after suicide: Understanding the consequences and caring for survivors* (pp. 371–379). Routledge.

Shneidman, E. S. (1993). Commentary: Suicide as psychache. *The Journal of Nervous and Mental Disease, 181*(3), 145–147. https://doi.org/10.1097/00005053-199303000-00001

Tedeschi, R. G., & Calhoun, L. G. (2004). *Helping bereaved parents: A clinician's guide*. Brunner-Routledge.

United States Catholic Conference. (1994). *Catechism of the Catholic Church* (2nd ed.). English translation. Libreria Editrice Vaticana. Pauline Books & Media.

Walter, T. (1999). *On bereavement: The culture of grief*. Open University Press.

CHAPTER TEN

Homicide

> It is the victim [of homicide] and those who love him who serve a life sentence.
>
> —Lula Moshoures Redmond (1989)

Redmond's (1989) work with homicide survivors in Florida led her to identify the cruel irony experienced by the loved ones of homicide victims. As she describes in the epigragh, loved ones' suffering is lifelong, regardless of the fate of the perpetrator.

CASE 10.A

James felt uneasy most of the day at work. He tried calling his teenage daughter, Jenn, several times and got no answer. It was a school holiday, so she should have been home, and it was unlike her not to respond to calls or text messages. A nagging sense that something was wrong plagued him.

James and Jenn had always been close. She was his only child, and their bond grew even stronger following his divorce from her mother years earlier. James readily embraced his role as custodial parent. He prided himself on being the kind of father who forthrightly handled all the physical changes and emotional challenges presented by an adolescent girl going through puberty. Jenn was his princess, and James vowed to always protect her.

James's uneasiness became horror when he turned down the road to his home. Yellow security tape cordoned off his driveway, and police vehicles were everywhere. Officers on the scene were circumspect in what they disclosed, responding only with, "Someone hurt Jenn, badly." Frustrated by this brush-off, James insisted on going inside to see his daughter. Finally, the police told him Jenn was deceased. The area was considered a crime scene, and therefore he could not be permitted access. Officers began asking James to account for his whereabouts that day. Their questions incensed James, who realized he was being treated as a potential suspect. Only after his supervisor verified by phone that James had worked a full shift at the plant did the officers become more accommodating.

When the ambulance arrived, tensions escalated again. James argued vehemently that he needed to see his daughter. With his background as a Navy Seal, James projected an intimidating presence as he threatened to cross the yellow tape. Finally, one compassionate detective agreed to let James look at Jenn on the stretcher to identify her body, but only on the condition that he not touch her. James complied. He described what he saw by saying that it "tore me up."

The investigation did not last long. The assailants turned out to be two juveniles who bragged to a friend that they had killed someone simply to see what it felt like. The alarmed friend told her parents, who subsequently contacted police. Arrests followed quickly.

As an overweight young woman, Jenn had not attracted much attention from males. When two boys she knew from school showed up at her door claiming they had car trouble, unsuspecting Jenn welcomed them and offered beverages as if it were a social visit. One boy brandished a knife and stabbed Jenn in the chest, severing her aorta. The other boy then shot her in the head.

The juveniles were tried separately. There were several pretrial hearings. James sat in the front row just behind the defendant's table. He described a powerful urge to exact revenge by crossing the rail and deploying military techniques to kill the defendant barehanded. He suppressed those violent impulses with the realization that "I could only get one" before deputies would likely subdue him.

Much of what tormented James was a feeling of abject failure as a father. He incurred tremendous guilt and self-recrimination, even as his rage toward the offenders boiled. In desperation, James sought grief therapy about three months after Jenn's murder, remorsefully reflecting, "I spent my whole life for my only child—it was centered around her, and now I don't have a life." Jenn's murder meant his mission as a parent had ended dismally.

Several of the general risk factors for complications in grieving (see Chapter 2, "What Makes Parental Grief So Difficult?") clearly applied to James. Jenn's murder was unexpected, traumatic in nature, and completely preventable. As so aptly articulated by Therese Rando (1991),

> In homicide, there is no question that the death was preventable. . . . No matter what rationale the murderer may have had . . . it is a senseless and unnecessary event. In such cases, no death is acceptable, no death is timely, no death is anticipated.
>
> (p. 110)

For James, Jenn's murder was a personal disaster of cataclysmic proportions. His relatively small social support system further contributed to a sense of isolation from the rest of humanity.

However, James was not without protective characteristics, as described in Chapter 3, "Helpful Factors." He demonstrated personal hardiness in his commitment to living authentically, influencing outcomes, and adapting to change. He possessed an intrinsic spirituality. That spirituality would later become a key factor in coming to terms with Jenn's death and developing a narrative account that provided at least a modicum of comfort. In a world radically changed by gratuitous violence, James initially lost hope, expressing, "I have no desire for living." Slowly, he became determined to go on and not let his daughter's killers take his life as well by rendering it meaningless. He did not want to serve the life sentence of bitterness described by Redmond (1989).

IMPORTANCE OF LANGUAGE

Laws against killing another person have been codified by civil societies for millennia, going back as far as Hammurabi in the second century B.C. (Pearn, 2016). When practitioners work with parents bereaved by homicide, using accurate language is important. *Murdered* or *killed* are the two main verbs in the English language describing the heinous act of taking the life of another person with malice aforethought. Murder invariably carries strong criminal penalties.

Yet not every homicide is murder. Current legal codes differentiate manslaughter from murder. Although both acts result in the unlawful killing of another person, manslaughter does not involve malicious intent on the part of the perpetrator and therefore usually warrants lesser punishment. In cases of manslaughter, the word *killed* is appropriate. Also, some instances of homicide involve killing another person in self-defense, for example, fending off a would-be assailant threatening one's life and killing the assailant in the process. Self-defense killings often involve considerable ambiguity and may result in complete exoneration of the actor. The word *killed* is also appropriate in these cases.

Practitioners should use direct language when speaking with parents whose children died by homicide. In most health-care and counseling-related settings, practitioners encountering such cases already know before the first interview that the child died by homicide. In the few instances where this fact may not be known ahead of time, practitioners who discover the child's death resulted from homicide can immediately pivot to follow these recommendations. Although using words such as *murdered* and *killed* may seem harsh, anything less could be offensive and perceived by the bereaved parents as invalidating the awful reality of what happened. Worse yet, avoiding direct language could be perceived by bereaved parents as implying less horror to the child's death or even connoting less responsibility by the perpetrator. Practitioners unable or unwilling to use clear language about homicide run the risk of alienating the parents and undermining rapport or being seen as unqualified for the task.

When practitioners surmise a softer approach is needed at the beginning, the interview could start with a request for information: "Tell me how your son [or daughter] died." Thereafter, using the terms *murdered* or *killed*—with appropriate tone modulation—respects the reality of what happened and signals the arduous nature of the bereavement journey ahead. Avoid euphemisms such as *passed away* or *lost*. Repulsive as it may seem, tactfully saying *murdered* or *killed* enables the practitioner to join the bereaved parents in confronting the abhorrent nature of these crimes and indicates the practitioner can handle the grisly work entailed.

Interestingly, during the early interviews with James, he used phrases such as, "When Jenn passed . . ." to describe her death. He seemed to prefer, or need, a layer of emotional insulation from the brutality of what happened. Noting this psychological defense, the practitioner chose not to challenge James's language or countermand his terminology. Instead, the practitioner slowly transitioned the session vocabulary. By deliberately not echoing the term *passed*, the practitioner avoided colluding with this defense. Instead, the practitioner used phrases such as, "Jenn's death" or "Jenn died." From there, the terms *killed* or *murdered* were intermittently introduced in the exchange, gradually transitioning the lexicon to the accurate terms. This way, James's defenses were gently dismantled at a pace he could tolerate as he confronted the full force of his rage over Jenn's murder.

ANGER AND REPRISAL FANTASIES

Many parents of murdered children find it disconcerting how primitive their anger is toward the assailant(s). The violent aggression of homicide engenders reciprocal rage and reprisal impulses among survivors. In their minds, bereaved parents may entertain a variety of schemes for exacting revenge on the parties responsible for their child's death, even if such behavior is inconsistent with their own moral code. Such violent urges may lead them to question if they are really any different from the killers themselves. It is important for practitioners to normalize the occurrence of such fantasies and to allow for dispassionate discussion of such material during consultation. Homicide cases are not for the squeamish. Practitioners need the death competence that enables them to listen to and tolerate descriptions of violent thoughts and feelings (Gamino & Ritter, 2009, 2012). At the same time, they must possess the objectivity and poise to deter bereaved parents from any intention of carrying out such reprisal fantasies and help them understand their anger as part of grief following homicide.

From his training as a Navy Seal, James's core identity was warrior and defender. He had little hesitation about verbalizing his urges to kill the thugs who murdered Jenn. His military knowledge of hand-to-hand combat made his fantasies eerily realistic. James found visualizing those scenarios satisfying because retaliation would restore the family (or tribal) honor by avenging his daughter's killing. Also, embracing his role as a societal defender meant preventing the juveniles from ever harming anyone else.

What can bereaved parents do with anger and reprisal fantasies? Harboring intense anger means living with a dreaded enemy as a constant presence in one's life. Strong hostility psychologically fuses the survivor with the target of their anger. In effect, one exists "in hate" with another person, and that enmity binds the two parties in an unhealthy emotional dyad. To disengage emotionally from the perpetrator, anger and rage toward that person must dissipate. Releasing the anger voluntarily—when psychologically ready—means limiting the perpetrator's influence over the parent's emotional and social landscape.

Working through this difficult choice of either hating the murderer or emotionally disengaging constitutes a thorny challenge for many parents of murdered children. Loyalty to their deceased child seems to demand maintaining a vigorously negative view of the perpetrator, yet at great price in permitting the perpetrator to dominate their subsequent existence. If everything is seen through the lens of the murder, then the assailant will always occupy a leading role. Alternately, making the parent-child relationship the central focus relegates the murderer to the periphery and reduces the amount of negative emotional energy consumed by hate. Practitioners should exercise great care when guiding bereaved parents through this dilemma. Their anger belongs to them, and they will release it only if, and when, they are ready.

James made his choice reluctantly. He acknowledged that reprisal killing of one, or even both, of Jenn's murderers would bring him only momentary gratification. It would not bring back his daughter. Instead, those actions would be followed by inevitable conviction and incarceration, making his figurative "life sentence" a literal imprisonment. He begrudgingly allowed his intense anger to ebb into more low-grade bitterness, avowing, "They're not worth it. I'm not going to let those two 'pissants' determine the rest of my life."

GUILT

Despite its oppressive nature, guilt can be difficult to dismiss. Persistent guilt draws its staying power from preserving an illusory sense of control one does not want to relinquish. The allure of this sense of control accounts for the seductiveness of counterfactual thinking (Shear, 2015; Neimeyer et al., 2021). Self-assigned guilt preserves the belief that an undesirable outcome such as homicide could have been prevented, either by choosing a different course of action or by taking definitive action instead of failing to do so. Helping parents of murdered children moderate persistent guilt requires sensitive exploration of the counterfactual thinking that supports it and reevaluation of the faulty assumptions of control embedded within it.

CASE 10.B

One bereaved mother experienced tremendous guilt thinking she could have done something different to prevent her 19-year-old son's murder during a disputed drug deal. Having raised her son with strong middle-class values and Christian ethics, she deplored his association with "street" friends. She tried unsuccessfully to warn him, fearing that his naivete would be quickly recognized and exploited.

Her son was killed on her birthday. The family's plan to celebrate at the mother's favorite restaurant was canceled because she had a bad migraine that evening. After confirming the birthday dinner had been postponed, her son left with one of his street friends. The mother had an ominous feeling about where her son might be going, but she did not try to detain him from leaving. Later that night, when her son tried to negotiate a drug purchase, he was shot in the back of the head by a member of the dealer's gang.

The bereaved mother's nagging guilt manifested in several lines of thought, all of which had roots in two main counterfactuals. First, the bereaved mother kept thinking she should have done more to dissuade her son from associating with unscrupulous friends or tried harder to restrict his movements, even though legally he was an adult. "I should have raised him better," she kept repeating to herself, implying she could have been more insistent about avoiding bad company and exercising good judgment. Next, the bereaved mother endlessly second-guessed the decision to postpone her birthday dinner. Over and over came the thought that, if she had just toughened up and gone out for the family dinner as planned, her son would never have embarked on his ill-advised drug mission and would still be alive. A more selfless decision by her could have shifted events that evening and averted her son's murder.

Methodically, the practitioner sought to clarify the boundary where her responsibility for the son's risky behavior ended and his accountability began. She was more comfortable weighing her own culpability or lamenting the depravity of the assailants than she was looking squarely at how her son had placed himself in danger. Slowly, she allowed herself to critique her son's actions. She became willing to parse her own guilt more objectively while acknowledging how her son took undue risks. In such delicate discussions, practitioners need to refrain from directly criticizing the child's behavior (see Chapter 2, "What Makes Parental Grief So Difficult?"). Only the bereaved parent has that right.

Later in treatment during an imaginal conversation using the Gestalt empty chair technique (see Chapter 12, "Non-Death Losses"), the mother scolded her son for not being more careful and reprimanded him for not adhering to the family's values. This maneuver brought a flood of emotion that had been suppressed until then. She went beyond righteous anger at the murderers, and beyond her own persistent guilt, to confront the underlying fracture in the parent-child relationship. Expressing disappointment in her son's ill-fated choices was a necessary step toward repairing what was broken between them, together with the tragic consequence of losing him forever. Only then could her internalized love connection be restored to the extent possible.

CRIMINAL JUSTICE SYSTEM

Many parents of murdered children feel betrayed by the criminal justice system. Shattered are their implicit assumptions that the legal system will enact a timely, fair, and proportional response to the great injustice of their child's murder. From the beginning, justice may seem elusive or nonexistent. For example, James found himself a potential suspect in his own daughter's murder, having to provide an alibi before he could even receive basic information about what happened.

Following a homicide death, bereaved parents may not be given clear options about viewing the body of their deceased child. When they are permitted to view the body, or required to do so for purposes of identification, families may not receive adequate preparation or support for what they will see (Mowll et al., 2017; Mowll et al., 2016). Some parents choose not to view the body of their deceased son or daughter. This choice sometimes leads to later fantasies that maybe it was someone else who was killed or that the child's injuries were worse than they were. Selective draping of the body and sensitive guidance by coroners and morgue personnel can help ensure bereaved parents view their child with a minimum of traumatic exposure.

For example, one funeral director recalled serving a family whose child was murdered. The bereaved mother did not want to see the damaged areas but only wanted to verify that the body under the sheet was "her baby." Because the child's feet were not injured in the fatal attack, the funeral director displayed only the deceased child's ankles and feet. That limited viewing provided all the confirmation needed because the mother immediately recognized those familiar feet that she had washed and put lotion on so many times.

Practitioners helping bereaved parents early in the aftermath of a homicide can play important roles in mitigating some of the perceived injustices in the criminal justice system. Educating parents about how the system works, and giving realistic timelines, can modify parents' idealistic assumptions about what should happen. For example, when the child's body is with the medical examiner or sent elsewhere for autopsy, delays can occur in scheduling funeral or memorial services. Also, murder trials typically have lengthy timelines due to preliminary hearings, evidence reviews, postponements, docket schedules, or other legal requirements. It is not unusual in the United States for murder trials to occur two to five years following the death. Coordinating with victim's services sometimes garners extra consideration for grieving parents. Contacting jurisdictional authorities on behalf of parents to express concerns or ask questions can be an important form of advocacy for bereaved parents who may feel too defeated to reach out themselves. Practitioners can also make a big difference by reminding parents to exercise their prerogatives about whether to accept or decline interview requests from media. They can also limit the range of disclosure to what they feel is appropriate.

Courts of law require a focus on proven facts and physical evidence to enact *legal justice*, a process often resulting in homicide survivors feeling shortchanged. Therefore, a critical early intervention is creating an opportunity for *therapeutic justice*, that is, providing a forum designed to give bereaved parents a full hearing about their child's homicide (cf. Gamino & Ritter, 2009). That hearing permits unrestricted discussion of all contextual factors: background, characteristics of the child, the parent-child relationship, conjecture about the events, collateral information, speculation about the perpetrators, and any other thoughts, feelings, or perceptions deemed pertinent. Therapeutic justice dispensed in a safe, supportive environment allows parents of murdered children to be heard and validated, not silenced or discounted. The validation that results from being seen by virtue of being heard (Graybar & Leonard, 2005) is critical for bereaved parents whose children die by homicide.

Later, when hearings start or the trial begins, practitioners can help prepare bereaved parents for what to expect. Prosecutors may not preview how testimony will unfold, and many times do not want to rehearse questioning, for fear of revealing their legal strategy. Yet from a psychological perspective, knowing how court proceeds enables bereaved parents to brace for the emotional rigors involved and make prudent decisions about their participation, such as choosing not to be present when graphic images are displayed or raw accounts of the murder given.

If a bereaved parent is expected to testify, behavioral rehearsal can help them prepare. Conversely, if the bereaved parent is listed as a witness by the defense in a legal maneuver to exclude them from being present in the courtroom and potentially swaying the jury, alternate ways of accessing what happened can be devised, such as enlisting a close friend to relay a detailed account of what occurred while the parent was out of the room.

Most jurisdictions allow victims to give an impact statement, sometimes called *allocution*, near the conclusion of the proceedings if there is a guilty verdict. Often the impact statement comes during deliberation of punishment and before sentencing. Although emotionally wrenching, this moment may be the bereaved parents' only chance to directly address the child's killer. With the entire court's attention, there is no better platform for expressing their thoughts and feelings about the homicide and its effect on them and the community.

Practitioners can provide invaluable assistance with victim impact statements by offering suggestions about content or delivery. Bereaved parents who represent their deceased child in court advocate for them in a manner that bolsters parental competence (Klass & Marwit, 1989) and facilitates long-term adjustment (see Chapter 3, "Helpful Factors"). Practitioners sometimes need to encourage reluctant parents to give a statement in court, stressing the potential benefits from "speaking for the child who cannot speak for themselves."

CASE 10.C

A school-aged girl was killed by a negligent boat operator trolling too close to a designated swimming area at a recreational lake. After the defendant accepted a plea bargain of involuntary manslaughter, the family had the opportunity to give an impact statement at his sentencing. The bereaved mother felt extremely anxious about public speaking. She was afraid of freezing up at a time of such high emotion. Alternate ways to manage the anxiety of the courtroom atmosphere were practiced, such as diaphragmatic breathing, squeezing her mother's hand (the girl's grandmother), or holding a comfort object. The practitioner explained how the bereaved mother might draw solace from speaking out in court on behalf of her deceased daughter, just like she would speak up if someone were trying to harm the girl in her presence.

The practitioner recalled how the bereaved mother once laughed when relating a playground incident where her precocious daughter tried to involve a withdrawn playmate by demanding, "Acknowledge me!" A parallel was drawn to the trial—not a time for silence but for acknowledgment. So, the mother resolved to tell the assailant and the court just how much her precious daughter meant to the family and everyone who knew her and how she would be missed because of this tragically avoidable killing.

SOCIAL DISPARITIES IN HOMICIDE

With homicide rates in the United States, two staggering disparities stand out. First, when compared with 30 other high-income countries in the world, the 2015 homicide rate in the United States was more than seven times higher overall (Grinshteyn & Hemenway, 2019). Nearly 73% of those homicides involved firearms, a finding the authors attributed to more guns per capita in the United States together with relatively permissive gun laws in many states. Circumstances leading up to gun homicides typically involve arguments, family violence, or personal crises (Fowler et al., 2021).

The second disparity in U.S. homicide rates pertains to racial and ethnic groups. Non-Whites sustain firearm homicides at a rate nearly six times as high as Whites, 11.5 versus 2 per 100,000 (Grinshteyn & Hemenway, 2019). Among Blacks between the ages of 15 and 34, homicide was the leading cause of death, surpassing accidents, which accounted for most deaths among White and Hispanic individuals in that age range (Centers for Disease Control and Prevention, National Center for Health Statistics, 2021). Of deaths by homicide occurring in the United States between 2003 and 2017, 52.3% of the victims were Black, 30.3% were White, and 13% were Hispanic (Fowler et al., 2021). Considering that African Americans represent only 14.4% of the entire U.S. population (Moslimani et al., 2024), the disparity is sobering.

One implication of these statistics for practitioners working with bereaved parents of homicide victims in the United States is they will likely be helping African American parents at some point. Demonstrating sensitivity to their specific plight is essential to good care.

Practitioners in the United States must recognize that societal factors rendering African American individuals, particularly young adults, more vulnerable to homicide deaths can further complicate the grief experience of African American parents.

Many scholars have identified stigma associated with homicide deaths in the African American community (Burke et al., 2010; Hannays-King et al., 2015; Sharpe & Boyas, 2011; Sharpe & Iwamoto, 2022; Wallace et al., 2018). Stigma emerges from unwarranted attributions about race, socioeconomic status, violence, criminal behavior, gang culture, drug use, or family dynamics. Stigma can engender negative feelings of shame, blame, and anger among those unfairly labeled. Additionally, systemic discrimination can lead to inequities in the provision of social and health-care services as well as differential treatment by law enforcement personnel and the legal system. These added pressures make the sad reality of grieving a murdered son or daughter even more dispiriting for African American parents.

Practitioners exercising cultural attunement can help counteract the effects of these biases. It starts with a searching self-assessment of any personal attitudes that may deleteriously impact one's interview style or case conceptualization when working with bereaved African American parents. Taking care to cultivate an atmosphere of therapeutic justice validates the personhood and dignity of grieving parents. Advocating for disadvantaged parents in their dealings with social systems that may ignore or impede their rights—police departments, coroner's offices, hospitals, courts of law—can be of inestimable value during the heartbreaking aftermath of homicide.

Conversely, culturally specific elements can facilitate adaptation among African American bereaved parents. One notable example is the intervention model for African American family members of homicide victims developed by Tanya Sharpe and colleagues (Sharpe & Boyas, 2011; Sharpe et al., 2018). Their program was tested on a sample consisting primarily of mothers of murdered sons, so their model is especially applicable for bereaved parents. After providing psychoeducation about grief and trauma, the program focused on four components characteristic of African American coping patterns following homicide deaths (Sharpe & Boyas, 2011).

1. *Spiritual coping and meaning making*—Fidelity to spiritual traditions grounded in prayer and relentless faith in God or a higher power helped grievers find a way to contend with the senseless murder of their loved ones. One bereaved mother explained her belief, "a faith in God, being able to help us get through anything, and that is one of the worst things to try to get through" (p. 862).
2. *Maintaining a connection to the deceased*—Tangible and concrete reminders of their loved ones, such as photos, videos, and keepsakes, proved to be quite practical for holding on to positive memories, or even to the pain itself, as a means of connecting.

3. *Collective coping and caring for others*—Based on a long history of communal support in the face of oppression, African American families relied on coming together collectively to meet each other's emotional and psychological needs during bereavement. One bereaved mother noted "that sharing helped carry me through" (p. 864).
4. *Concealment*—Compartmentalizing and suppressing emotions surrounding the murder was normative. Deliberate avoidance of mentioning the deceased family member was intended to not burden others and to dissociate oneself from the pain.

The latter point about concealment has important implications for practitioners trained in standard psychotherapy paradigms emphasizing disclosure of detail and expression of emotion. With African American parents whose children have been killed, there may be moments to respect silence and honor the choice to not disclose or moments to refrain from seeking comprehensive accounts of the death and focusing on subjective feelings. Not revealing everything may be normative. Deliberate pauses or shifts in topic do not necessarily represent "resistance" as described in traditional psychotherapy models. Sharpe et al. (2018) concluded that African American parents bereaved by homicide were more inclined to seek support from trusted family and friends versus clinicians or doctors. The following case exemplifies several coping strategies used by African American parents of murdered children.

CASE 10.D

Nevaeh received a call that her 25-year-old son, Jamal, who lived out of state, had been killed. He had purchased a mattress from a private seller but found it defective. When Jamal confronted the seller demanding a full refund, an argument led to a fistfight. Ultimately, the other man drew a gun and shot Jamal, who died from his injuries. The man who killed him had previously been incarcerated for murder.

Nevaeh was inconsolable. At the same time, she knew Jamal's temperament and had to contend with the realization he may well have thrown the first punch. Regardless, his killing seemed senseless, especially when she found out the disputed amount was $300. She protested in outrage, "My son lost his life over $300?" That figure grossly devalued Jamal's life.

> Nevaeh and her husband both traveled to Jamal's home state for the trial only to find the assailant had accepted a last-minute plea bargain of 35 years in prison on a manslaughter charge. No one had attempted to notify them of this development. At the family's opportunity to address the assailant at sentencing, Nevaeh declined, "I have nothing to say [to him]." Her husband spoke, but she chose not to remain in the courtroom to hear his comments.
>
> Nevaeh went to a mental health clinic for treatment 18 months later. She was assigned to a therapy group for bereaved mothers. Unsure whether a group suited her, Nevaeh returned to the second session mostly out of a sense of loyalty toward other the group members, some of whom were also Black. She appreciated the psychoeducational aspects of the group, such as learning about the Dual Process Model of grief (Stroebe & Schut, 1999, 2010), along with suggestions for handling anniversary and holiday observances. Nevaeh's spirituality was a major source of solace. Also, she kept Jamal's Mickey Mouse key ring and found it to be a meaningful token for remembering him and feeling closer to him.
>
> Nevaeh's mother was extremely supportive. They talked about almost everything, except their grief over Jamal's murder. Her husband kept his sorrow to himself and never mentioned it. Nevaeh compartmentalized at home to avoid burdening the family. The therapy group became one of the few outlets she had for discussing her grief. Sometimes she found it helpful but other times not so much. When the time-limited therapy group terminated, Nevaeh did not seek further treatment.

MULTIPLE-VICTIM HOMICIDES

In the United States, the Centers for Disease Control and Prevention reported that more than 90% of homicide deaths involved only one victim (Fowler et al., 2021) compared to multiple homicides (defined as two or three victims) and mass homicides (defined as four or more victims). Mass homicides generally fell into one of two scenarios: multiple family members, especially children, killed during a dispute between intimate partners or other family members, or multiple victims who were strangers to the perpetrator or connected to an acquaintance or friend of the killer, consistent with incidents in schools, workplaces, houses of worship, or retail settings. Certain mass killings designated as hate crimes target specific groups identified by immigration status, racial or ethnic identity, religious affiliation, sexual preference, or political party. Mass homicides often receive widespread media attention and pose special challenges for bereaved parents.

When children are killed because of lethal quarreling among adult family members, the complex interplay of love and hate toward the assailant can generate a spectrum of emotions difficult to reconcile. Surviving parents try to comprehend why their child or children were killed by a coparent, stepparent, dating partner, sibling, or relative. Adult children who are killed may well have been a vital source of support to the bereaved parents—providing emotional support, financial assistance, or personal care—so their absence poses significant coping challenges. Grieving grandparents may be required to assume a parental role for surviving grandchildren, even while contending with their own grief over a murdered son or daughter (see Chapter 7, "Death of an Adult Child").

When children are killed randomly by strangers targeting some other individual (i.e., "in the wrong place at the wrong time"), the repercussions are tectonic. The death of children killed because they happen to be part of a targeted group shatters a parent's trust in a safe and predictable world. Following mass homicide perpetrated by a stranger, many bereaved parents do not even know where to begin picking up the pieces of their lives. Approximately one-third of mass killers complete suicide at the conclusion of their rampage, leaving many questions permanently unanswered (Fowler et al., 2021).

Besides blaming the perpetrator's heinous actions in mass homicides, bereaved parents may deem law enforcement personnel or other officials at fault for not ensuring their children's safety, particularly if warning signs were disregarded. Along with the killer, these civil servants may become recipients of anger and reprisal fantasies. The sensationalism of such killings often leads to intrusive or voyeuristic inquiries by media that go far beyond responsible journalism, as if the parents' private grief is considered part of the public domain.

ROLE OF FORGIVENESS

An egregious example of mass homicide occurred in 2006 in West Nickel Mines, Pennsylvania, in the United States, when a gunman barricaded himself and ten Amish girls in a one-room schoolhouse. Evidence indicated the attacker, who lived locally, planned to sexually assault the victims before killing them and himself. The killer left suicide notes for his wife and living children. Ironically, the killer was a bereaved parent whose infant daughter had died shortly after birth nine years earlier. Had his daughter lived, she would have been approximately the age of the girls he attacked (Kasdorf, 2007).

These killings received widespread publicity because the Amish are nonviolent people who neither own guns nor embrace modern technology. Consistent with their strong Christian values, the Amish community chose forgiveness as a response to the killings. Amish community leaders expressed condolences to the bereft family of the killer, indicating they held no ill will toward them on account of the killings. Many of the Amish even attended the killer's funeral. The radical nature of these actions drew admiration, as well as criticism, from the broader culture, where retaliation responses of anger and revenge are much more prevalent and perhaps seen as justified (Metcalfe, 2019).

Forgiveness can play a key role for some bereaved parents following the homicide death of a son or daughter. It goes far beyond the concept of emotionally disengaging from the killer. However, in no way is forgiveness a necessary component of every bereaved parent's grief journey following homicide. Those who do embrace forgiveness as a value—typically as a function of intrinsic spiritual beliefs, as with the Amish—will generally make that fact known to practitioners. Consistent with principles of cultural attunement, practitioners need to respect the attitude of grieving parents toward forgiveness regardless of the practitioner's own sensibilities. When bereaved parents are not inclined toward forgiveness, they should not be pressured in that direction.

For bereaved parents motivated to forgive their child's killer, practitioners can help educate them about what it involves. Psychological definitions of forgiveness incorporate two key dimensions. First, the victim voluntarily and unilaterally relinquishes any anger or revenge strivings toward the offender. In choosing not to carry such negativity any longer, victims unburden themselves from the obligation to remain angry. It is important to remember that releasing the anger does not mean the offender is undeserving of blame. Second, instead of an attitude of hostility or indifference toward the offender, the victim adopts a stance of benevolence—wishing well for the offender (McCullough et al., 2001). Understood in this dual way, genuine forgiveness represents a lofty aspiration. Yet considerable scientific evidence shows there are tangible psychological and physical health benefits that accrue from practicing forgiveness (Rasmussen et al., 2019).

Forgiveness is a process rather than a single action. Worthington (2003) provided a useful perspective by contrasting "decisional" forgiveness with "emotional" forgiveness. Decisional forgiveness means pledging not to seek revenge against or maintain avoidance of the offending party. After the Amish killings, decisional forgiveness was evident in their non-retaliatory stance and their seeking out conciliatory contact with the killer's family. Decisional forgiveness does not necessarily result in victims feeling differently toward the offender. Such a change of heart, or emotional forgiveness, involves a longer-term process wherein negative emotions associated with the offender gradually subside in favor of more positive responses.

Bereaved parents striving to forgive their child's killer can start with decisional forgiveness. Actions should be performed only when the bereaved parents' sense of timing indicates they can be tolerated. Behavioral steps may include reaching out to the killer, or the killer's family, to express forgiveness (via written messages, conversation, or an intermediary). Sometimes bereaved parents reserve this step until criminal prosecution has been accomplished, for example, extending verbal forgiveness during their victim impact statement. In cases where the perpetrator also died, as with a suicide death at the end of a killing spree, forgiveness can be expressed in alternate ways, such as telling a trusted confidant about one's decision to forgive or writing a letter or journal entry articulating forgiveness. Reminding others (and oneself) of the intent to forgive might require interrupting social conversations about revenge or redirecting internal fantasies about retaliation rather than nursing them. Other possible forgiveness steps include adopting an attitude of compassion toward the offender, praying for the offender, or performing acts of kindness toward the offender's family. What these various steps have in common is walking the path of decisional forgiveness, hoping those behaviors will foster emotional forgiveness over time.

TIMING TREATMENT STEPS

Because homicide deaths are inherently violent and transgressive, practitioners working with parents of murdered children need familiarity dealing with trauma. When and how practitioners approach trauma material in a treatment sequence is vitally important for outcome (cf. Resnick et al., 2010). Consistent with the ten key therapeutic elements elucidated in Chapter 4, "Contemporary Treatment Approaches," educating bereaved parents about the effects of trauma and teaching them distress-reduction methods precedes direct work with the trauma itself. With self-regulation skills in place, bereaved parents can safely explore the trauma to defuse its emotional intensity and rework their mental images and internal narrative. When applied properly, these techniques promote coping and adaptation.

Rynearson et al.'s (2015) Restorative Retelling model uses principles from trauma protocols in its structure and pacing. Returning to the case of James, whose teenage daughter, Jenn, was murdered, excerpts from his clinical treatment are recounted to illustrate how maneuvers from RR were applied.

CASE 10.A (Continued)

James's background as a Navy Seal and his disposition as a "man's man" influenced his response to treatment. During his military years, James had seen several comrades develop posttraumatic stress disorder, so he considered himself well versed in what trauma can do to the mind. He was not very patient with psychoeducation. He already knew he was mired in his trauma.

James was also accustomed to physical ways of relieving stress: shooting at the range, riding his motorcycle, working around his property. He did not take immediately to quieting methods for reducing tension and stress. However, his practitioner recognized that James needed some way of downregulating in an office setting before undertaking the more intense retelling and reconstruction steps of the treatment. The act of shooting provided the metaphor. James could relate very well to the need to regulate his breathing while aiming and squeezing a gun's trigger in order to hit a target accurately. The term *triggering* took on a double meaning for James during treatment—both an indication that his emotions were escalating and a reminder to use breath control to steady himself. The shooting metaphor also appealed to James because he could imagine the killers on the paper targets at the range.

During the reunion step prior to retelling, James spoke at length about how close he was to Jenn. He felt proud about bringing her through the aftermath of the divorce and functioning as a single father. Yet he yearned to have his precious daughter back. His world was a void without her.

The pivotal moment in James's treatment came during the detailed in-session recounting of Jenn's murder, based on what he had learned about the events. In statements to the police, the boy who stabbed Jenn described how her eyes had widened with fear and her stare went blank as he raised the knife. In visualizing the scene, James riveted on that split second before the attack.

Protocol-based suggestions called for James to imagine to himself in the scene performing compensatory actions such as comfort, care, rescue, or retaliation. However, James altered the images in a different fashion. Rather than interpreting Jenn's blank stare as shock from realizing she was about to be stabbed, James invoked a meaning based on his Christian beliefs. He recalled a scripture passage pertaining to that final moment: "We will all be changed, in an instant, in the blink of an eye, at the last trumpet" (1 Corinthians 15:51–52). Even though he had not been there to protect Jenn, James concluded that God had called his daughter home "in the blink of an eye" before the knife ever penetrated her body. Therefore, Jenn did not suffer. The assailants may have killed her body, but Jenn was already safe with her Creator.

This reworking of the narrative brought James consolation. It neutralized much of his reenactment imagery because it disarmed Jenn's killers. With this alternate narrative, James did not have to torment himself over Jenn's agonal struggles. The killers could not prevail over God. The remainder of the scripture passage bolstered his interpretation.

> And when this [body] which is corruptible clothes itself with incorruptibility and this which is mortal clothes itself with immortality, then the word that is written shall come about: "Death is swallowed up in victory. Where, O death, is your victory? Where, O death, is your sting?" . . . Thanks be to God who gives us the victory through our Lord Jesus Christ. (1 Corinthians 15:54–57)

In the later steps of treatment, inducing James to consider how he could go on living and find some sense of joy was not easy. He battled depression. He remained cynical and fatalistic about life. James existed primarily to attend court and see justice served. He expressed gratitude for help received from the practitioner. After the two trials delivered guilty verdicts, James relocated out of state to escape painful reminders of Jenn's murder, a form of situational avoidance. Treatment concluded with mixed gains.

SUMMARY

Homicide constitutes a reprehensible crime and inflicts untold suffering on bereaved parents and families. This chapter surveyed several important topics for practitioners working with parents whose son or daughter was murdered. From the importance of using accurate language to handling bereaved parents' anger and reprisal fantasies, from exploring persistent guilt to negotiating the criminal justice system, from managing social disparities to dealing with mass homicides, from understanding forgiveness to timing treatment steps, the subject matter is exhaustive. Because dealing with homicide deaths can be emotionally demanding, practitioners must have the foundational qualifications of death competence and cultural attunement to appropriately serve parents whose children die by homicide. Daunting as the challenges may be for these bereaved parents, the case illustrations show that there are pathways to adaptation and resilience.

REFERENCES

Burke, L. A., Neimeyer, R. A., & McDevitt-Murphy, M. E. (2010). African American homicide bereavement: Aspects of social support that predict complicated grief, PTSD, and depression. *OMEGA-Journal of Death and Dying, 61*(1), 1–24. https://doi/abs/10.2190/om.61.1.a

Centers for Disease Control and Prevention, National Center for Health Statistics. (2021). *Mortality 2018–2021 on CDC WONDER Online Database*, as compiled from data provided by the 57 vital statistics jurisdictions through the Vital Statistics Cooperative Program. http://wonder.cdc.gov/ucd-icd10-expanded.html

Fowler, K. A., Leavitt, R. A., Betz, C. J., Yuan, K., & Dahlberg, L. L. (2021). Examining differences between mass, multiple, and single-victim homicides to inform prevention: Findings from the National Violent Death Reporting System. *Injury Epidemiology, 8*, 1–15. https://doi.org/10.1186/s40621-021-00345-7

Gamino, L. A., & Ritter, R. H., Jr. (2009). *Ethical practice in grief counseling*. Springer Publishing Company.

Gamino, L. A., & Ritter, R. H., Jr. (2012). Death competence: An ethical imperative. *Death Studies, 36*, 23–40. https://doi.org/10.1080/07481187.2011.553503

Graybar, S. R., & Leonard, L. M. (2005). In defense of listening. *American Journal of Psychotherapy, 59*, 1–18. https://doi/abs/10.1176/appi.psychotherapy.2005.59.1.1

Grinshteyn, E., & Hemenway, D. (2019). Violent death rates in the US compared to those of the other high-income countries, 2015. *Preventive Medicine, 123*, 20–26. https://doi.org/10.1016/j.ypmed.2019.02.026

Hannays-King, C., Bailey, A., & Akhtar, M. (2015). Social support and Black mothers' bereavement experience of losing a child to gun homicide. *Bereavement Care, 34*(1), 10–16. https://doi/abs/10.1080/02682621.2015.1028199

Kasdorf, J. S. (2007). To pasture: "Amish forgiveness," silence, and the West Nickel Mines school shooting. *CrossCurrents*, 328–347. www.jstor.org/stable/24462390

Klass, D., & Marwit, S. J. (1989). Toward a model of parental grief. *OMEGA-Journal of Death and Dying, 19*(1), 31–50. https://doi.org/10.2190/BVUR-67KR-F52F-VW35

McCullough, M. E., Pargamet, K. I., & Thoresen, C. E. (2001). *Forgiveness: Theory, research, & practice*. Guilford.

Metcalfe, D. (2019). The West Nickel Mines Amish school murders and the cultural fetishization of "Amish Forgiveness." *Religions, 10*(9), 524. https://doi.org/10.3390/rel10090524

Moslimani, M., Tamir, C., Budiman, A., Noe-Bustamante, L., & Mora, L. (2024). *Facts about the U.S. Black population*. Pew Research Center's Social & Demographic Trends Project. Retrieved March 20, 2024, from www.pewresearch.org/social-trends/fact-sheet/facts-about-the-us-black-population/

Mowll, J., Adams, G., & Darling, J. (2017). Facilitating access to scene photographs and CCTV footage for relatives bereaved after violent death. *Bereavement Care, 36*, 11–18. https://doi.org/10.1080/02682621.2017.1305042

Mowll, J., Lobb, E. A., & Wearing, M. (2016). The transformative meanings of viewing or not viewing the body after sudden death. *Death Studies, 40*, 46–53. https://doi.org/10.1080/07481187.2015.1059385

Neimeyer, R. A., Pitcho-Prelorentzos, S., & Mahat-Shamir, M. (2021). "If only . . .": Counterfactual thinking in bereavement. *Death Studies, 45*(9), 692–701. https://doi.org/10.1080/07481187.2019.1679959

Pearn, J. (2016). Hammurabi's code: A primary datum in the conjoined professions of medicine and law. *Medico-Legal Journal, 84*(3), 125–131. https://doi.org/10.1177/0025817216646038

Rando, T. A. (1991). *How to go on living when someone you love dies*. Bantam.

Rasmussen, K. R., Stackhouse, M., Boon, S. D., Comstock, K., & Ross, R. (2019). Meta-analytic connections between forgiveness and health: The moderating effects of forgiveness-related distinctions. *Psychology & Health, 34*(5), 515–534. https://doi.org/10.1080/08870446.2018.1545906

Redmond, L. M. (1989). *Surviving when someone you love was murdered: A professional's guide to group grief therapy for families and friends of murder victims* (p. 1). Psychological Consultation and Education Services.

Resnick, P. A., Monson, C. M., & Chard, K. M. (2010). *Cognitive processing therapy: Veteran/military version*. Department of Veterans' Affairs.

Rynearson, E. K., Correa, F., & Takacs, L. (2015). *Accommodation to violent dying: A guide to restorative retelling and support*. Virginia Mason Clinic. www.vmfh.org/content/dam/vmfhorg/pdf/legacy-vm/workfiles/Manual_Accommodation_Violent_Dying.pdf

Sharpe, T. L., & Boyas, J. (2011). We fall down: The African American experience of coping with the homicide of a loved one. *Journal of Black Studies, 42*, 855–873. https://doi/abs/10.1177/0021934710377613

Sharpe, T. L., & Iwamoto, D. K. (2022). Psychosocial aspects of coping that predict post-traumatic stress disorder for African American survivors of homicide victims. *Preventive Medicine, 165*, 107277. https://doi.org/10.1016/j.ypmed.2022.107277

Sharpe, T. L., Iwamoto, D. K., Masey, J. M., & Michalopoulos, L. M. (2018). The development of a culturally adapted pilot intervention for African American family members of homicide victims: A preliminary report. *Violence and Victims, 33*, 708–720. https://doi.org/10.1891/0886-6708.VV-D-17-00052

Shear, M. K. (2015). *Complicated grief treatment*. Columbia Center for Complicated Grief.

Stroebe, M., & Schut, H. (1999). The Dual Process Model of coping with bereavement: Rationale and description. *Death Studies, 23*, 197–224. https://doi/abs/10.1080/074811899201046

Stroebe, M., & Schut, H. (2010). The Dual Process Model of coping with bereavement: A decade on. *OMEGA—Journal of Death and Dying, 61*, 273–289. https://doi/abs/10.2190/OM.61.4.b

Wallace, C. M., McGee, Z. T., Malone-Colon, L., & Boykin, A. W. (2018). The impact of culture-based protective factors on reducing rates of violence among African American adolescent and young adult males. *Journal of Social Issues, 74*(3), 635–651. https://doi/abs/10.1111/josi.12287

Worthington, E. L., Jr. (2003). *Forgiving and reconciling: Bridges to wholeness and hope*. InterVarsity Press.

CHAPTER ELEVEN

Military or Combat Death

> Do not seek death. Death will find you. But seek the road which makes death a fulfillment.
>
> —Dag Hammarskjöld (1964)

CASE 11.A

Carole's son Dayton was killed by insurgent fire during deployment overseas. The grandson of a World War II combatant and son of an Air Force veteran, Dayton's lifelong dream was military service. Dayton joined the U.S. Army after the September 11, 2001, attacks. During his second overseas deployment, Dayton was killed in action. With his unit under fire, Dayton heroically ignored his own safety while directing and saving several other soldiers. A rocket-propelled grenade took his life.

Posthumously, Dayton was awarded the Silver Star, as "his gallant actions and dedicated devotion to duty, without regard for his own life, were in keeping with the highest traditions of military service and reflect great credit upon himself, his unit, and the United States Army." He also received a Legislative Medal of Honor. A highway near his hometown was named after him. These tributes and honors did not bring Carole much comfort.

Dayton left behind a wife, two children, his grieving parents, and a brother. Carole bluntly described her roller-coaster emotions during the aftermath of Dayton's death, commenting, "Some days are great, and some days are crap." Instead of taking leave, she returned to work as an educator. However, Carole's preoccupation with Dayton's death diminished her passion for teaching. School administrators were superficially sympathetic, but their underlying dissatisfaction was evident. She struggled to get by. At family gatherings where their widowed daughter-in-law and grandchildren were present, Carole felt grateful when her other son took an active role with the two fatherless grandchildren (his nephew and niece). Yet she also felt terribly sad that Dayton was not there to do those things himself.

Carole and her husband leaned on their Christian faith and belief in an afterlife. They also attended monthly support group meetings for Gold Star families who experienced the death of a family member on active duty (www.operationwearehere.com/FallenWarriors.html/). She found those meetings helpful. Carole later helped facilitate Gold Star meetings. She reflected, "That was good, to give my story [where] others benefitted, it gave some value to others." They received an invitation to record an oral history of Dayton's life and military career as an archive for the Library of Congress. They found that activity meaningful.

A significant complication in Carole's grief over Dayton was the fact that her daughter had died 11 years earlier from a rare autoimmune disease. Dayton's subsequent death meant that two of her three children were now deceased. Her daughter had not monitored her health condition very conscientiously and suffered a massive stroke, which proved fatal. Carole's internal narrative included lament and irritation over her daughter's lack of regard for her own health. Similarly, she had bitter thoughts about Dayton because he "chose to protect [his] comrades when he had two children at home."

Three years after Dayton's death, Carole's physician expressed concern about depression and referred her for psychological treatment. Carole chose a practitioner whom she had met at a bereavement meeting sponsored by the Tragedy Assistance Program for Survivors (TAPS). She attended five therapy sessions. Curiously, she spent much of the time talking about her deceased daughter, acknowledging it was easier to focus away from Dayton's death. Ultimately, what Carole found more helpful than therapy was her own research on how trauma affects the brain. That information gave Carole permission "not to bypass my emotions" over Dayton's death, which was not just a loss but a trauma. Years later she described herself as doing "pretty well."

Most military deaths involve a young or middle-aged adult, making their deaths untimely and premature from a life-cycle perspective (Drescher, 2013). In addition, military deaths, especially combat deaths, can occur in a violent fashion where bodily remains may not be intact due to dismemberment, burns, or mutilation. Added distress is generated when military deaths happen far from home in war theaters around the world, especially following lengthy periods of separation from family and friends. These factors of untimeliness, traumatic death, and physical separation intensify the grief response of bereaved parents (see Chapter 2, "What Makes Parental Grief So Difficult?"). In Carole's case, contemplating the horrors of Dayton's death in a firefight was something she eschewed precisely because of how her son died. She did not want to think about it.

MILITARY CULTURE AND THE WARRIOR ETHOS

When working with parents whose son or daughter died while serving in the armed forces, cultural attunement requires practitioners to have some knowledge of the basic tenets of military culture and the warrior ethos because they form the sociological context for how military deaths are viewed. Bereaved parents will vary in the extent to which they endorsed their child's military service or the warrior ethos. When the bereaved family holds values consonant with military life, their acceptance of service-based protocols will likely be greater and their meaning-making efforts can incorporate military ideals. However, when bereaved parents either do not understand or do not agree with the values of the warrior ethos, additional suffering can ensue as they attempt to assimilate their child's death into a worldview at variance with military culture.

Christian et al. (2009) outlined key dimensions of military culture that differ significantly from civilian culture, particularly in Western industrialized democracies such as the United States where rugged individualism and personal autonomy are sacrosanct. In contrast, military culture is inherently *collectivist*, *hierarchical*, and based on *core values* of serving as guardians and fighters. Among other things, military life explicitly regulates the expression of emotion in most circumstances.

Collectivism in the military means that the unit or force to which the warrior belongs is more important than any individual fighter within it. The unit always comes first. Rigorous training acculturates recruits and officers alike to subordinate self to the group, draw their identity from the group, and prioritize group goals ahead of any personal aspirations. They are taught that the individual is of limited value whereas the unit can accomplish anything. Collectivism leads to high social cohesion, critically important for relying on one another

MILITARY OR COMBAT DEATH

and entrusting one's life to other unit members in potentially mortal situations such as live-fire combat. That tight social cohesion—the sense of being in it together—also serves a protective function against the inevitable stresses of military life.

The hierarchical structure of the military, often misunderstood by those outside of it, features a rigid rank system designed to promote effective leadership and accomplish critical objectives. Unit commanders issue orders based on achieving the mission's purpose. Sometimes that means putting specific fighters in harm's way. Respect for and trust in leadership enables fighters to respond to battlefield orders and perform dangerous activities in the interest of completing their mission. Proscribing fraternization between officers and enlisted recruits is intended to preserve rank structure and prevent personal feelings from interfering with assignment of potentially risky duties.

Core military values include honor, courage, and commitment to duty. Honor means operating with integrity and observing rules of engagement so that one's actions always support the designated mission in a manner meriting pride in a job well done. Even while vanquishing an enemy, harm to civilian noncombatants is avoided wherever possible. Courage means bravery in the face of life-threatening conditions, including the willingness to sacrifice one's life if necessary to advance the cause. Suppressing emotion and learning to tolerate pain are necessary for displaying courage (Brim, 2013). Commitment means warriors discharge their duties faithfully and competently, understanding their role in the overall mission to which they have been assigned. Prioritizing the mission means other considerations—such as personal wishes, family circumstances, or individual ego—are secondary. Fighters who die in combat or in the line of duty are seen as paying the ultimate price to uphold their commitment to military values and the mission to which they dedicated themselves, the fulfillment referenced in Hammarskjöld's quote (1964) at the beginning of this chapter.

At its essence, military service is about maintaining and using controlled aggression to guard and protect one's country and citizenry from hostile forces. Sometimes that objective necessitates preemptive strikes or even offensive campaigns designed to prevent enemies from attacking the homeland or a nation's important allies. Everyone serving in the military, whether arms-bearing combatants or those performing duties to support the mission, understands their activities are part of this overall effort. Believing their cause to be just validates the use of controlled aggression.

Even families strongly supportive of military culture and the warrior ethos can have misgivings about military deaths. Carole's responses to Dayton's combat death showed that parental bereavement is rarely a categorical response. Carole came from a family where military service was applauded and honored, yet she watched her own father struggle with shell shock after World War II. When Carole looked at things from the viewpoint of her two young grandchildren now fatherless because her son sacrificed his own life to save unit members, she felt unsettled and privately questioned the justice of it. These facets of Carole's grief illustrate how nuanced bereavement can be when parents lose a son or daughter to a military or combat death. Accommodating all the different facets, including contradictory ones, is part of the challenge when working with bereaved parents such as Carole.

DYING WITH HONOR

Given the nature of the warrior ethos, a critically important variable in the aftermath of a son or daughter's military death is whether their child died with honor. In Dayton's case, his self-sacrificial death was universally lauded by the army, the legislature, his home community, and countless other individuals and organizations. His designation as a hero accounted for this enormous groundswell of accolades and social support. Having others affirm the deceased child's gallantry and altruism offers bereaved parents some compensatory comfort in the aftermath of a combat death.

Dying honorably in military service can also lend substantial meaning when parents develop a durable narrative about the death of their child and its impact on them and others. Particularly if their child's death meant a noble cause was served or other lives were saved, as with Dayton, a clear path to legacy is evident. These elements can help buffer bereaved parents' distress. Yet even then, once the fanfare has quieted and time goes on, bereaved parents are still left with the permanent reality of living without their beloved son or daughter, hero or not. They may experience the same factors that make loss of a child difficult for other bereaved parents (see Chapter 2, "What Makes Parental Grief So Difficult?"). Practitioners can certainly highlight the honorable and heroic aspects of a military death when working with bereaved parents while at the same time avoiding any suggestion that the bereaved parents, or the world at large, are better off without the presence of their deceased son or daughter.

Not every military death happens during combat or occurs in heroic fashion. Active-duty military members sometimes lose their lives in accidents, during training maneuvers, or from criminal assault. As a counterpoint to Carole's story, consider the following example of an accidental military death that occurred on base. Its bereavement dynamics strongly resemble those described in Chapter 8, "Accidental Death."

> **CASE 11.B**
>
> A soldier died at an overseas supply depot when a delivery truck accidentally backed over him. Human error was the cause. Though still afforded military honors at burial, the context of that soldier's death was devoid of the recognitions and tributes bestowed on soldiers killed in combat. Instead, his death seemed senseless and unnecessary. Finding meaning after the loss was much more difficult for that soldier's family, thus making their grief more onerous.

Military deaths during training exercises present a complex picture. No doubt combat simulations are risky, especially when they involve live fire. However, if fatalities result from inadequate planning, faulty logistical support, equipment malfunction, or questionable command decisions, factors of negligence and preventability enter the equation and can negatively affect bereaved parents. Military investigations into fatal training accidents can be lengthy and shrouded in secrecy (for purposes of not disclosing operational errors or strategic blunders). Even when investigations are completed and bereaved families are briefed about the results, unanswered questions often persist. Such accidental training deaths often generate anger among bereaved parents frustrated with an impersonal, bureaucratic system seen to withhold information to cover its own mistakes. This righteous anger complicates the grief response of bereaved parents, similar to accidental deaths resulting from negligent, reckless behavior, such as driving while intoxicated.

Sadly, some active-duty military personnel die from homicides perpetrated either by another service member or by a civilian. Murders can occur either on or off a military installation. These deaths are typically not seen as honorable but as shameful and deplorable. A complex set of military justice regulations govern jurisdictional authority for prosecuting such crimes, sometimes with overlapping responsibility among military, federal, and civilian courts (U.S. Department of the Army, 2024). These complexities can be very difficult to comprehend. Practitioners must work patiently with bereaved parents of murdered service members as they navigate the different bureaucracies involved in bringing their child's killer to justice (see Chapter 10, "Homicide").

An additional consideration determining whether military deaths are viewed as honorable comes from public attitudes and societal context. Some armed conflicts may be unpopular or controversial at home (Rolls & Harper, 2016). For example, when political expediency or questionable alliances with other nations (rather than defense of the homeland) seem to motivate a government's decision to commit its military to a particular conflict, public support for the war effort may be lacking. Societal criticism or opposition of an armed conflict can detract from, or even negate, any sense of honor connected with a military death, even one that occurs heroically in combat such as Dayton's death. Bereaved parents can be left disenfranchised in their grief when society views the military action that caused their child's death as unjust or wrong.

One final form of military death to be considered is the case of fighters missing in action, called "suspended deaths" by Kaplan (2008). Parents of these missing warriors experience a form of ambiguous loss (Boss, 2016; see Chapter 12, "Non-Death Loss"). Even though their missing son or daughter may be viewed in an honorable light for their service, parents feel relegated to a limbo state of not knowing whether their child is alive or dead. The angst of that uncertainty may outweigh any compensatory benefit associated with military honor.

MILITARY PROTOCOL

Regulations govern how the military handles the line-of-duty deaths of service members (U.S. Department of the Air Force, 2021; U.S. Department of Defense, 2015). Adherence to military protocol can have certain benefits for bereaved parents. On one hand, the care and respect shown by the military in retrieving the body of a fallen comrade and transporting that service member's remains from a foreign battlefield back to the United States assume an almost reverential tone. Salutes, flag draping, honor guards, and other visible signs convey respect for the ultimate sacrifice made by the fighter. Strict regulations pertaining to body preparation and casketing further convey dignity to a fallen warrior. Personal support extended by a casualty assistance officer together with financial coverage for burial and disposition of remains, including a military headstone or memorial marker, can relieve many burdens associated with the military death of an adult child. Usually, a death benefit is paid to the family as well. In the United States and other countries around the world, a permanent resting place of honor awaits veterans whose families choose interment in military cemeteries.

Procedures for death notification, typically done in person, emphasize a formal yet compassionate approach to bearing news of the worst order to a parent whose son or daughter has died in the line of duty. Personnel are trained to show sensitivity to bereaved families, regardless of the circumstances of death. For parents, notification of a child's death (regardless of age) can activate protective responses arising from their unique role as the child's first attachment figures. For single young adults who die in military service, parents may still be the official next of kin and the requisite decision-makers. Spouses are primary next of kin for married warriors. Yet with some young military couples, the spouse may be a relative newcomer to the family. In those instances, bereaved parents may still feel a possessory obligation toward their deceased son or daughter yet have no legal standing to make decisions about funeral or burial arrangements. Alternately, or in addition, custodial control exercised by the military in "taking care of our own" sometimes generates competitive responses by bereaved parents who would prefer to handle arrangements themselves. Practitioners should remain cognizant of such emotional crosscurrents that could affect parental grief in these situations. Rolls and Harper (2016) commented on conundrums that can arise following some military deaths:

> The method of notification of the death and subsequent investigation procedures restrict access to and control over their son or daughter's body. This lack of control can be exacerbated where there is a struggle to exert parental care and protection over the body and the personal effects of their still young "child" if the parent(s) has not been designated next of kin, or when the legal and military regulations, processes, and procedures are at odds with their needs.
>
> (p. 89)

Burial or interment with military honors is one of the most universally recognized and emotionally evocative aspects of protocol extended to a fallen warrior. For U.S. service members, full military honors include uniformed pallbearers, a firing party for a 21-gun salute, a bugler to play "Taps," and a color guard to fold and present the American flag to the family. Some families prefer to provide their own pallbearers or may not want to hear guns firing at such a sad moment, so these elements may be omitted. At a minimum, a color guard for flag presentation and the traditional playing of "Taps" are required. When the officer in charge presents the folded flag to the chief mourner, the following message is delivered aloud: "On behalf of the President of the United States, the [specific military branch], and a grateful nation, please accept this flag as a symbol of our appreciation for your loved one's honorable and faithful service" (U.S. Department of Air Force, 2021, p. 46). For many bereaved parents, military honors at burial are an indispensable ritual that symbolizes recognition by their country of their deceased child's service and sacrifice (cf. Hoy, 2025).

A striking example of resilience was displayed by the bereaved mother in the following case.

> **CASE 11.C**
>
> As a native of Puerto Rico, Lucia proudly served on active duty in the U.S. Navy and then continued her military service in the Navy Reserves. Her son Mateo served briefly in the military as well. Sadly, he died a few years later as a young adult. His car stalled on a major interstate highway. When Mateo attempted to cross the high-speed thoroughfare on foot to seek assistance, he was struck and killed by another vehicle. Because Mateo was a veteran in good standing, he qualified for military honors at burial. Lucia found great comfort in the protocol performed at the cemetery by the military honor guard.
>
> As a way of working out her grief, Lucia volunteered for honor guard duty at the burials of other service members. Lucia explained how she had served at more than 100 funerals since Mateo's death. In folding and presenting the flag to other mourners, Lucia relived her experience of burying Mateo and came more and more to accept her own loss. Her empathy for the devastation that grieving families feel (especially bereaved parents) at the moment of committal made Lucia acutely sensitive while performing those solemn duties.

American haiku poet Nick Virgilio (1928–1989) was a World War II veteran whose brother died in combat during the Vietnam conflict. Virgilio composed a series of haiku rendering poignant snapshots of his parents' experience with death notification and military burial. The following short verses communicate the intense emotion stirred by such events.

> *telegram in hand,*
> *the shadow of the marine*
> *darkens our screen door*

> *the autumn wind*
> *has torn the telegram and more*
> *from my mother's hand*

> *into the blinding sun . . .*
> *the funeral procession's*
> *glaring headlights*

flag-covered coffin
the shadow of the bugler
slips into the grave

my gold star mother
and father hold each other
and the folded flag

Thanksgiving dinner:
placing the baby's high chair
in the empty space

(reprinted with permission from the
Nick Virgilio Haiku Association)

MILITARY SUICIDES

Suicide among military service members has become an undeniable mental health problem that confounds surviving families and the military alike. Given its cohesive culture, military commanders and unit members share much of the same consternation experienced by grieving families when a warrior dies by suicide—a death seemingly needless and preventable. Current estimates of the problem, based on data from 2020 to 2022, indicate approximately 500 U.S. military personnel (including active duty, reserves, and national guard) died annually from suicide (U.S. Department of Defense, 2023). Given the preponderance of young males below age 30 serving in the armed forces, the report argued that the active-duty military suicide rate mimics rates in the general U.S. population when factors of age and gender are controlled statistically. However, recent data from the Department of Veterans Affairs (2023a) showed that the suicide rate among veterans is significantly higher than the civilian population, especially for younger veterans aged 18 to 34 years.

What causes this vexing problem? The U.S. Department of Defense (2023) identified several factors associated with military suicides: coexisting behavioral health problems (such as substance misuse, depression, anxiety, and trauma), intimate partner conflicts, workplace difficulties, administrative or legal issues, financial strain, and access to firearms. When several of these factors are present, service members become more vulnerable. Specifically, two pernicious conditions exhibited by individuals contemplating suicide may be evident: *perceived burdensomeness*, where self is seen as a burden to others who would be better off without them, and *thwarted belongingness*, where one feels isolated, rejected, or unimportant to others (Joiner et al., 2009; see Chapter 9, "Suicide"). Joiner also identified a third characteristic, *the capacity to act on a desire for death*, developed from progressive tolerance for painful or fear-inducing experiences.

Unfortunately, the nature of armed conflict repeatedly exposes fighters to horrific scenes of carnage and suffering, including the violent deaths of close comrades. Bryan et al. (2015) performed a meta-analytic review of combat deployment and found a definite relationship between exposure to killing or atrocities and subsequent suicide-related outcomes (death by suicide, suicide attempts, and suicidal ideation). Subsequent studies suggested combat exposure leads to higher levels of posttraumatic stress disorder (PTSD), a mental health condition leading to higher suicidality (Glenn et al., 2020; LeardMann et al., 2021; Orak et al., 2023). Lifetime rates of PTSD among veterans who served in war zones since the Vietnam conflict have been estimated between 10% and 29% (U.S. Department of Veterans Affairs, 2023b). Consider the following case example.

CASE 11.D

Faith's son, Quinton, shot and killed himself on a remote mountain road several miles from the military installation where he was stationed. A determined African American mother, Faith raised her family while also working because the children's father abandoned them early in the marriage. As a result, Faith and Quinton were always close. Quinton was never academically inclined, but he thrived in army life, which became his "path to manhood." After two overseas tours on active duty, Quinton enjoyed the esteem of his unit members, who described him as a good soldier. However, war trauma took a toll on Quinton, and domestic problems at home proved unbearable. He returned from his second deployment to find his wife pregnant by another man, living with a female lover, withholding the stepson, and wanting a divorce.

Quinton confided in Faith how emotionally distraught he was over his disintegrating marriage. She encouraged him in every way she could, insisting, "I too have known rejection. You have to go on." Returning to post after a contentious holiday visit with his wife, Quinton wrecked his car, totaling it. In hindsight, Faith wondered if Quinton's crash may have been a suicide attempt or rehearsal. A week later, Quinton texted his mother and sister in the middle of the night, saying, "I'm sorry. It's not your fault. I'm broken." He shot himself in the head.

Faith described the impact of Quinton's suicide as "devastating, like a tsunami." His unit commander approved holding a memorial service on post. Faith and her daughter traveled to attend the out of state service, with an official escort. The military then transported Quinton's body back to his home state for burial in a veteran's cemetery with full honors. Some of his unit members made the long drive to be present at his funeral and interment. Even though Quinton and his wife were emotionally estranged at the time of his death, she remained the official next of kin and made all decisions about his arrangements. Knowing how their marital struggles contributed to Quinton's desperation, it was all Faith could do to be civil during the ceremonies.

Faith sought grief therapy several months after Quinton's death. Once comfortable with the practitioner, Faith let down her defenses and wailed loudly, releasing the intense visceral pain she carried from Quinton's tragic suicide. Subsequently, Faith learned methods to self-regulate her emotions. In the safety of the therapy, she slowly unpacked the traumatic details of Quinton's death and conducted a psychological inquest into what happened (cf. Jordan, 2011). Faith began formulating a "good enough" narrative about Quinton's suicide based on the idea that he had become overwhelmed. In the process, she acknowledged her feelings of exasperation toward Quinton's wife as well as her disappointment in Quinton's father, who had been absent from the picture for so long.

Faith's emotions fluctuated, with some bad days and some better ones. On Mother's Day about 18 months after Quinton's suicide, Faith visited the cemetery intending to leave flowers at his grave. When she attempted to force the plastic flower holder into the sunbaked ground, it broke. Faith collapsed in a river of tears, finding the episode emblematic of the whole regrettable scenario of a "broken" son and shattered dreams. Too distraught to drive home, Faith called her daughter to come get her.

Several months later, Faith agreed to drop a friend at the local airport to catch a flight. Unexpectedly, seeing the terminal reminded Faith of her most recent trip, the one to Quinton's out-of-state post for the unit memorial service. That association triggered an overwhelming grief upsurge, including panic and suicidal ideation. Faith "fought through it." She mobilized her breathing methods, prayed, and recited her mantra, "You can do this." She called her daughter, but this time Faith kept driving as they spoke. Ironically, this frightening experience increased Faith's compassion for Quinton in his final desperate moments, believing she had felt some semblance of his excruciating pain. It also stoked her anger at Quinton for not fighting through the pain. Eventually, Faith came to describe herself this way, "I'm not a victim. I'm a survivor."

Quinton's case illustrates how suicide can be multifactorial, with several influences leading to that fateful decision. To what degree Quinton's war service contributed to his self-perception of being "broken" is impossible to verify. Faith believed Quinton's combat exposure demoralized him, eroded his natural zest, and left him less capable of enduring the extreme marital discord he encountered, a hypothesis supported by research findings (Glenn et al., 2020; LeardMann et al., 2021; Orak et al., 2023). Certainly Quinton could be seen as experiencing thwarted belongingness via rejection by his wife (Joiner et al., 2009). Marris (2019) described how "suicidogenic" relationships characterized by conflict of high volatility and intensity are often associated with a person's decision to kill themselves. Regardless of how these various factors contributed to Quinton's suicide, Faith was left with the inescapable reality of his permanent absence. Cataloging the tragic events leading up to that moment—a task that seemed so essential for understanding—could not change the outcome. Gradually, Faith embraced the idea of living again while never forgetting how wonderful Quinton was.

SUMMARY

Bereaved parents whose son or daughter died while serving in the military face a unique set of circumstances during their grief journey. Parents and practitioners need to recognize military culture and the warrior ethos that dictate how these deaths are viewed and handled in a military context: whether fighters die in combat or away from active war theaters, whether a military death is considered heroic or honorable, whether fighters are killed accidentally or during training maneuvers or in criminal attacks or are designated missing in action. Death notification and burial arrangements may be largely determined by military protocol, sometimes leaving bereaved parents relegated to a bystander role. Suicide deaths among service members contradict military collectivist values and create untold havoc for bereaved parents. Fortunately, each branch of the U.S. military offers specific support for Gold Star families who suffer a military or combat death of an adult child. In addition, other support organizations such as Operation Here We Are (www.operationwearehere.com/FallenWarriors.html/) and TAPS (www.taps.org/) offer practical information and useful programs specifically geared for bereaved parents.

REFERENCES

Boss, P. (2016). The context and process of theory development: The story of ambiguous loss. *Journal of Family Theory & Review, 8*, 269–286. https://doi.org/10.1111/jftr.12152

Brim, W. L. (2013). Impact of military culture on the clinician and clinical practice. In B. A. Moore & J. E. Barnett (Eds.), *Military psychologists' desk reference* (pp. 31–36). Oxford University Press.

Bryan, C. J., Griffity, J. E., Pace, B. T., Hinkson, K., Bryan, A. O., Clemans, T. A., & Imel, Z. E. (2015). Combat exposure and risk for suicidal thoughts and behaviors among military personnel and veterans: A systematic review and meta-analysis. *Suicide and Life-Threatening Behavior, 45,* 633–649. https://doi.org/10.1111/sltb.12163

Christian, J. R., Stivers, J. R., & Sammons, M. T. (2009). Training to the warrior ethos: Implications for clinicians treating military members and their families. In S. M. Freeman, B. A. Moore, & A. Freeman (Eds.), *Living and surviving in harm's way: A psychological treatment handbook for pre- and post-deployment of military personnel* (pp. 27–49). Routledge.

Drescher, K. D. (2013). Grief, loss, and war. In B. A. Moore & J. E. Barnett (Eds.), *Military psychologists' desk reference* (pp. 251–255). Oxford University Press.

Glenn, J. J., Dillon, K. H., Dennis, P. A., Patel, T. A., Mann, A. J., Calhoun, P. S., Kimbrel, N. A., Beckham, J. C., & Elbogen, E. B. (2020). Post-traumatic symptom severity mediates the association between combat exposure and suicidal ideation in veterans. *Suicide and Life-Threatening Behavior, 50,* 1167–1172. https://doi.org/10.1111/sltb.12678

Hammarskjöld, D. (1964). *Markings* (p. 159). L. Sjöberg & W. H. Auden (Trans.). Faber & Faber.

Hoy, W. G. (2025). *Creating meaning in funerals: How families and communities make sense of death.* Routledge.

Joiner, T. E., Van Orden, K. A., Witte, T. K., Selby, E. A., Ribeiro, J. D., Lewis, R., & Rudd, M. D. (2009). Main predictions of the interpersonal-psychological theory of suicidal behavior: Empirical test in two samples of young adults. *Journal of Abnormal Psychology, 118,* 634–646. https://doi.org/10.1037/a0016500

Jordan, J. R. (2011). Principles of grief counseling with adult survivors. In J. R. Jordan & J. L. McIntosh (Eds.), *Grief after suicide: Understanding the consequences and caring for survivors* (pp. 179–223). Routledge.

Kaplan, D. (2008). Commemorating a suspended death: Missing soldiers and national solidarity in Israel. *American Ethnologist, 35*(3), 413–427. https://doi.org/10.1111/j.1548-1424.2008.00043.x

LeardMann, C. A., Matsuno, R. K., Boyko, E. J., Powell, T. M., Reger, M. A., & Hoge, C. W. (2021). Association of combat experiences with suicide attempts among active-duty US service members. *JAMA Network Open, 4*(2), e2036065. https://doi.org/10.1001/jamanetworkopen.2020.36065

Marris, R. W. (2019). *Suicidology: A comprehensive biopsychosocial review.* Guilford.

Orak, U., Yildiz, M., Aydogdu, R., Koenig, H. G., & Pietrzak, R. H. (2023). The relationship between combat exposure and suicide risk in U.S. military veterans: Exploring the role of posttraumatic stress symptoms and religious coping. *Journal of Affective Disorders, 341,* 77–87. https://doi.org/10.1016/jad/2023.08.115

Rolls, L., & Harper, M. (2016). The impact of practical support on parental bereavement: Reflections from a study involving parents bereaved through military death. *Death Studies, 40,* 88–101. https://doi.org/10.1080/07481187.2015.1068247

U.S. Department of the Air Force. (2021). *Survivor continuum of care: Commander's Guide*. www.afpc.af.mil/Portals/70/documents/AIRMAN%20AND%20FAMILY/Survivor%20Continuum%20of%20Care%20Commander's%20Guide%20v12.pdf

U.S. Department of the Army. (2024). *Military justice: Army regulation 27-10*. https://armypubs.army.mil/epubs/DR_pubs/DR_a/ARN38919-AR_27-10-000-WEB-1.pdf

U.S. Department of Defense. (2015). *Directive—mortuary affairs policy*. www.esd.whs.mil/Portals/54/Documents/DD/issuances/dodd/130022p.pdf

U.S. Department of Defense. (2023). *Annual report on suicide in the military: Calendar year 2022*. www.dspo.mil/

U.S. Department of Veterans Affairs. (2023a). *2023 national veteran suicide prevention: Annual report*. www.mentalhealth.va.gov/suicide_prevention/data.asp

U.S. Department of Veterans Affairs. (2023b). *How common is PTSD in veterans?* www.ptsd.va.gov/understand/common/common_veterans.asp

CHAPTER TWELVE

Non-Death Loss

> Not all losses get headstones, but they are inscribed on our hearts.
> —John Greg Adams (personal communication, 2024)

CASE 12.A

Donna always wanted to be a mother. She was thrilled to become pregnant after marrying Lanny. Their son, Samuel, was an only child whom Donna treasured as the fulfillment of her lifelong dream. However, storm clouds gathered over the family when Samuel reached adolescence and began using illicit drugs. Various attempts to enforce "tough love" went nowhere. He started stealing from his parents to supply his addiction. When Samuel pawned some heirloom jewelry for cash, Donna and Lanny were able to buy it back. But when those same items were pawned a second time, Donna angrily confronted Samuel. He replied sarcastically, "You should have hidden them better." They finally concluded their son was a sociopath whom they could not trust, so he was no longer welcome in their home.

Samuel left to live in a nearby city and stopped all communication with his parents—no text messages, no phone calls, no visits, no response at all. Occasional secondhand reports from relatives and friends confirmed that Samuel continued to live an addictive lifestyle. Their estrangement continued for years until Lanny became ill with cancer. Word that Lanny was dying reached Samuel through a cousin, so he came to the hospital.

> The final straw was his request for money from his dying father. Lanny's last interaction with Samuel was an angry rebuke. Donna lost any remaining respect for her son after that encounter. She told him not to come to the funeral. She never saw Samuel again.
>
> Donna tried to go on with her life. She found some degree of solace in affiliations with her extended family, her "work family," and her church congregation. She became an honorary grandmother to a local family with young children who enthusiastically embraced her participation in their lives. But Donna never stopped grieving the loss of what might have been if Samuel had not estranged himself. She had hoped for grandchildren of her own and for an adult relationship with her son, thinking she would be able to count on him through widowhood and old age. As the years passed, Donna was left with intangible emptiness and chronic depression, a sad story with no definite conclusion.

Not every loss is visible to the social eye. Some parents grieve losses pertaining to their children even in the absence of physical death. Non-death losses—situations where nobody has died (Harris, 2020)—can trigger grief responses in parents similar to grief over a deceased child, as with Donna and her estranged son. Three theoretical concepts help practitioners understand the plight of parents bereaved by non-death loss.

AMBIGUOUS LOSS

Pauline Boss (2002, 2016, 2020) coined the term *ambiguous loss* to describe situations where the loss is incomplete or uncertain and therefore unending. Her original work focused on soldiers missing in action and presumed dead. Without official verification of death, societal acknowledgment of grief and rituals of finality were held in abeyance. Such ambiguous losses defy resolution, and the unacknowledged grief associated with them can be complicated and ongoing.

Boss (2002, 2016) classified two different forms of ambiguous loss. Applied to bereaved parents, Type I happens when a child is physically absent but still very much psychologically present, "gone but still here." Examples of Type I ambiguous losses would be family estrangement, a child with addiction remanded to a rehabilitation program where no family contact is permitted, incarceration, or a missing or kidnapped child. Type II occurs when the child is still physically alive but is psychologically or emotionally absent, "here but not here." Personality changes or the limitations of disability illustrate Type II forms of ambiguous loss. Resilience in the face of ambiguous loss requires living with uncertainty and shifting from binary thinking—either alive or dead—to dialectical thinking with "both-and" suppositions, such as, "She is gone but present in our hearts" or "He is here yet not himself."

Mechling et al. (2018) described how some situations involve both types of ambiguous loss—physical absence and psychological absence. For example, a child suffering from addiction could be physically unavailable due to being on an alcohol bender or a drug binge, confined in jail or prison, or lost on the street and homeless. Even when accessible, the child remains in a compromised condition due to intoxication or preoccupation with obtaining alcohol or drugs and may be uncharacteristically moody and quarrelsome, "Not here and not himself."

DISENFRANCHISED GRIEF

Ken Doka (1989) first introduced the concept of *disenfranchised grief* to describe losses not openly acknowledged, socially validated, or publicly mourned. Lack of social recognition or validation of a loss results in grievers being denied the benefit of comforting social support critical for adaptation. His original framework, refined later (Doka, 2002, 2020), identified three common circumstances that lead to disenfranchised grief.

- First, the *nature of the loss* itself may not be acknowledged. Examples of disenfranchised child loss might be a miscarriage that is discounted, illustrated by statements such as, "Well, you can always have another one," or an elective pregnancy termination that remains undisclosed due to concern over moral disapproval or hectoring (see Chapter 5, "Pregnancy Loss and Infant Death").
- Second, the *relationship between the griever and the deceased person* may not be socially recognized or accepted. Examples of disenfranchised grief arising from an invalidated relationship include a divorced stepparent grieving the death of a stepchild, grief by a birth parent after surrendering a child for adoption, or feelings of loss on the part of a non-biological surrogate parent who helped raise the deceased child.
- Third, the *griever as a person* may be discounted or excluded and thus disenfranchised. Parents seen as not fully capable of grief, by virtue of physical disability such as a head injury or mental illness, may not be accorded the same consideration or level of social support that might otherwise be rendered.

In all three cases, the grieving parent, or parent figure, remains isolated, and that nonrecognition impedes their coping. Still, these invisible losses remain inscribed on their hearts (J. G. Adams, personal communication, February 6, 2024).

CHRONIC SORROW

Roos (2002, 2020) identified *chronic sorrow* arising from the loss or absence of crucial aspects of another living person with whom there is a deep attachment. Examples include having a child with genetic defects, disabling deformities, psychiatric disorders, neuromuscular diseases, or a host of other limiting conditions. In these instances, parents face losses that are profound, ongoing, and indefinite.

Chronic sorrow resembles the Type II form of ambiguous loss (Boss, 2002, 2016, 2020) in that the child is alive but compromised in a manner that undermines key human functions or capacities, with no foreseeable end. Chronic sorrow focuses on the affective consequences for parents—how they react and feel while living with such a nonfinite loss. Additionally, Roos (2002, 2020) argued that chronic sorrow by its nature is disenfranchised, that is, underrecognized by others. It involves not only loss of the "other," as in hoped-for capacities or experiences for the disabled child, but also loss of "self," as in never witnessing a child fulfill life dreams or being deprived of grandparenting. Practitioners will recognize elements of ambiguous loss, disenfranchised grief, and chronic sorrow when working with parents bereaved by non-death losses.

SEVEN TYPES OF NON-DEATH LOSS PARENTS GRIEVE

Estrangement

Health-care professionals and mental health practitioners regularly encounter family situations like Donna's where estrangement has occurred. Parent-child estrangements happen for a multitude of reasons. Resentments, irreconcilable conflicts, or differences in cultural values and sensibilities often figure prominently in these situations. In the case of estranged children, parents often feel disrespected or demeaned in their position as elders. They want to be accorded a certain level of deference for bearing and raising the estranged child, but it is not forthcoming. The children in these disputes frequently see their parents as irresponsible, judgmental, intrusive, or even abusive; therefore, they want to insulate themselves and their own families from such treatment. Persistent mistrust and fear of additional hurt keep both sides apart.

Contentious issues that frequently contribute to parent-child estrangement are listed here as examples.

- *Abuse*—A history of abuse in the family, allegations of abuse, childhood traumas disclosed in adulthood, or family members being deemed unhealthy or unsafe can estrange parent-child relationships, sometimes permanently.

- *Money or property*—Loans not repaid, houses inhabited without permission or rent paid, investments disputed, shares in the family business challenged, inheritances or estates distributed unevenly—an array of financial inequities or the perception of such—can create enduring ill will.
- *Religion*—Matters of faith can divide parents and children: marrying someone of another faith, converting to a different religion, unwelcome proselytizing or condemnation, forsaking any belief system at all. Prioritizing God or deities can overlap with bids for control and tear families apart.
- *Politics*—Different political views can polarize.

CASE 12.B

One family's estrangement started during the COVID-19 pandemic. The adult daughter endorsed vaccination and insisted on it for anyone in contact with her children (the patient's grandchildren). The adult son decried vaccinations as a hoax and criticized his sister as politically spineless and gullible. The parents agreed to be vaccinated to ensure access to their daughter's children. Incensed, the son boycotted family gatherings and held out for acknowledgment by everyone that he was right all along.

- *In-laws*—Once children find life partners and marry, whole other family systems come into play and sometimes rupture parent-child relationships. Tensions can spring from jealousy over how or where time is spent, perceived possessiveness, attitudinal differences, cultural misunderstandings, or unfamiliar traditions that are not valued.
- *Sexuality* — Contentious issues regarding human sexuality can estrange families.

CASE 12.C

An only child (born female) announced an intention to transition to a man after partnering with another trans man. The child insisted on male pronouns and pursued reassignment surgery. The parents could not accept these developments. They perceived transgender as unnatural and regarded the proposed surgery as mutilation. They blamed the situation on unhealthy influence from the child's partner. They wanted their child to "come to her senses" and "be the daughter" they raised. Otherwise, they declined to endorse an "alternate lifestyle," which they considered grossly misguided.

The first step for practitioners working with parents estranged from a child is to acknowledge the reality of their loss. Approaching estrangement as a genuine loss worthy of the practitioner's attention helps parents feel understood and counteracts any sense of disenfranchisement they may have already encountered. The relationship loss in estrangement may be largely invisible to the grieving parent's social network. After all, the child is alive, not dead. What may seem like a simple act of acknowledgment by the practitioner can mean a great deal to the suffering parents. Consultation may be one of the few places where a distressed parent can discuss the estrangement candidly.

Unpacking the origin of the dispute to understand what happened often provides clues about how to guide the discussion. The ability to see both sides is important. Allowing parents to explore their own contribution(s) to the estrangement, without judgment, can help assess any prospects for reconciliation and prevent aggravating already entrenched divisions. Any focus on the shortcomings of the child should be handled carefully and compassionately, recognizing that any criticism is the purview of the parents, not the practitioner. Finally, it is prudent to maintain modest expectations and not assume long-standing estrangements can be readily resolved with a fresh look and a novel approach. Some cutoffs prove to be permanent. Interventions that resemble befriending distressed parents in their grief, consistent with the expert companionship model of Tedeschi and Calhoun (2004), can be constructive. Never rule out hope for the future.

Regardless of the specific cause of estrangement, the following metaphor can be useful. Parents are asked to visualize a hotel room featuring a pass door to an adjacent room. Pass doors permit access between rooms, replicating a home environment and facilitating caregiving or socializing. To establish such a connection, both parties must unlock and open their respective pass doors. Estrangement is the equivalent to the child (or sometimes the parent) closing and locking the pass door from their side, a move that effectively suspends any ongoing connection. Even if the parent knocks on the door or calls out verbally to the child, there may be no response.

Extending the metaphor, it is crucial that bereaved parents refrain from concluding the situation is hopeless, therefore shutting and locking their own pass doors either out of resignation or reprisal, the equivalent of breaking ties. If the parents close their door, they shut off the possibility of reconnection should the estranged child decide to reopen the pass door from their side. Rather, keeping their own door open and maintaining an ongoing invitation is what Boss (1999) called the "still-open door." It holds out hope for positive change and a restored relationship. This metaphor assumes the parent-child bond to be more akin to a covenant than a contract based on reciprocity. Even if the child gives up on the parent, the parent never gives up on the child.

However, as Case 12.A with Donna and Samuel shows, estrangements can be very thorny, and parents may feel a need to protect themselves from the child, in effect keeping their pass door closed for their own security. Even in these instances, practitioners can usually help parents engineer creative ways to keep open a channel for communication in the event the estranged son or daughter ever seeks to reestablish ties. For example, sometimes a third party can serve as a go-between or help mediate initial contacts to ensure both parties feel safe. Donna indicated she would accept a phone call from Samuel but would only agree to meet with him in a public place, with a friend or relative present, so she could access support if needed and exercise her right to withdraw should the encounter not go well.

Addiction

Addiction constitutes an enormous public health problem. An annual report from the U.S. Department of Health and Human Services' Substance Abuse and Mental Health Services Administration (SAMHSA, 2023) showed 17.3% of the population met criteria for a substance use disorder in the past year: 29.5 million people with an alcohol use disorder, 27.2 million people with a drug use disorder, and 8 million classified with both. Broadening the scope of addiction to include related problems such as pathological gambling, compulsive spending, or sexual proclivities such as pornography further extends the web of addiction. The long-term rift between Donna and Lanny and their son Samuel certainly illustrates how destructive addiction can be.

Parents whose children fall prey to addiction experience helplessness in the face of a menace they cannot control, compounded by a perception of preventability (see Chapter 2, "What Makes Parental Grief So Difficult?"). Boss's (2002, 2016) concept of ambiguous loss helps practitioners understand what parents experience when a child is addicted: perceptions of their child as physically absent (such as on a bender or a drug trip), psychologically absent (not the child they once knew), or both. Feelings of shame and stigma associated with addiction cause many parents to suffer in silence lest their secret become known (see the section on unintended overdoses in Chapter 8, "Accidental Death"). Nondisclosure by parents who fear judgment or indifference from others results in disenfranchised grief.

Tuning in to underlying assumptions embedded in a parent's attitude toward addiction enables practitioners to respond more adroitly. Speaking the conceptual language of parents will appeal to their sensibilities and maximize the chance of having a therapeutic impact.

For example, some parents endorse a disease model of addiction. They see their child as having a medical disorder or sickness, much like cancer. The addiction is not seen as the child's fault but rather as a misfortunate afflicting them. These parents tend to feel sadness and despair. They want to help their "sick" child. They may be receptive to assistance from recovery programs such as Al-Anon (https://al-anon.org) that seek to support and empower family members of alcoholics and addicts. These programs guide family members toward regaining a sense of personal agency in the face of an uncontrollable addiction. Al-Anon also discourages parents from enabling their child's addiction through well-meaning efforts that only sustain the cycle. Distraught parents learn to distinguish between actions genuinely benefiting the health and welfare of their child and ones surreptitiously abetting the addiction. For example, most parents would readily feed a hungry child who appears at their door while at the same time declining requests for cash (ostensibly for food or other amenities) that could finance alcohol or drug purchases.

On the other hand, some parents view drinking or using as a conscious, albeit lamentable, choice about how to live. They see the child with addiction making bad, immoral, or even illegal choices, like a delinquent teenager led astray by undesirable peers. Along with disapproval, these parents often feel betrayed by the alienated child who prioritizes a drug of choice over family ties. Those perceptions often create feelings of anger, resentment, and blame. Donna viewed Samuel's addiction and wayward behavior in this way—as a series of bad choices resulting from a lack of conscience or a character defect. She was unwilling to relinquish the idea that Samuel could make better, prosocial choices and turn his life around. Predictably, she remained angry and hurt.

One cognitive reframe often useful with distraught parents is defining addiction as a condition in which the addict's primary affiliation in life is with their chemical (or other object of addiction). An addict will always serve the addiction first and privilege it above all other relationships, including the one with parents. Understood this way, parents can sometimes depersonalize what feels like an intentional repudiation. They come to see addiction as the equivalent of enslavement to an impersonal master that has invaded and entrapped their child. While heartache and pain may be undiminished, this reframe can reduce the intensity of parents' anger. Parents may adopt a more compassionate posture if they view their child as an enslaved person rather than a renegade deliberately choosing a chemical over a relationship with them.

Incarceration

Having a child in jail or prison, not dead but "gone" and largely inaccessible for an in-person, real-time relationship, brings a special kind of agony to parents. As with addiction, the pain of missing the incarcerated child is mixed with consternation that their son or daughter violated societal laws and forfeited their rights to a free life (unless parents believe their child is unjustly detained). Coming to terms with these mixed emotions is much of the challenge.

Inequities based on race and ethnicity exist in U.S. federal and state justice systems. Expressed as numbers per 100,000 adults, disproportionately higher rates of incarceration occur among African Americans (1,196), American Indians or Alaska Natives (1,042), and Hispanics (603) compared to Whites (229), according to the Bureau of Justice Statistics (Carson & Kluckow, 2023). These sharp differences reflect, in part, socioeconomic factors that disadvantage groups showing higher incarceration rates. Also, some inmates confined in jails or prisons have been wrongly accused or convicted. Practitioners sensitive to these disparities will understand why many parents grieving the non-death loss of an incarcerated child, particularly among disproportionately affected groups, feel righteous anger over injustices contributing to that outcome.

Another demoralizing factor for parents of inmates is the obvious restriction on participating in family events where the imprisoned child would otherwise be present. Parents of incarcerated children most acutely feel their absence at milestone moments like births, weddings, graduations, reunions, special trips, and even funerals, resulting in heightened pining for their absent child. Their longing can be intensified by empathic awareness of how much their imprisoned child aches as well by virtue of being excluded.

Even when others are aware of the parent's longing for an imprisoned child to be present, their judgments can be invalidating of the parent's loss, as described by Doka (1989, 2002). Allusions to their sentence being deserved, or merely the logical consequences of their mistakes, or something they should have pondered before committing the crime are off putting. Adopting those positions undermines any attempt to sympathize. For parents of an incarcerated child, that son or daughter is still their child who is remembered and wanted. Practitioners can best support these grieving parents by focusing on the relational aspects of the underlying attachment with the incarcerated child—the bond that continues even when physical presence is precluded by imprisonment. To paraphrase Pauline Boss, "gone (behind bars) but still here (in my heart)."

Missing or Kidnapped Children

The reality of a child gone missing or kidnapped strikes terror in the hearts and minds of their parents. An infinity of unknowns generates a multitude of awful fantasies. At the same time, anxious parents nurture desperate hope that it is all a mistake, that the absent son or daughter will walk through the door at any moment and declare it all a misunderstanding. Criminal suspicions lead to anger and outrage, similar to feelings experienced by parents bereaved by homicide (see Chapter 10, "Homicide").

Because many children are never reported missing, statistical estimates of the problem vary widely. Once a missing child is reported to law enforcement in the United States, the report is entered into the FBI's online National Crime Information Center. In 2023, more than 38,000 juveniles under the age of 21 were actively missing with no resolution of their case (National Crime Information Center, 2024). The private, nonprofit organization National Center for Missing & Exploited Children (NCMEC, 2023) assisted law enforcement with almost 29,000 cases of missing children. Their data included endangered runaways, family abductions, lost children, and missing young adults. Most children reported to NCMEC as missing or exploited were recovered. Yet some were never located, leaving their parents in a perpetual limbo of waiting and wondering if today the call will come announcing that their child has been found alive and unharmed—or dead as they feared.

Wayland et al. (2016) reported events in certain South American countries (Argentina, Brazil, Columbia), as well as Northern Ireland, Kosovo, and Nigeria, where large numbers of people, including children, were abducted or missing due to political unrest. Their whereabouts were never revealed, resulting in the term *desaparacido* ("the disappeared") being used to describe these missing persons. The terror and grief experienced by parents whose children are caught in such dragnet schemes know no national boundaries. The "disappeared" are never gone from the minds and hearts of their mothers and fathers.

Events such as the unexplained disappearance of a child gone missing or kidnapped trigger the grief of ambiguous loss (Boss, 2002, 2016). Not knowing what happened accentuates the emotional distress of separation. Lacking credible information, anxious parents have little basis for engaging action-based coping strategies (Lazarus & Folkman, 1984) beyond reporting their child missing and working with law enforcement officers investigating their case. In desperation, some parents hire private investigators or take on the search themselves at great personal risk or expense, often fueled by movies or media stories about improbable rescues.

Emotion-based coping methods may prove more feasible for parents, especially as the duration of the child's disappearance lengthens. Examples of emotion-based coping strategies include self-calming techniques such as breathing from the diaphragm, meditation, and mindfulness practices. Setting limits on catastrophic thinking may be helpful, such as telling oneself, "I only know what I know today, I can only control what I am given today" or similar efforts to forestall ruminative worry. Learning to hold the paradox that a loved child can be physically absent but emotionally present at the same time helps parents manage the elongated trauma of a child gone missing or kidnapped (Boss, 1999).

Parents of missing and kidnapped children remain committed to protecting their children and ensuring their survival. The internal struggle between a parent's urge to do something instrumental to recover a missing child and the realization of how few workable options exist creates a sense of powerlessness.

Individuals who support grieving parents of missing and kidnapped children, including professional practitioners, may readily empathize with their fears and trauma but have difficulty working with the open-ended timeline of their ambiguous grief, especially if the disappearance remains unsolved. Tedeschi and Calhoun's (2004) admonition to "stick with it" clearly applies to the treatment relationship needed by parents of missing or kidnapped children.

Disability

Every expecting parent hopes for the best—a viable, healthy child born without complications or anomalies. But not every child is born healthy. Some children are born with obvious congenital disabilities, conditions sometimes detected during prenatal ultrasound tests. Other children may appear healthy at birth only later to manifest developmental delays, effects of undetected genetic disorders, or impairments associated with underlying physical diseases or mental health disorders. In the United States, approximately 3% of babies are diagnosed with birth defects (Centers for Disease Control and Prevention, Birth Defects, 2024), some of which are fatal, such as major heart defects, while others can be repaired, such as club foot or cleft palate. Some birth defects become lifelong disabling conditions. Raising a child with special medical needs or mental disability requires a continuously evolving level of adaptation to a series of progressive losses that those outside the family may never fully grasp or appreciate. Peer-based resources for parents of disabled children are available through the Courageous Parents Network (https://courageousparentsnetwork.org).

Not all disabilities are congenital. Some are acquired because of accidents, tragic events, or even war trauma. For example, head injuries or spinal cord injuries can have devastating physical consequences for the rest of the child's life, leaving parents to contend with the chronic medical problems that result. The life their child had started, or that the parents had orchestrated, is permanently changed in an instant. Acquired disabilities can engender a grief response in parents much like a sudden, unexpected death. The proverbial rug is pulled from beneath their feet in one rapid movement, leaving the parents off balance and struggling to find psychological and emotional equilibrium.

Most parents of disabled children persevere in loving them, accommodating their unique needs, and finding joy in their specialness. Yet these adjustments do not happen without incurring many losses. Parents of disabled children grieve the loss of dreams, the "what might have been" for their children and themselves. Yet parental grief over a child's disability—whether congenital or acquired—is often endured quietly. Parents rarely, if ever, give voice to the many-layered disappointments they harbor. With a living child, regardless of the degree of disability, parents may feel guilty or selfish acknowledging the non-death losses inherent in the reality that life has not turned out the way they hoped, either for their disabled child or for themselves.

Roos's (2002, 2020) concept of chronic sorrow has special pertinence in these cases. Chronic sorrow embodies both the ongoing timeline presented by the permanent disability of a child and a predominant affective response of sadness in their parents who struggle to find meaning in a world that no longer makes sense. Roos cogently observed how professional helpers need to be comfortable working with the existential questions that inevitably arise, such as, "How can God allow such devastation to an innocent child? Am I being punished? What kind of universe metes out such unthinkable tragedy?" Because these questions have no definitive answers, assisting bereaved parents to develop a coherent perspective about their disabled child's condition can be one of the practitioner's most important contributions.

Infertility

Infertility presents a wrenching form of non-death loss for parents or potential parents. The desire to start one's own family, so central to the hopes and dreams of many human beings, can be a powerful physical and psychological drive. Bearing children constitutes an indisputable part of the human quest for fulfillment, including biological continuity and personal legacy. Therefore, infertility as a form of non-death loss carries weighty ramifications.

Problems conceiving or carrying a pregnancy through to live birth affect a significant percentage of couples. Because medical definitions of infertility vary, estimating the statistical prevalence of the problem becomes tricky. Among women in the United States between ages 15 and 49, approximately 13% experience problems with conception or gestation—the ability to get pregnant or carry a pregnancy to term (National Center for Health Statistics, Centers for Disease Control and Prevention, 2023). Men also suffer infertility, either lack of sperm or other anatomical impediments to virility. However, male infertility is not universally reported and therefore difficult to quantify. Agarwal et al. (2015) used statistical methods to estimate the worldwide prevalence of male infertility at 2.5% to 12%.

While the notion of infertility is most often associated with couples unable to have any children of their own, the problem can also affect couples who already have one or more children. Couples with children who yearn for another baby also experience the loss of dreams, and their corresponding grief should be validated as well.

How does an individual grieve the "loss" of a person who never existed, as in the case of potential parents unable to conceive due to infertility? Do they even have a basis to grieve if there never was a baby? Technically, they are not even parents at all, yet their aspirations and deep desires for a child remain. Certainly their dream is lost.

Scholarly work on nonfinite loss (Bruce & Schultz, 2001) and living losses (Schultz & Harris, 2011) helps sensitize practitioners to the challenges facing couples who suffer infertility. Grief associated with infertility is continuous and ongoing, with considerable uncertainty regarding what will happen next. Infertility frustrates the couple's convictions about what life should be or could be. Often, couples who are childless due to infertility suffer shame, embarrassment, and self-doubt. They feel conspicuously different from their childbearing peers because their predicament represents an exception to what is considered mainstream or "normal." Their grief is disenfranchised because the magnitude of their loss is not recognized. There are no societal rituals to grieve the intangible losses inherent in infertility.

Practitioners will best connect with couples who are childless due to infertility by approaching them as *intentional parents*. These individuals desperately want children and see parenthood as an integral part of their personhood. They ache over not having the son or daughter they hoped for and whom they have likely imagined in vivid detail. In this way, their mindset and emotional makeup parallel their peers who have living children. The non-death loss of infertility is as real to them as the grief of parents whose children die. Treating them as intentional parents who are bereaved honors that fundamental aspect of their nature, regardless of whether they eventually bear children, adopt children, or remain childless.

Adoption Loss

Birthparents who surrender a child for adoption may experience grief over this non-death loss for years afterward. Although their lives go on, the experience of delivering a child, making the difficult decision to give the baby to another family to raise, then relinquishing their parental rights is never forgotten. Knapp (1986) used the term *shadow grief* to describe the emotional haze hovering on the periphery of a parent's consciousness years after the loss of a child. Knapp's description of shadow grief corresponds closely with the experiences reported by many birth mothers and birth fathers who gave up a child for adoption. Although each parent's experience will be different, their shadow grief may contain unmistakable traces of sadness, remorse, guilt, low self-esteem, shame, and anger (Deykin et al., 1984, 1988; Lapidus et al., 2023; Weinreb & CodyMurphy, 1988). Birth parents' grief is often disenfranchised because it is not openly acknowledged, socially accepted, or publicly mourned.

Adoption may be elected due to a variety of circumstances: a young unmarried women who unexpectedly finds herself pregnant, a partner unprepared and unready for fatherhood, lack of family or societal support for raising a child as a single parent, limited or uncertain economic means, lack of health insurance or access to health care, or pressure from medical professionals, agency staff, or their own families to make a decision for adoption. Other parties often counsel birth parents to "move on" with their lives as quickly as possible after placement. Their advice is proffered as what is best for the emotional and psychological health of the surrendering parent but often camouflages unspoken concern that the birth mother will change her mind and want the baby back. Even when birth parents do set their sights on the future, in their hearts they still look over their shoulder at what they have done.

The era of open adoptions has changed much of the secrecy and shame associated with confidential adoptions (Wiley & Baden, 2005). Open adoptions allow for ongoing contact in the triad of birth parents, surrendered children, and their adoptive parents, yet ongoing challenges must be negotiated in each situation (Grotevant, 2020). Henney et al. (2007) found that birth mothers showed better grief adjustment when adoptions were open versus confidential. In addition, while the majority of birth mothers still report some amount of grief in relation to the adoption 12 to 20 years after the placement, their grief distress declined over time to where they were not suffering extensively and felt relatively resolved about the adoption. March (2014) reported on birth mothers contacted by a child surrendered for adoption who had reached adulthood and desired reunion. Those mothers felt "resurrected emotional pain" from their past pregnancy and placement experiences; however, they also gained emotional healing from the contact and realized a sense of relief from knowing their adopted child's life situation.

CASE 12.D

Rhonda, a married mother with four children, sought marital therapy together with her husband, Ethan. With Rhonda as an at-home mother and Ethan as sole breadwinner, finances were tight. They quarreled over decision-making, and those struggles brought them to treatment. During initial history taking, Rhonda revealed that she had been sexually assaulted during college and became pregnant as a result. Her bombastic father was furious. He called her a slut and refused any suggestion that she could keep the baby and raise the child as a single parent with the family's help. Not knowing what else to do, Rhonda gave up the baby boy in an open adoption arranged by a faith-based agency. The birth father was never involved. Even though Rhonda knew the adoptive parents would give the baby boy his legal name, she named him Paul.

> Ethan had been "only a friend" at the time of this ordeal, but he was consistently supportive and admired Rhonda's choice as consistent with her moral compass. Their shared values were a big element in bringing them together as a couple. They eventually married and had their own family. As a tribute to Rhonda's child who had been adopted, they named their youngest son Paul.
>
> Rhonda acknowledged remorse and sadness when she thought about giving up her adopted child. There was no doubt in her mind that she would have kept the baby had her father been more supportive. She opined, "I would have figured it out." While the open adoption permitted communication between her and the adoptive family, she had discontinued contact because the adoptive parents appeared uncomfortable with her intentions.
>
> Unexpectedly, Rhonda received word that the son, now age 18, wanted to meet her. Suddenly, her story of adoption loss took center stage. The therapist helped Rhonda sift through long-deferred emotions and prepare for a face-to-face meeting. It became an opportunity for Ethan to be supportive and to strengthen their relationship by facing the events together. The meeting went well. The son seemed satisfied with her explanations. They prayed together and hugged goodbye. Prospects for future contact, on their own terms, now seemed possible. Rhonda felt immensely relieved and more validated in her decision.

Birth parents experience the Type 1 form of ambiguous loss defined by Boss (2002, 2016): the child has "gone" to the adoptive family but is "still here" and psychologically present for the surrendering parents. In Rhonda's case, she never forgot her firstborn child. She even showed signs of psychologically merging that experience with subsequent childbearing by giving her youngest son the same name, Paul. Her case also illustrates how adoption loss, like other forms of non-death loss, may not be the identified reason for mental health treatment. Yet when non-death loss emerges as a therapeutic focus, it warrants attention from practitioners providing holistic care to parents bereaved in this manner. Finally, the reunion meeting between Rhonda and her son placed for adoption shows the power of such contact for redressing feelings of uncertainty and regret held by grieving parents who surrendered their child for adoption many years earlier.

GESTALT-BASED CHAIR WORK

The common denominator with instances of estrangement, addiction, incarceration, missing or kidnapped children, and post-adoption loss is that parents have lost the connection with their child who, although still living (or presumed living), is unavailable or inaccessible. With disability, it is the idealized child who is lost and unattainable. With infertility, it is the desired child who cannot be realized. Parents bereaved by these non-death losses often feel defeated. They see their conundrum as a two-party problem but with only one party—themselves—willing or able to address it.

Gestalt-based chair work using the empty chair technique (Dayton, 2005; Perls, 1969) offers practitioners several options for conducting an imaginal conversation between the bereaved parent and the lost child (cf. Shear, 2015; see Chapter 7, "Death of an Adult Child," and Chapter 8, "Accidental Death"). Even though the grieving parent is the only party physically present in the consultation, chair work allows the psychological and emotional presence of the absent child to be introduced into the encounter, thus simulating the two-person exchange sought so desperately by the bereaved parent. In effect, both parties become "present" for the therapeutic maneuver.

In a typical empty chair exercise, the bereaved parent is the participant and the practitioner functions as the facilitator or director. If bereaved parents are seen conjointly, they can alternate turns or choose to do the exercise in tandem, with each one contributing to the flow. The simulation sequence includes three phases: warm-up, action, and reflection (Dayton, 2005).

During warm-up, previously discussed issues, concerns, or questions that distress the bereaved parent are clarified or reiterated: "What would you really like your son to hear about your anger over his withdrawal from the family?" "Addiction stole your daughter from you, and you want her back." "No matter the reasons he is in prison, you still love him, and he will always be your son." "You need forgiveness for letting her down; perhaps you could ask her for it." Two chairs are placed opposite one another. The parent occupies one chair. Sometimes a pillow or inanimate object is placed in the empty chair to represent the absent child. The practitioner assumes a position behind the parent or to the side, out of the parent's sight line with the empty chair so as not to distract from the flow of the encounter.

Once the action phase starts, the parent is prompted to verbalize their thoughts and feelings to the absent child, using first-person language and a conversational voice, just as they would speak if their child were sitting directly in front of them. Should the parent hesitate or become tongue-tied, the practitioner can gently encourage them with some simple prompts, such as, "Tell Susan how it affected you when she cut herself off from the family" or "Express to John how sorry you feel about overreacting like you did." The time interval for speaking is flexible. Sometimes parents signal when they have finished speaking. Or a natural pause may indicate when the parent has fully expressed what is on their mind or has articulated the essence of their concerns.

At that point, the action shifts and the parent is invited to switch chairs. Now occupying the "child's seat," the parent is instructed to assume the persona of their absent son or daughter and respond to what the parent has said. Again, first-person voice is used. This part of the exercise is usually unexpected by the participant and is not disclosed ahead of time to ensure spontaneity. Switching chairs can generate considerable anxiety, sometimes leading to protest or doubt. Yet it constitutes a crucial ingredient—enacting a dialogue between the two parties. Chair work lacks its full impact if this step is skipped. However, following the principle of dosing (Jordan, 2011; see Chapter 9, "Suicide"), parents should never be pushed beyond their tolerances. Reluctant parents can usually be persuaded to attempt this maneuver when practitioners point out how unlikely it is that anyone would know the mind and heart of their absent child better than them. Once the absent child has been given a voice in this manner, the parent switches back to their original chair and continues the dialogue by responding to the child's comments. Switching chairs may be repeated two or more times until the communication sequence seems complete.

Tears frequently flow during both parts of this two-chair simulation. Emotional catharsis is important to the treatment. Reassurance and a calm, caring demeanor on the part of the practitioner are needed to maintain a space of psychological safety for parental emotion to be expressed, whether sadness, anger, guilt, love, regret, gratitude, or other affect.

Reflection is the final phase of the exercise. With the two chairs returned to their usual place in the room indicating the action phase is over, practitioner and parent resume a therapeutic conversation in which they process what was said, heard, and felt during the chair work—the internal narrative mode (Angus et al., 1999; Neimeyer, 2019). Thoughtful discussion allows the bereaved parent to recover from the emotional aspect of the exercise and begin integrating their insights and realizations—the reflexive narrative mode. One of the most vital therapeutic outcomes of chair work is helping the bereaved parent discover how to connect again with their child who has been lost.

Practitioners contemplating chair work with bereaved parents need preparation to use this technique effectively. Like an orchestra conductor, knowing how to prompt for more disclosure, sensing when to switch chairs, detecting key themes, recognizing when a participant has reached their limit, and a myriad of other nuanced decisions are involved. As with death competence in general, chair work in particular can be learned with appropriate training and supervision. Because these exercises can evolve in so many unforeseen directions, a spirit of rational confidence in one's ability is needed (cf. Roos, 2002).

For practitioners willing to incorporate chair work as an intervention, the potential rewards for the grieving parents they serve are unlimited.

SUMMARY

Part II of this book cataloging various types of child deaths and death circumstances concludes with a discussion devoted to the phenomenon of non-death losses—situations where the child is not technically dead but lost to the parents in some critical way. These losses can occur from estrangement, addiction, incarceration, children gone missing or kidnapped, disability, infertility, or adoption loss. Bereaved parents suffering non-death losses mourn the loss of relationship, loss of access, or loss of parental dreams. Although prospective parents willingly take on a lifetime commitment to their children, most never anticipate events producing cutoffs or impasses that may be permanent. The psychology of non-death loss can be understood using theoretical lenses of ambiguous loss, disenfranchised grief, and chronic sorrow. Gestalt-based chair work holds great therapeutic potential for addressing and salving parental pain generated by the vexations of non-death loss.

REFERENCES

Agarwal, A., Mulgund, A., Hamada, A., & Chyatte, M. R. (2015). A unique view on male infertility around the globe. *Reproductive Biology and Endocrinology, 13*, 1–9. https://doi.org/10.1186/s12958-015-0032-1

Angus, L., Levitt, H., & Hardtke, K. (1999). The narrative processes coding system: Research applications and implications for clinical practice. *Journal of Clinical Psychology, 55*, 1255–1270. https://doi.org/10.1002/(SICI)1097-4679(199910)55:10<1255::AID-JCLP7>3.0.CO;2-F

Boss, P. (1999). *Ambiguous loss: Learning to live with unresolved grief*. Harvard University Press.

Boss, P. (2002). Ambiguous loss: Working with families of the missing. *Family Process, 41*(1), 14–17. https://doi.org/10.1111/j.1545-5300.2002.40102000014.x

Boss, P. (2016). The context and process of theory development: The story of ambiguous loss. *Journal of Family Theory & Review, 8*, 269–286. https://doi.org/10.1111/jftr.12152

Boss, P. (2020). Understanding and treating the unresolved grief of ambiguous loss: A research-based theory to guide therapists and counselors. In D. L. Harris (Ed.), *Non-death loss and grief: Context and clinical implications* (pp. 73–79). Routledge.

Bruce, E. J., & Schultz, C. L. (2001). *Nonfinite loss and grief: A psychoeducational approach*. Paul H. Brookes.

Carson, E. A., & Kluckow, R. (Bureau of Justice Statistics). (2023). *Prisoners in 2022-statistical tables*. (NCJ No. 307149). U.S. Department of Justice, Office of Justice Programs. https://bjs.ojp.gov/document/p22st.pdf

Centers for Disease Control and Prevention, Birth Defects. (2024). *Data & statistics on birth defects*. https://www.cdc.gov/birth-defects/data-research/facts-stats/index.html

Dayton, T. (2005). *The living stage: A step by step guide to psychodrama, sociometry and experiential group therapy*. Health Communications.

Deykin, E. Y., Campbell, L., & Patti, P. (1984). The postadoption experience of surrendering parents. *American Journal of Orthopsychiatry, 54*(2), 271–280. https://doi.org/10.1111/j.1939-0025.1984.tb01494.x

Deykin, E. Y., Patti, P., & Ryan, J. (1988). Fathers of adopted children: A study of the impact of child surrender on birthfathers. *American Journal of Orthopsychiatry, 58*(2), 240–248. https://doi.org/10.1111/j.1939-0025.1988.tb01585.x

Doka, K. J. (1989). *Disenfranchised grief: Recognizing hidden sorrow*. Lexington.

Doka, K. J. (2002). *Disenfranchised grief: New directions, challenges, and strategies for practice*. Research Press.

Doka, K. J. (2020). Disenfranchised grief and non-death losses. In D. L. Harris (Ed.), *Non-death loss and grief: Context and clinical implications* (pp. 25–35). Routledge.

Grotevant, H. D. (2020). Open adoption. In G. M. Wrobel, E. Helder, & E. Marr (Eds.), *The Routledge handbook on adoption* (pp. 266–277). Routledge. https://doi.org/10.4324/9780429432040-19

Harris, D. L. (2020). Introduction. In D. L. Harris (Ed.), *Non-death loss and grief: Context and clinical implications* (pp. 1–6). Routledge.

Henney, S. M., Ayers-Lopez, S., McRoy, R. G., & Grotevant, H. D. (2007). Evolution and resolution: Birthmothers' experience of grief and loss at different levels of adoption openness. *Journal of Social and Personal Relationships, 24*(6), 875–889. https://doi.org/10.1177/0265407507084188

Jordan, J. R. (2011). Principles of grief counseling with adult survivors. In J. R. Jordan & J. L. McIntosh (Eds.), *Grief after suicide: Understanding the consequences and caring for survivors* (pp. 179–223). Routledge.

Knapp, R. J. (1986). *Beyond endurance: When a child dies*. Schocken.

Lapidus, E. P., Watkins, C. L., & Farr, R. H. (2023). Birth mothers' experiences of support before, during, and after adoptive placement. *American Journal of Orthopsychiatry, 93*(6), 543–556. https://doi.org/10.1037/ort0000701

Lazarus, R. S., & Folkman, S. (1984). *Stress, appraisal, and coping*. Springer Publishing Company.

March, K. (2014). Birth mother grief and the challenge of adoption reunion contact. *American Journal of Orthopsychiatry, 84*(4), 409–419. https://doi.org/10.1037/ort0000013

Mechling, B. M., Ahern, N. R., & Palumbo, R. (2018). Applying ambiguous loss theory to children of parents with an opioid use disorder. *Journal of Child and Adolescent Psychiatric Nursing, 31*(2–3), 53–60. https://doi.org/10.1111/jcap.12209

National Center for Health Statistics, Centers for Disease Control and Prevention. (2023). *Infertility*. www.cdc.gov/nchs/fastats/infertility.htm

National Center for Missing & Exploited Children. (2023). *Our impact 2023—Recovery*. www.missingkids.org/ourwork/impact

National Crime Information Center. (2024). *2023 National Crime Information Center (NCIC) missing person and unidentified person statistics pursuant to the requirements of the crime control act of 1990*. (Pub. L. No. 101-647, 104

Stat. 4789). Federal Bureau of Investigation. https://le.fbi.gov/file-repository/2023-ncic-missing-person-and-unidentified-person-statistics.pdf/view

Neimeyer, R. A. (2019). Meaning reconstruction in bereavement: Development of a research program. *Death Studies, 43*(2), 79–91. https://doi.org/10.1080/07481187.2018.1456620

Perls, F. S. (1969). *Gestalt therapy verbatim*. Real People Press.

Roos, S. (2002). *Chronic sorrow: A living loss*. Brunner-Routledge.

Roos, S. (2020). Chronic sorrow. In D. L. Harris (Ed.), *Non-death loss and grief: Context and clinical implications* (pp. 193–204). Routledge.

Schultz, C. L., & Harris, D. L. (2011). Giving voice to nonfinite loss and grief in bereavement. In R. A. Neimeyer, D. L. Harris, H. R. Winokeur, & G. F. Thornton (Eds.), *Grief and bereavement in contemporary society* (pp. 235–245). Routledge.

Shear, M. K. (2015). *Complicated grief treatment*. Columbia Center for Complicated Grief.

Substance Abuse and Mental Health Services Administration. (2023). *Key substance use and mental health indicators in the United States: Results from the 2022 national survey on drug use and health*. (HHS Publication No. PEP23-07-01-006, NSDUH Series H-58). Center for Behavioral Health Statistics and Quality, Substance Abuse and Mental Health Services Administration. www.samhsa.gov/data/report/2022-nsduh-annual-national-report

Tedeschi, R. G., & Calhoun, L. G. (2004). *Helping bereaved parents: A clinician's guide*. Brunner-Routledge.

Wayland, S., Maple, M., McKay, K., & Glassock, G. (2016). Holding on to hope: A review of the literature exploring missing persons, hope and ambiguous loss. *Death Studies, 40*(1), 54–60. https://doi.org/10.1080/07481187.2015.1068245

Weinreb, M. L., & CodyMurphy, B. (1988). The birth mother: A feminist perspective for the helping professional. *Women & Therapy, 7*(1), 23–36. https://doi.org/10.1300/J015V07N01_03

Wiley, M. O. L., & Baden, A. L. (2005). Birth parents in adoption: Research, practice, and counseling psychology. *The Counseling Psychologist, 33*(1), 13–50. https://doi.org/10.1177/0011000004265961

Part III

CHAPTER THIRTEEN

Long-Term Adaptation and Resilience

> Bereaved parents carry the weight of loss throughout their lives, hoping it will get lighter over time, but knowing it never completely disappears.
> —Ben Wolfe (personal communication, 2024)

CASE 13.A

Eleven years after the murder of her son, Janette continued altering the trajectory of her life as part of a long-term effort to cope with Robert's death. None of it came easy, but she was determined not to allow the "evil" that killed her son to overtake her also.

Janette's father was a university professor, and her mother taught high school. Unfortunately, her father suffered from bipolar disorder and drank alcohol excessively to self-medicate his mood spirals. Her mother became addicted to pain pills while contending with chronic medical problems. Coming from chemically dependent parents, Janette experimented with alcohol and drugs as a teenager and later became addicted. She was arrested for driving while intoxicated (DWI) twice in her early 20s. Janette's two daughters were born during those turbulent years, each to different alcoholic fathers. After both parents died, Janette moved back into the family home where she had grown up.

Several years later, Janette became pregnant again. This time, she stopped drinking immediately, ended the relationship with child's father (also an alcoholic), and started recovery. Janette found that the 12 steps of Alcoholics Anonymous (aa.org) synchronized well with her Christian beliefs and gave traction to her efforts. Her son, Robert, was born without complications, and she raised him in a nondrinking environment with a husband she married after becoming sober (Robert's stepfather). Janette managed to stay sober until Robert became a teenager. She relapsed, received a third DWI, and went to prison for several months.

Meanwhile, Robert began drinking and dabbling with street drugs. His behavior brought Janette considerable worry as she witnessed "the family curse" continue to play out. Robert graduated from high school but still lived at home with Janette and her husband. When her middle daughter was about to have her first baby, Janette traveled out of state to be there. She unsuccessfully tried to convince Robert to accompany her to keep him out of trouble. When the grandchild's birth was delayed, Janette even sent Robert money for a plane ticket, but he still declined.

Apparently, Robert had visions of becoming a drug dealer himself and tried to negotiate a "wholesale" purchase (using the plane ticket money). He invited a dealer to the family home to complete a transaction. The anticipated sale soured when it became apparent the other man brought no merchandise (street drugs) and intended only to steal Robert's cash. A fistfight erupted and spilled over to the front porch, where the assailant shot Robert and walked away with the money. Robert left a bloody silhouette on the front door as he attempted to reenter the house but ultimately collapsed and died on the porch. The macabre scene was discovered by the stepfather when he returned home from his night shift.

When Janette received the terrible news by telephone, she wailed. She asked officers on the scene to hold the phone next to Robert's ear so she could tell him goodbye. They initially resisted the idea, declaring that he was "already gone." Janette insisted emphatically, and they relented, allowing her to express a final goodbye before Robert's body was removed. Janette immediately went to a 12-step meeting, fearing she may otherwise relapse. When Janette got home, the house and porch had already been professionally cleaned. But she could still see the outline of Robert's body on the front door because the cleaning chemicals left that area brighter than the rest of the door.

Beside herself with grief, Janette sought help. She talked with a crime victims' advocate for several sessions and attended a grief support group. However, before the assailant's trial several months later, Janette relapsed and was hospitalized for detoxification. Once sober again, she restarted a recovery program. The assailant was eventually convicted of murder and sentenced to life in prison. Janette read a victim's impact statement at trial, extending forgiveness to the assailant "not because he deserved it but because God asked me to."

Subsequently, depression set in. Janette consulted a grief therapist about 18 months after Robert's murder. Staying sober was a priority for Janette, as was dealing with persistent reenactment imagery of Robert dying alone on the porch. The therapist's approach combined recovery principles with Restorative Retelling methods aimed at helping Janette regulate her emotions and rework her internal narrative of Robert's death.

These latter efforts came to full fruition during an incident at home. Janette's dogs were raising a ruckus at the back door, so she let them loose in the yard even though she could not see what was making them bark. A few minutes later, Janette heard the dogs pawing to come back inside. Only when opening the door could she see what happened—the dogs had trapped a squirrel and brought it to the porch to display their prey. Janette could see that the squirrel was still alive, gasping its last breaths.

Horrified, Janette immediately thought of Robert dying alone. She sat down to pet the squirrel, talked to it soothingly, and comforted it with the kind of caregiving she would have shown Robert had she been there when he died. Recounting this incident in therapy helped Janette finally revise how she pictured Robert's last moments. Invoking her spiritual beliefs, Janette mentally reconstructed the death scene and concluded that Robert had not really been alone but rather accompanied and comforted by his Creator, who was always with him.

Another powerful change came when Janette announced that the big oak tree in her front yard looked unsightly and needed to be removed. In its prime, the large tree had provided much shade and served as the central location for family barbecues and outdoor gatherings. In the spring following Robert's murder, the oak never leafed out again and died "from the sadness," Janette concluded. Later, lightning struck the tree, and it declined into an eyesore. Yet Janette was reluctant to dispatch the oak tree because of the many positive memories associated with it, including happy times with Robert.

At the therapist's suggestion, Janette contacted the art department at the university to ask if someone would accept a commission to paint or sketch the oak tree before she cut it down. That way, Janette could preserve memories associated with the tree via a portrait but could also plant a young tree to restart the cycle of life. Upon hearing the story, one of the professors volunteered to paint a portrait of the tree. Janette was pleased with how the painting turned out, with flecks of sparkle worked into the trunk, hints of life emanating from within the bare tree consistent with her Christian beliefs in the afterlife and a world beyond this one. In the background, the artist included the massive adjacent oak from which the dead tree may well have been a sapling. The portrait brought Janette great comfort.

When Janette finally cut down the oak, she was astonished to find the stump formed the outline of a heart, just like the heart tattoo on Robert's chest that had "Mom" emblazoned over it. The striking symbolism moved Janette to tears. She could feel the love still there between Robert and her. She went and got a heart tattoo to match, with "Robert" emblazoned on it. By doing so, Janette not only extracted meaning from the heart-shaped stump as a reflection of the continuing bond with Robert, but she consolidated this meaning by acquiring the matching tattoo. She would always carry Robert in her heart—figuratively, emotionally, and decoratively.

Dark moments recurred periodically for Janette when she felt Robert's physical absence most acutely and conjured up what might have been had he lived longer. Janette's emotional state gradually improved over the course of therapy, and she never relapsed again. From feeling completely broken by her grief at the outset, Janette came to see herself as "stronger and victorious" because she did not fall into abject hatred or cynical negativity or retreat into addiction. Rather, Janette managed to carry on and experience the joys of life as best she could with her husband, daughters, and grandchildren.

Her husband's subsequent decline due to chronic illness made Janette understandably sad, but she could readily differentiate that sadness from the grief she felt after Robert's murder. Anticipating widowed life in the future, Janette began to envision how she could survive and function as a bereaved mother and a widow. She planned to tear down the family house where the murder happened and rebuild a smaller residence for herself at the back end of their large city lot. Janette wanted to salvage hand-hewn beams from the 100-year-old structure to be repurposed in building her new home as an homage to the past. In addition, she

> planned to build some small apartments on the property that she could rent to university students in need of affordable housing, in the process giving her the opportunity to serve as a surrogate parent to promising young adults with bright futures ahead of them, like Robert. Finally, on the site of Robert's bedroom, she planned to install a fountain, benches, and ornamental shrubbery to create a gathering space in his memory, one that honored the fingerprint he left on the world in the very spot that was his "footprint" in life.
>
> Behind it all was Janette's drive to keep going, to not be crushed by the sadness and rage brought on by Robert's tragic murder, to not relapse into the trap of chemical dependency but to go beyond parental grief to regrowth and evolution as a person. She was attentive to the world around her—both nature and events—that she could readily imbue with symbolic meaning and significance, finding in them an expression of loving connection to her deceased son. New life could still come from old life, and hope could be found even in the face of the grimmest loss. In the long term, Janette continued to generate loving, life-giving energy toward those around her and honor Robert's memory through meaningful symbols and connections, exemplary service to others, and personal decorum superseding the treachery that destroyed her son's life.

"Resolved as much as it will be" is a phrase echoed by bereaved parents acknowledging that their grief over a child's death is never concluded (Klass, 2001). Ultimately, what may be most important for bereaved parents' adaptation are the interior changes forged out of a seismic life crisis such as loss of a child. Positive personal transformation can be a source of consolation and one of the most important ways to honor a deceased child.

POST-BEREAVEMENT PERSONAL GROWTH

No bereaved parent can return to their previous life unchanged. Revisiting Tedeschi and Calhoun's (2004a) metaphor, exile to the foreign land of child loss is permanent. There is no going back to how things were. Assimilation and accommodation are the only possible forward paths. Practitioners committed to working with bereaved parents take on the dual roles of helping relieve distress as well as promoting personal growth and resilience.

The concept of post-bereavement personal growth received empirical support from the work of Hogan et al. (2001), who developed a psychometric measure of how adults respond to loss of a loved one—the Hogan Grief Reaction Checklist (HGRC). Their findings are especially relevant because they intentionally included bereaved parents in their focus groups where item content was generated. Their validation samples consisted largely of bereaved mothers and fathers. Thus, the voices of bereaved parents speak poignantly through their instrument. Their 61-item questionnaire contains five scales measuring grief distress—despair, panic behavior, blame and anger, detachment, and disorganization—as well as one additional scale measuring positive perceptions of self, called post-bereavement personal growth. Growth was evidenced by statements indicative of being a *stronger person*, becoming *more loving and caring*, and finding *hope for the future*. Hogan and colleagues (2001) argued that bereaved parents demonstrating higher levels of post-bereavement personal growth had wrestled with deep introspection and existential questions yet emerged transformed because of grieving their child's death:

> Out of that suffering they sensed they had become different than they had been before death. They now viewed themselves as more tolerant, forgiving, compassionate, resilient, and loving . . . personal growth is an integral component of the grieving process.
>
> (p. 23)

Because the HGRC (Hogan et al., 2001) maintained strong fidelity to the lived experience of bereaved parents, the items from its Personal Growth subscale form a roadmap to resilience (see Table 13.1). They provide a granular exposition of specific attitudes and behaviors comprising post-bereavement personal growth in the aftermath of child loss.

Subsequent work by Hogan and Schmidt (2002) revealed how personal growth results from struggling with grief. Social support—either offered by others or sought out by bereaved parents—helps them move past pain and avoidance and toward salutary growth. Assistance provided by medical professionals and trained practitioners constitutes a culturally recognized form of social support (cf. Kosminsky & Jordan, 2024).

Clearly, post-bereavement personal growth is aspirational. Not all bereaved parents can "get there," so practitioners should not expect this kind of transformation in every case. Yet it is a professional obligation to foster movement toward personal growth. Practitioners can validate attitudinal and behavioral signs of growth when they appear spontaneously and recognize moments of opportunity where bereaved parents may be gently guided that direction.

In Janette's case, signs of post-bereavement personal growth emerged in several ways. She saw herself as "stronger and victorious" because she chose

TABLE 13.1 Post-Bereavement Personal Growth Subscale Items (n = 12) from the Hogan Grief Reaction Checklist

I have learned to cope better with life.
I feel as though I am a better person.
I have a better outlook on life.
I have more compassion for others.
I am stronger because of the grief I have experienced.
I am a more forgiving person.
I am more tolerant of myself.
I am more tolerant of others.
I have hope for the future.
I reached a turning point where I began to let go of some of my grief.
I am having more good days than bad.
I care more deeply for others.

Reprinted with permission from Hogan et al. (2001).

not to dwell in a state of angry retribution that would have been a reciprocal response to the perpetrator's aggression that killed Robert. Janette's resolve to grow beyond the tragedy of Robert's murder through attentiveness to people and appreciation for the natural world heightened her caring and compassion toward others and herself. Her plans for the property were based on hope for the future, hope that she could nurture the next generation of young people as a legacy to Robert. The practitioner affirmed and encouraged Janette's strivings for post-bereavement personal growth.

POSTTRAUMATIC GROWTH

The concept of post-bereavement personal growth (Hogan et al., 2001; Hogan & Schmidt, 2002) paralleled the notion of posttraumatic growth championed by Tedeschi and Calhoun (1995, 1996), defined as positive psychological change that results from struggling with highly adverse life circumstances. Their paradigm-shifting work moved the treatment emphasis beyond considerations of how to cope with trauma distress to a new horizon featuring growth and change. These respective contributions from the fields of thanatology and traumatology converged to yield a more robust understanding of how people can adapt and grow in response to monumental life obstacles or unspeakable personal disasters. Both concepts arc toward resilience.

Originally, trauma work focused on the psychological aftermath of harrowing, life-threatening events such as sexual assault, criminal attacks, combat experiences, weather-related catastrophes, motor vehicles crashes, and even medical emergencies. Diagnostic symptoms of posttraumatic stress included intrusive flashbacks or nightmares of the event, high anxiety paired with physiologic hyperarousal, and guarded hypervigilance toward the environment (American Psychiatric Association, 2022). Treatment focused on reducing the terror associated with the traumatic episode, regaining a sense of personal safety, and developing a revised narrative of how the world works. The genius of Tedeschi and Calhoun (1995, 1996) was recognizing the potential for positive personal transformation amid recovery from trauma. They proposed five key dimensions to their construct of PTG, later verified through confirmatory factor analysis (Taku et al., 2008).

1. Discovering latent personal strengths
2. Realizing new possibilities from unwelcome change
3. Relating to others more closely, with new valuing
4. Deepening one's spirituality
5. Appreciating life more and discerning what is really important

The paradoxical nature of PTG can be summarized in this brief phrase: "out of loss there is gain" (Tedeschi & Calhoun, 2004b, p. 6).

How does the notion of PTG apply to working with bereaved parents? First, the chapters in Part II of this book illustrate repeatedly how often child deaths occur in a heinous manner that complicates parental grief (see Chapter 2, "What Makes Parental Grief So Difficult?"). Second, regardless of the mode of death, bereaved parents consider the death of their child to be a traumatic event. Calhoun et al. (2010) emphasized how it is the level of disruption to the core beliefs and worldviews held by bereaved persons—sometimes called their *assumptive world*—that drives both trauma distress and the potential for PTG. In other words, only deaths that force significant reexamination of people's understanding of the world and their place in it, such as the death of an innocent child, create the conditions necessary for PTG.

Bereaved parents who see the deaths of their children as unnatural, untimely, unthinkable, or unforgiveable find their assumptive worlds greatly disrupted. Practitioners can help bereaved parents moderate their emotional distress and manage unwanted, intrusive thoughts. At the same time, practitioners can engage parents in a reflective dialogue leading to a reconstructed worldview where bereaved parents find some meaning in the weighty burden they carry. That burden of grief never completely disappears, as so eloquently stated at the beginning of this chapter (B. Wolfe, personal communication, January 22, 2024). Rather, Klass (2001) described the psychological "destination" of a bereaved parent's journey as a vanishing point where there is always more beyond the horizon.

Returning to Janette's case, her recollections of being notified of Robert's death and her reenactment imagery of what he must have suffered generated classic trauma responses. Mirroring interventions from Restorative Retelling (Rynearson, 2018; Rynearson et al., 2015), Janette reworked the final scene of Robert's death by petting and comforting the dying squirrel on her back porch. This real-life replay of a creature's death brought a belated sense of peace to Janette, together with her strong faith convictions that Robert had not died alone but had been accompanied all along by his Creator. Similarly, the artist's rendering of the tree that died after Robert's murder brought solace because the artist portrayed the dead tree with an otherworldly illumination suggesting Robert's spirit resided in the afterlife in a manner not fully comprehensible. Also, from seeing the "mother tree" in the background, Janette could identify her reality of remaining grounded on earth still loving and remembering Robert. These images helped reduce her distress and set the stage for more reflective adapting.

Janette's grief trajectory following Robert's death exemplified all five dimensions of PTG. Although Janette had found some measure of personal strength during her earlier recovery from addiction, nothing prepared her for the magnitude of grief experienced over Robert's murder. Yet she discovered even *more strength* needed to face and forgive her son's murderer and carry on with her own life rather than have it end "in a bottle" or from intractable depression. Replanting a tree in the yard as well as her plans for converting her property to housing for college students showed Janette's openness to *new possibilities*. No doubt Janette also reinvigorated her attentiveness to her two daughters, and her grandchildren, by *better cherishing* their presence in her life as living children. *Deepening spirituality* was a mainstay. Janette's trust in the spiritual realm helped her maintain a sense of metaphysical connection with Robert and provided a compensatory framework for anticipated reunion in the afterlife where evil does not exist. Heightened awareness of the fragility of life led Janette to *living more fully in the present moment*, taking time to appreciate beauty and wonder in people and nature. As Calhoun et al. (2010) noted, practitioners encourage movement toward PTG so positive changes are not lost over time but become a tribute or memorial to the person who died, a conduit to continuing connection with the deceased, and a source of meaning amid the suffering, "recognition that the loss has set in motion a reconsideration of life that has wrought valuable changes" (p. 138).

RESILIENCE

Researchers who study resilience describe it as the capacity to maintain a balanced perspective in the face of adversity, persevere through stress, believe in one's ability to cope, find purpose and value despite hardships, and accept that some things in life must be faced alone (Wagnild, 2009; Wagnild & Young, 1993). Wagnild and Young's Resilience Scale features items such as,

> I usually manage one way or another. I can usually find something to laugh about. I can usually look at a situation in a number of ways. When I'm in a difficult situation, I can usually find my way out of it.
>
> (p. 169)

In related bereavement literature, Bonanno (2004) analyzed a large data set of widowed persons to see how they fared after the deaths of their spouses. He found *resilience* to be the most common pattern of adjustment, displayed by nearly half the sample. Resilient widowers universally experienced distress over their spouse's deaths, but those perturbations tended to be transient, so they were still able to function. Many grievers describe such perturbations as "having a moment" of emotional letdown but one from which they could pick themselves up and go on. Resilient widowers maintained a capacity for positive emotion. Even during acute grief, they could still smile and laugh. They took comfort in memories of the deceased. Most resilient widowers did not need professional treatment to cope. They managed to manage.

As noted in Chapter 3, "Helpful Factors," several conceptual terms, such as *hardiness* (Campbell et al., 1991; Kobasa et al., 1982; Maddi, 2006; Mund, 2016), are often used interchangeably with *resilience*. To recap, both hardiness and intrinsic spirituality were identified as inherent strengths possessed by some bereaved parents, attributes that aid coping and adaptation after death of a child. Yet these attributes are not static traits. Parents can cultivate these attributes during and after the death of a child. For example, developing hardiness requires engagement (commitment) rather than avoidance, expectancy of personal agency (control), and determination to adapt to change (challenge). The following case exemplifies a bereaved parent displaying both hardiness and intrinsic spirituality.

CASE 13.B

In her 80s, Hazel found herself recuperating from heart bypass surgery. She became tearfully upset because her postsurgical healing was not progressing as planned, so the surgical team requested consultation with a psychologist. When the consultant arrived at her hospital room, Hazel denied any consternation about the heart operation. "This is nothing,"

> she declared, gesturing to the staples on her chest and dismissing her earlier crying jag as a moment of weakness. Hazel's principal concern was returning home as expeditiously as possible to resume watching over her husband, who suffered from dementia and relied on her, not for physical care but for guidance and direction throughout the day. When the consultant inquired about other difficult experiences she had endured in her lifetime, Hazel responded, "My cancer treatment, that was hard. And the loss of my son."
>
> Hazel's middle-aged son had been presumed healthy and had no known medical conditions. He worked hard as a skilled craftsman. His shop's security camera showed him busy on a typical afternoon before he laid down for a nap, as was his custom. However, this time he never woke up. Her daughter-in-law declined an autopsy, so the cause of death was listed as "natural." Hazel inferred her son had a fatal heart attack. She took some comfort in knowing he did not suffer.
>
> Now in her ninth decade, Hazel had seen her share of life difficulties and had come through them with a conviction of personal durability (hardiness). She also relied heavily on her faith to get through tough times (intrinsic spirituality). When the consultant offered the option of follow-up care to address any lingering distress related to her son's death, her surgery, or anything else, Hazel politely declined, saying, "If I have a problem, I take it to God, and we work it out."

Hazel's case illustrates how bereaved parents can be encountered in a variety of health-care settings and situations, even if child loss is not their chief complaint or the focus of treatment. Besides the ubiquity of child loss, this example also shows how many bereaved parents find ways to cope without professional assistance or psychotherapy. Hazel clearly embodied the key features of hardiness, tackling life challenges head on and with a presumption of effectiveness. How Hazel responded to the death of her son was no different. Intrinsic spirituality was evident in her assertion God would be her saving grace in the event she reached her limits in coping. Resilience of this nature should be validated and encouraged by health-care professionals, never contested or discounted. Should bereaved parents overestimate their ability to handle things on their own and subsequently require professional help, it will be easier for them to accept care if their most recent experience was positive. Savvy practitioners leave the door open for bereaved parent to seek help in the future, if needed, always promoting the inherent resiliencies of parents dealing with the long-term proposition of life without their beloved child.

Albuquerque et al. (2016, 2018) studied the interrelationship between PTG and several positive psychological variables in a sample consisting primarily of bereaved mothers. *Resilience showed the strongest correlation* with PTG. Other key resiliency variables included an internalized form of continuing bond with the deceased child and the partner's ability to articulate the stresses of child loss together with a willingness to request emotional or practical support. Self-disclosure and open communication between bereaved fathers and mothers enhanced closeness and mutual understanding, which in turn positively influenced both partners on their respective grief journeys after the loss of a child. The work of Albuquerque and colleagues is especially relevant because of the widespread belief that loss of a child frequently leads to divorce. While some scholars disavow this assertion as a myth with no empirical basis (Murphy et al., 2003; Schwab, 1998), evidence from some large-scale quantitative studies suggests bereaved couples may indeed be at higher risk for separation and divorce (Bolton et al., 2013; Lyngstad, 2013; Rogers et al., 2008). Therefore, helping bereaved couples enhance their communication and closeness following child loss can pay double dividends—strengthening their union and promoting resilience.

Practitioners can further foster resilience by encouraging bereaved parents to practice the adaptive behaviors listed in Chapter 3, "Helpful Factors." Consider the following case example of a bereaved father plagued by mourner characteristics of someone destined to struggle after child loss who nonetheless progressed toward resilience.

CASE 13.C

Brendan's son Patrick—an athletic young man who enjoyed hiking the mountains of Colorado—was diagnosed in his late 20s with a rare bone cancer that chemotherapy could not cure. When the cancer advanced, Brendan served as caregiver during the last several months of Patrick's life. Although Brendan had stopped his heavy drinking some years earlier, the addiction resurfaced as sedative dependence during the strain of Patrick's terminal illness. Within a month after the funeral, Brendan could barely function due to his sedative misuse. He was admitted to a psychiatric hospital for detoxification and treatment.

> Brendan presented for a group therapy session in the hospital looking disheveled and shaky, in the throes of sedative withdrawal. He mentioned that the family intended to go to Colorado to spread Patrick's cremains in approximately two weeks. He doubted his health would permit him to make the trip, so he envisioned staying home instead to recuperate. Intuiting unhealthy avoidance at play and knowing the proven benefits of funeral participation, the therapist bluntly told Brendan he needed to go, "even if someone has to drive you all the way to Colorado and carry you up the mountain."
>
> Over the course of four days in the hospital, Brendan reconsidered and decided to make the trip. Besides his wife and three living children, plus their families, seven close friends of Patrick planned to fly in from around the country to attend the service. A particular meadow in Patrick's favorite national park was designated as the location. After some remarks about Patrick's life, each participant was given a small receptacle containing some of Patrick's cremains to spread. When Brendan released his son's ashes into the brisk wind, he recalled that they formed "a bigger cloud than I anticipated," resembling an ethereal image of a humanlike figure kneeling in prayer. His wife captured the image in a photo snapped at that precise moment. They found the symbolism staggering. That treasured photo became part of a memory corner at home, placed next to a picture of Patrick in good health before cancer and his favorite baseball cap.

Brendan had contended with anxiety problems his entire life, and dealing with Patrick's death from cancer led to a relapse of his chemical addiction. Yet, on the positive side, he stepped in to care for Patrick as he died. He also agreed to hospitalization and psychotherapy to treat his addiction when things became unmanageable. He listened to the input of a therapist during group sessions. In making the Colorado trip, Brendan enacted seven of the nine adaptive behaviors listed in Chapter 3, "Helpful Factors." Spreading Patrick's cremains in Colorado meant seeing his son all the way to his final resting place and *saying goodbye*. At the same time, it was a valuable *ritual of remembrance* generating *positive memories* of his treasured son, in conjunction with *accessing social support* from those people who loved Patrick the most. Because the mountain meadow was personally significant to Patrick, choosing that location gave special *meaning* to depositing his son's physical remains in a place so evocative of Patrick's spirit. In the family's resolution to return each year to Colorado for an anniversary observance, the foundation was laid for *continuing connection*. Brendan's openness to these possibilities and changes signaled the beginning of *personal growth and transformation*.

Brendan's story shows it is never too late to start coping better. Astute practitioners can almost always find seams of opportunity for guiding bereaved parents in the direction of growth and resilience. Once Brendan changed his mind about making the trip and conveyed details about the planned ritual to spread Patrick's cremains, the therapist made an additional suggestion. Transposing the hiker's credo of "take only pictures, leave only footprints," the therapist proposed distributing pocket-sized photo cards of Patrick to all attendees as a keepsake, that is, "leave only ashes, take only memories."

The kind of positive life changes and adaptive behaviors exhibited by all three bereaved parents described in this chapter—Janette's response to Robert's murder, Hazel's accommodation to her son's midlife heart attack, and Brendan's efforts to honor Patrick's memory—required a level of *belabored acceptance* that did not come easily. This stance was well summarized in another bereaved mother's reflection on her stepdaughter's death: "Let it be broken." Her tone carried neither angry resentment nor fatalistic resignation. Rather, it conveyed a sad recognition of the child's death combined with a willingness to embrace the awful reality that the loss could not be reversed—belabored acceptance. Growth and resilience do not supplant parental grief after the death of a child; they coexist with it.

Contemplating how a bereaved parent juxtaposes belabored acceptance of a child's death along with the possibility for growth and resilience recalls the ancient Japanese art form *kintsugi*, literally meaning gold (*kin*) joint (*tsugi*) (Santini, 2019). Developed in Japan in the 15th century, this technique consists of repairing broken pottery by accentuating its cracks with gold rather than trying to conceal them. The shattered pieces are first gathered, then carefully cleaned and reassembled. Once fused back together with epoxy, the wet crack lines are dusted with gold powder. After drying, they are lacquered and polished for a brilliant final shine. The restored piece is prized as even more beautiful than its original unblemished form.

Metaphors and lessons abound in the imagery of *kintsugi*. Bereaved parents are tasked with picking up the shattered pieces of their lives following the death of a child. They must acknowledge being broken and accept that reality. The brokenness forces them to take stock of their situation and evaluate what can be salvaged. As they begin reassembling their lives, the pain of loss and missing their child—the brokenness—is omnipresent. Yet between and around those broken edges, shining forth from the cracks, can be new and beautiful elements. The true gold consists of positive changes such as post-bereavement personal growth and PTG. These veins of gold frame the brokenness and hold the whole together with a coherency and beauty that did not previously exist. A new and different harmony results with its own special history and meaning—resilience from brokenness. As with a *kintsugi* vase, the restored life of bereaved parents incorporates precious aspects of the deceased child but in a different, still beautiful way.

SUMMARY

This entire book is about promoting resilience among bereaved parents. Their lifetime journey never ends but has a psychological "destination" that is merely a vanishing point where there is always more beyond the horizon (Klass, 2001). Bereaved parents must live with this uncomfortable reality. Belabored acceptance opens the door to the possibilities of post-bereavement personal growth, posttraumatic growth, and ultimately a sense of resilience, exemplified by the analogy to Japanese *kintsugi*. Applying lessons learned from individuals who are more naturally resilient can aid the recovery process for bereaved parents struggling to find a place of emotional and personal equilibrium following the loss of a child. In the end, adopting such positive changes may be one of the most important ways a bereaved parent can honor and remember their deceased child. While no bereaved parent would ever willingly trade their child's life for post-loss gains, regardless of how admirable those changes may be, it is still possible to go on living, loving, and enjoying life after the death of a child.

REFERENCES

Albuquerque, S., Narciso, I., & Pereira, M. (2018). Posttraumatic growth in bereaved parents: A multidimensional model of associated factors. *Psychological Trauma: Theory, Research, Practice and Policy*, 10(2), 199–207. https://doi.org/10.1037/tra0000305

Albuquerque, S., Pereira, M., & Narciso, I. (2016). Couple's relationship after the death of a child: A systematic review. *Journal of Child and Family Studies*, 25(1), 30–53. https://doi.org/10.1007/s10826-015-0219-2

American Psychiatric Association. (2022). *Diagnostic and statistical manual of mental disorders, text revision DSM-5-TR* (5th ed., text revision). Author.

Bolton, J. M., Au, W., Leslie, W. D., Martens, P. J., Enns, M. W., Roos, L. L., Katz, L. Y., Wilcox, H. C., Erlangsen, A., Chateau, D., Walld, R., Spiwack, R., Seguin, M., Shear, K., & Sareen, J. (2013). Parents bereaved by offspring suicide: A population-based longitudinal case-control study. *JAMA Psychiatry*, 70(2), 158–167. https://doi.org/10.1001/jamapsychiatry.2013.275

Bonanno, G. A. (2004). Loss, trauma, and human resilience: Have we underestimated the human capacity to thrive after extremely aversive events? *The American Psychologist, 59*(1), 20–28. https://doi.org/10.1037/0003-066X.59.1.20

Campbell, J., Swank, P., & Vincent, K. (1991). The role of hardiness in the resolution of grief. *OMEGA—Journal of Death and Dying, 23*(1), 53–65. https://doi.org/10.2190/QVHR-5FWW-74LA-F884

Calhoun, L. G., Tedeschi, R. G., Cann, A., & Hanks, E. A. (2010). Positive outcomes following bereavement: Paths to posttraumatic growth. *Psychologica Belgica, 50*(1–2), 125–143. https://doi.org/10.5334/pb-50-1-2-125

Hogan, N. S., Greenfield, D. B., & Schmidt, L. A. (2001). Development and validation of the Hogan Grief Reaction Checklist. *Death Studies, 25*(1), 1–32. https://doi.org/10.1080/07481180125831

Hogan, N. S., & Schmidt, L. A. (2002). Testing the grief to personal growth model using structural equation modeling. *Death Studies, 26*(8), 615–634. https://doi.org/10.1080/07481180290088338

Klass, D. (2001). The inner representations of the dead child in the psychic and social narratives of bereaved parents. In R. A. Neimeyer (Ed.), *Meaning reconstruction & the experience of loss* (pp. 77–94). American Psychological Association. https://doi.org/10.1037/10397-004

Kobasa, S. C., Maddi, S. R., & Kahn, S. (1982). Hardiness and health: A prospective study. *Journal of Personality and Social Psychology, 42*, 158–167. https://doi.org/10.1037/0022-3514.42.1.168

Kosminsky, P. S., & Jordan, J. R. (2024). *Attachment-informed grief therapy: The clinician's guide to foundations and applications* (2nd ed.). Routledge.

Lyngstad, T. H. (2013). Bereavement and divorce: Does the death of a child affect parents' marital stability? *Family Science, 4*(1), 79–86. https://doi.org/10.1080/19424620/2013.821762

Maddi, S. R. (2006). Hardiness: The courage to grow from stresses. *The Journal of Positive Psychology, 1*(3), 160–168. https://doi.org/10.1080/17439760600619609

Mund, P. (2016). Kobasa concept of hardiness: A study with reference to the 3Cs. *International Research Journal of Engineering, IT & Scientific Research, 2*(1), 34–40. https://sloap.org/journals/index.php/irjeis/article/view/243

Murphy, S. A., Johnson, L. C., & Lohan, J. (2003). Challenging the myths about parents' adjustment after the sudden, violent death of a child. *Journal of Nursing Scholarship, 35*(4), 359–364. https://doi.org/10.1111/j.1547-5069.2003.00359.x

Rogers, C. H., Floyd, F. J., Seltzer, M. M., Greenberg, J., & Hong, J. (2008). Long-term effects of the death of a child on parents' adjustment in midlife. *Journal of Family Psychology, 22*(2), 203–211. https://doi.org/10.1037/0893-3200.22.2.203

Rynearson, E. K. (2018). Disabling reenactment imagery after violent dying. *Death Studies, 42*(1), 4–8. https://doi.org/10.1080/07481187.2017.1370411

Rynearson, E. K., Correa, F., & Takacs, L. (2015). *Accommodation to violent dying: A guide to restorative retelling and support*. Virginia Mason Clinic. www.vmfh.org/content/dam/vmfhorg/pdf/legacy-vm/workfiles/Manual_Accommodation_Violent_Dying.pdf

Santini, C. (2019). *Kintsugi: Finding strength in imperfection*. Andrews McNeel.

Schwab, R. (1998). A child's death and divorce: Dispelling the myth. *Death Studies, 22*(5), 445–468. https://doi.org/10.1080/074811898201452

Taku, K., Cann, A., Calhoun, L. G., & Tedeschi, R. G. (2008). The factor structure of the posttraumatic growth inventory: A comparison of five models using confirmatory factor analysis. *Journal of Traumatic Stress, 21*(2), 158–164. https://doi.org/10.1002/jts.20305

Tedeschi, R. G., & Calhoun, L. G. (1995). *Trauma and transformation.* Sage.

Tedeschi, R. G., & Calhoun, L. G. (1996). The posttraumatic growth inventory: Measuring the positive legacy of trauma. *Journal of Traumatic Stress, 9*(3), 455–471. https://doi.org/10.1007/BF02103658

Tedeschi, R. G., & Calhoun, L. G. (2004a). *Helping bereaved parents: A clinician's guide.* Brunner-Routledge.

Tedeschi, R. G., & Calhoun, L. G. (2004b). Posttraumatic growth: Conceptual foundations and empirical evidence. *Psychological Inquiry, 15*(1), 1–18.

Wagnild, G. M. (2009). A review of the Resilience Scale. *Journal of Nursing Measurement, 17*(2), 105–113. https://doi.org/10.1891/1061-3749.17.2.105

Wagnild, G. M., & Young, H. M. (1993). Development and psychometric evaluation of the Resilience Scale. *Journal of Nursing Measurement, 1*(2), 165–178.

CHAPTER FOURTEEN

Practitioner Resilience

> We don't choose the work. The work chooses us.
> —Rabbi Earl Grollman (2013)

Grollman (2013) posited an intuitive truth about grief professionals. Working with bereaved persons is not merely a job or an occupation, even one requiring advanced training. Practitioners may refer to it as a calling, a mission, a sense of purpose, or a vocation. Vocation links *who* a person is to *what* a person does, making it integral to one's professional identity (Norcross & VandenBos, 2018). Many grief professionals would simply say it is work they *must* do. Such dedication to a cause is rarely mentioned in academic circles or corporate settings where advancement is based on objective measures of success. Trauma specialists Saakvitne and Pearlman (1996) spoke to this intangible element as an important prerequisite for longevity as a trauma therapist:

> You must love your work or some important aspect of your work. It must be more than a job. This work is too difficult and too personally demanding to do without a sense of mission or conviction. Without a passion for the work, an individual will most likely leave the field . . . your work must be meaningful to you.
>
> (p. 72)

That passion and intrinsic meaning drives the choosing of which Rabbi Grollman spoke.

PRACTITIONER SELF-CARE

It is incumbent on practitioners called to bereavement work to exercise appropriate self-care, both for personal preservation and for optimizing their effectiveness, especially when working with bereaved parents. Skovholt and Trotter-Mathison (2016) defined practitioner resilience as the ability to bounce back and adapt in positive ways when faced with work-related adversities. Similarly, Gamino and Ritter's (2009, 2012) concept of death competence (see Chapter 1, "Introduction") included an important tenet of self-care for helping professionals—the ability to unwind from work in healthy ways.

How do practitioners unwind? Perhaps Sir William Osler (1849–1919), Canadian physician and revered medical educator at Johns Hopkins Hospital in Baltimore, Maryland, had the best advice: "Saddle up a hobby and ride it hard." Avocational pursuits using a different part of self by tapping into other cognitive capacities or personal interests best serve practitioners seeking to unwind. Paths will be as different as the individuals pursuing them. Common outlets include gardening, traveling, enjoying nature and the outdoors, socializing with family and friends, reading for pleasure or curiosity, meditating, playing or watching sports, exercising, cooking, caring for animals, attending concerts or performances, and laughing as much as possible. For individuals blessed with creative ability, practicing their craft is one of the best ways to unwind: playing music, singing, dancing, painting, sculpting, writing, designing, building, throwing pots, crocheting, knitting, sewing, remodeling, restoring, or imagining. The formula only needs to work for you.

Conversely, maintaining resilience also requires practitioners to avoid unhealthy ways of escaping the pressures of professional work. Relying on alcohol or drugs, or engaging in problematic habit behaviors (such as gambling, compulsive spending, binge eating, pornography viewing, or reckless risk taking), signal trouble—one's life is out of balance. In these instances, honest self-reflection is needed. Practitioners who find themselves mired in unhealthy attempts to unwind need to reevaluate and make a change—either find a different field of endeavor that is less draining or make an intentional shift toward healthy outlets. Failure to make salutary changes can result in personal harm to the practitioner and the likelihood of disservice to the very individuals one intends to help—bereaved parents.

Norcross and VandenBos (2018) compiled an impressive list of strategies for psychotherapist self-care in their book, *Leaving It at the Office*. Most important among these strategies is respecting yourself as the person doing the work of treatment. Indispensable for helping bereaved parents is a robust therapeutic alliance between practitioner and patient. While practitioners dispense expert knowledge and counsel, it is largely the therapeutic relationship that impacts treatment outcomes (Wampold & Imel, 2015). Norcross and VandenBos decried industry's efforts to reduce practitioners to nameless, disembodied "providers" who perform a technical task by applying manualized treatment packages and who are seen as readily interchangeable with the next candidate possessing a similar educational pedigree.

Monetized and depersonalized providers will not cut it with bereaved parents. Mothers and fathers whose children are deceased require more than prescribed techniques and rote responses. Parents' broken hearts and waning spirits will connect only with someone willing to open their own heart in empathy to the tragic loss of a child. Helping bereaved parents starts with empathy and compassion. It also requires appropriate professional training to ensure the necessary death competence, which includes an obligation to care for oneself so as to remain vibrant and effective. Practitioner resilience depends on responsible self-care of the human being who performs the work and resistance against industry's efforts to objectify the therapist as an anonymous technician.

Norcross and VandenBos's (2018) list of self-care strategies for professional therapists included many other insightful recommendations. Their list gives much food for thought to practitioners contemplating how to both survive and thrive doing professional work with bereaved parents. While their major ideas are summarized here, readers are encouraged to explore the original source for more detail.

- *Refocusing on the rewards*—Take time to ponder the privilege of serving; recognize the enormous professional and personal satisfactions realized from making a profound difference in the lives of others.
- *Recognizing the hazards*—Embrace the grueling and demanding parts of therapeutic work with realistic expectations; avoid cynicism over the "grind" or setting impossibly high self-expectations. No practitioner cures every patient, every time.
- *Minding the body*—Care for yourself as a physical creature by meeting your body's basic needs for restorative sleep, tension release, healthy nutrition, regular exercise, and contact comfort (including sexual gratification).
- *Nurturing relationships*—Cultivate supportive peer relationships at work with mentors, coffee buddies, or supervision groups; spend time with the most important people in your life: spouse or partner, children and grandchildren, good friends.
- *Setting boundaries*—Say yes to maintaining good professional and personal boundaries and no to burdensome requests or inappropriate variances; follow the 90% rule (filling only 90% of your available schedule) thus leaving time for brief breaks and unforeseen events.

- *Restructuring cognitions*—Beware of fallacious thinking (what Norcross and VandenBos call "must-urbations"): must be the best, must be brilliant, must be liked and respected, must get results, must enjoy every second of the work. No practitioner or practice is perfect.
- *Sustaining healthy escapes*—Unwind from professional work in healthy ways (enumerated earlier in this section) and eschew unhealthy habit behaviors where escape is illusory or damaging.
- *Maintaining mindfulness*—Build on therapeutic skills of focused attention, watchful observation, and thoughtful reflection to enhance your own in-the-moment meditative awareness and sense of appreciation.
- *Creating a flourishing environment*—Strive for a welcoming, aesthetically pleasing workspace; promote a practitioner-friendly organizational culture; delegate business responsibilities to administrative staff.
- *Profiting from personal therapy*—Acknowledge that the life problems experienced by therapists are nearly identical to the problems of an educated clientele who seek mental health help; consider periodic therapy for purposes of self-monitoring.
- *Cultivating spirituality and mission*—Evaluate the sources of meaning and fulfillment in your own life, including transcendent dimensions; approach spirituality with ecumenical, pluralistic, and universal frames.
- *Fostering creativity and growth*—Deliberately diversify your professional activities to foster personal growth and development; participate in professional societies for continuing education and peer support.

PRACTICE RISKS

Some specific practice risks pose a threat to practitioner resilience. These liabilities include workaholism, burnout, helper secrets, and compassion fatigue.

Workaholism and Burnout

Workaholism and burnout represent the polar opposite of resilience. Yet they are endemic risks in the health-care professions, where putting in longer hours and going the extra mile are admired and rewarded. Workaholism and burnout have been linked not only to impaired health and well-being but also to conflicts with family life (Andreassan, 2014). In organizations where demands for increasing productivity and performance metrics seem endless, practitioners may feel compelled to work beyond advisable limits. Practitioners who incorporate sound self-care strategies in their everyday work rhythms, especially boundary setting, buffer themselves against the tides of workaholism and burnout.

Norcross and VandenBos's (2018) admonition to diversify one's professional activities to enhance personal growth and development has huge implications for avoiding burnout and promoting resilience. Practitioners choosing to work with bereaved parents do themselves and their patients a favor by not working exclusively with this population. Diversifying one's caseload, alternating individual sessions with family or group work, or taking on nonpsychotherapy roles such as teaching, supervising, consulting, or writing help ensure one will be refreshed and energized for arduous work with bereaved parents. Keeping a keen clinical edge comes from constantly exposing oneself to new challenges, new ideas, and new methods.

Helper Secrets

For health-care professionals who work with dying persons and bereaved individuals, Larson's (2020) metaphor of the helper's journey aptly depicts how practitioners encounter various obstacles and pitfalls over the course of their professional lives. In the interest of practitioner resilience, Larson encouraged open confrontation of "helper secrets" often considered shameful. Examples of these common yet corrosive helper secrets include the following reactions.

- *Feeling inadequate* doing professional work, such as the "imposter syndrome," and not wanting anyone to know.
- *Distancing* from grieving patients and families to protect yourself from the intensity of their emotional distress.
- *Experiencing anger* toward patients and families, considered an unacceptable therapeutic response.
- *Wanting recognition* ("What about me?") in the form of gratitude or praise.
- *Feeling overwhelmed* by the patient's loss when you are expected to empathize with their grief.
- *Hoping death would come sooner* to the dying patient because of their acute suffering or poor quality of life.
- *Believing you acted inappropriately* in some way, contrary to your professional ethics and values.

Undisclosed secrets sow doubt and erode one's motivation for doing bereavement work. Helper secrets undermine personal resilience and interfere with professional satisfaction and fulfillment.

Reviewing this list, one can see how self-care strategies such as nurturing relationships (especially with a collegial "buddy"), healthy escapes, making use of one's own therapy, and seeking personal growth and transformation can remedy dispiriting helper secrets. Pulling back the curtain on these embarrassing and painful secrets enables practitioners to view themselves more objectively and see helper secrets for what they are—byproducts of fallible human beings performing an immensely personal form of human care. Practitioners working with bereaved parents are not immune to professional doubts and fears. Resilient practitioners confront their flaws honestly and seek practical assistance managing them. According to Larson (2020), the best escape from this suffocating echo chamber of shame is disclosing one's helper secrets to a trusted and compassionate confidant.

Compassion Fatigue

Figley (1995, 2002) first identified compassion fatigue as a potential problem for mental health practitioners working with traumatized individuals. Compassion fatigue results from absorbing and personalizing the patient's suffering as a consequence of extending empathy and care. By witnessing the patient's distress, professionals can be traumatized by association, as Figley (2002) so astutely observed: "In our effort to view the world from the perspective of the suffering we suffer" (p. 1434).

Since Figley's (1995) original work, the term *compassion fatigue* has been used interchangeably with concepts such as secondary or vicarious traumatization (Sprang et al., 2024), overidentification (Wogrin, 2013), and countertransference (Redinger & Gibb, 2020). All these risks lurk when working with bereaved parents. For example, this book is replete with cases of children who died in traumatic and horrific ways, stories that can shock even the most seasoned professional. Death competence demands practitioners know how to receive such accounts in an empathic manner without distancing, shutting down, or panicking. As described in Chapter 1, "Introduction," death competence means *listening from the heart* and *hearing with the mind*, all the while remaining present and engaged.

When combatting burnout and compassion fatigue or coping with secondary or vicarious traumatization, the self-care principles outlined previously form the backbone of practitioner resilience. Nikel and Gildenblatt (2023) described an initiative to mitigate burnout and compassion fatigue among family medicine residents working in large medical centers in two midwestern cities in the United States. Their intervention program utilized meditation training, gratitude practices, guided support groups, and intentional exercise. A compelling feature for stakeholder buy-in was making all these components available during scheduled work shifts.

An antidote for practice risks such as compassion fatigue and vicarious or secondary traumatization is *compassion satisfaction*—the intrinsic reward of helping, such as the professional satisfaction experienced by providing care to patients. When describing compassion satisfaction, Stamm (2002) referred to the "payments of caring" in contrast to the "costs of caring" associated with burnout, compassion fatigue, and vicarious traumatization. Larson (2020) described an optimal "zone of compassion" where practitioners empathize yet remain emotionally regulated without caring too much (distressing) or too little (withdrawing).

A survey of hospice palliative care workers in Canada who operate daily on the edge between life and death showed compassion satisfaction inversely related to burnout and compassion fatigue (Slocum-Gori et al., 2013). Similarly, Naert et al. (2023) suggested that compassion satisfaction among maternal-fetal medicine physicians in the United States—professionals regularly exposed to pregnancy loss and infant death—may be a protective factor against burnout and compassion fatigue. Other reviews have shown that compassion satisfaction among health-care workers co-occurs with secondary traumatization (Sprang et al., 2024). Compassion satisfaction appears to be important for rebuffing work stress and enhancing practitioner resilience (Larson, 2020). Practitioners can enhance compassion satisfaction by refocusing on the rewards of the profession and cultivating a sense of mission (Norcross & VandenBos, 2018).

PERSONAL EXPERIENCE

Psychologists and other mental health professionals are taught the theory-research-practice triangle (see Figure 14.1). These three arms of professional endeavor inform and stimulate each other. Theory generates research ideas and practice initiatives. Research tests theory and validates practice methods. Practice produces hunches that become theory and develops techniques for research protocols. These bilateral influences are illustrated by the outside triangle in Figure 14.1.

Yet the lives of health-care professionals provide a fourth dimension—personal experience. Human beings know what they have lived. That personal experience provides practitioners with a double advantage. One's lived experiences can inform professional efforts with theory development, research

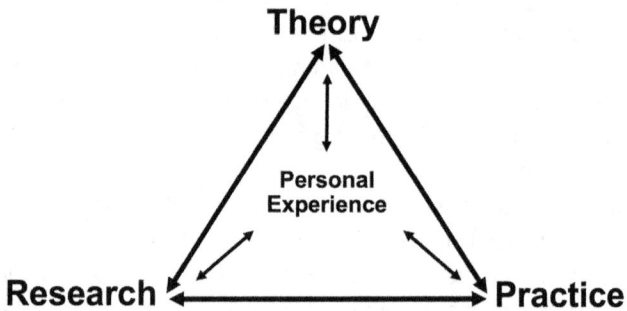

FIGURE 14.1 Theory-Research-Practice Triangle with Personal Experience

questions, and practice interventions if the professional reflects thoughtfully on those experiences. On the other hand, practitioners can draw upon their hard-earned professional knowledge when contending with difficult events and developmental transitions in their own lives. This fourth dimension is represented by the central elements in Figure 14.1.

The laboratory of life constantly supplies new challenges and requires new learning. Integrating one's personal experience as a knowledge source for professional endeavors means comparing it and contextualizing it with theory, research, and practice as reference points. Doing so demands candid self-awareness. Judicious application of knowledge gained from personal experience may or may not involve explicit self-disclosure. Fluidly employing all four knowledge sources in an ongoing, real-time manner is a strong indicator of practitioner resilience.

SUMMARY

To summarize, certain imperatives for practitioner resilience are clear. Resilient practitioners are dedicated to their work, unwind in healthy ways, incorporate a variety of self-care strategies, and deal with practice risks in adaptive ways. The stresses and pressures inherent in working with bereaved parents call for intentional action by practitioners to nurture and preserve their most precious professional resource—themselves. Honoring personal experience as an additional knowledge source can further enrich one's understanding of the human condition and translate into more sensitive and effective treatment interventions.

AUTHOR'S LOSS OF A CHILD

In the final sections of this chapter, I switch to first-person voice to tell my own story of child loss and enumerate what factors made the most difference to my wife, Marla, and me in coping with the death of our son. I chronicle how this personal experience has changed me, how I continued my work as a grief professional, and how my own path toward resilience continues to evolve. I can think of no better way to end this book than by conveying what I have come to learn about parental bereavement through my own experience, refracted by the lenses of theory, research, and practice.

Anthony's Story

In 1997, six words changed our lives forever: "There's a problem with the baby." When the doctor made this pronouncement at a routine 15-week sonogram, sudden alarm nullified our excitement. An unwanted journey of grief and adaptation began. Physical anomalies detected at that time and subsequent testing confirmed our baby's condition to be trisomy 18, a chromosomal disorder that laid down a faulty blueprint for growth and development. Our child had a one-chamber heart incapable of oxygenating blood. As long as Marla supplied his needs through the umbilical cord, he could live. Beyond the uterus, his prospects were nil. "Incompatible with life" was the textbook prognosis. I called my parents with the terrible news and wept uncontrollably as they tried to comfort me.

Even though the doctor mentioned pregnancy termination as an option, our Catholic Christian beliefs did not permit such action. Rather, we believe God is the author of life and we are stewards—life should be protected and nurtured, not taken. Besides, Marla had already felt the baby's quickening movements verifying his existence. We resolved to go on with the pregnancy and see things through to their natural conclusion. We also learned our child was a boy. We named him Anthony Francis.

All the while Marla carried our son, we began preparing for his birth and death. Yet uncertainty surrounded us. Would the pregnancy go full term? Would Anthony be born alive? If so, how long might he live? How would we handle it? Slowly, answers emerged. The duration of the pregnancy was not for us to know. We declined in advance any heroic life-saving attempts. With whatever time we were given, we would hold Anthony, make him comfortable, and let him know how much he was loved. We prayed, not for a miracle but for the strength to cope with what was to come.

Marla's primary care doctor agreed to deliver Anthony according to our wishes. We found a sensitive funeral director who charged us only for the tiny coffin we selected. She assured us she would come to the hospital herself and personally transport Anthony to the funeral home so he would never go to the morgue. Marla sewed an elaborate burial gown. I wrote an obituary and planned the funeral service. We decided to hold visitation hours at our house because it would be the only chance for Anthony to "come home." We purchased burial plots (for him and us) and arranged to close the grave ourselves, by hand, with shovels. We wanted to do everything we could for the baby in the short amount of time he would be in our care.

Grief was omnipresent. With Marla clearly showing, it was difficult to sidestep conversations about the baby. Fear awakened us in the night and kept us wondering what would happen. We told our two young children, Gabriel and Claire, that the baby was sick and probably would not come home from the hospital.

I was angry. I wanted a son without a fatal health condition. As it happened, two men who had lost children ministered to me during a church retreat. With their help, I came to see how lamenting over what might have been interfered with seeing what was—I had a son alive at that moment whose conception was not a medical mishap but a living testament of God's procreative power. Anthony's life was touching me, and everyone who became aware of him, in profound ways. I vowed to bear the sorrow involved with as much grace and dignity as possible.

Anthony was born alive at 38 weeks. He opened only one eye, moved just a little, and never made a sound. We had just enough time to baptize him, hold him, and take pictures. Anthony slipped away quietly with Marla holding him, surrounded by the love of his parents, his brother and sister, his godmother, and all four grandparents. The hospital staff was incredibly sensitive, giving us all the time and space we needed. Several shared our tears.

Two days later, at the visitation, Marla's milk had come in. Her body had no way of knowing the baby had died. Sympathizers wanted to hug Marla, of course, without realizing how her breasts hurt. She had also gained an inordinate amount of weight during the pregnancy, which seemed disproportionate to Anthony's small size, a cruel irony. A wise family doctor later told us, "Oh, her body was trying to feed the baby," a reframing invaluable for gaining perspective and healing.

Anthony's funeral Mass was beautiful and comforting. Just as Marla carried Anthony in life, I carried him in death—I was the only pallbearer needed. Several priests we knew officiated, including one family friend who made a special trip to deliver the homily. The music included the contemporary hymn "Eye Has Not Seen" by Marty Haugen (1982) based on 1 Corinthians 2:9–10. Its lyrics summarized our theology: "Our lives are but a single breath, we flower and we fade, yet all our days are in your hands as we return in love what love has made." (Lyric excerpt reprinted by permission. ©1982 GIA Publications, Inc.)

Our own minivan served as the hearse so we could drive Anthony ourselves to the cemetery. My brothers (Anthony's uncles) were tasked with lowering his small coffin into the grave. But when the moment came, I was mortified to realize the hole dug ahead of time by the workers was too small. My brothers were paralyzed with confusion. Finally, a friend grabbed a shovel, got down on his knees, and beat the earth until the hole was big enough. Those visceral sounds represented the shearing hearts of everyone present. It seemed no hole, no matter how big, could contain the enormity of grief felt not only by our family but by the whole community.

As a grief professional, I was concerned about returning to work after Anthony's birth and death. I was afraid of breaking down. I did not want my own grief to pervade sessions inappropriately. Oppositely, I worried defensive impassivity might render me robotic and unengaged. I decided to wear mourning garb—a simple black lapel ribbon affixed by a tiny gold angel pin—to signal others of my bereavement status. If anyone inquired, brief self-disclosure could occur. If I had an untoward moment, I could reference the ribbon. Most patients said nothing, but those who noticed were extremely understanding and kind.

My personal network of fellow thanatologists lent tremendous support during this ominous time. Jogging (now walking or cycling) was always a physical outlet and mental respite for me, even before Anthony's birth and death. I relied on it more than ever during those trying days.

Marla and I drew closer as a result of parenting Anthony in life and death. Desperately wanting something good to come out of this tragedy, we requested memorial contributions to create a children's library at our church. The funds received vastly exceeded our expectations. To make the space inviting, we commissioned a local artist to paint a wall mural of biblical scenes. We stocked the library with many spiritual and inspirational children's books and purchased appropriately sized tables and chairs. A sympathetic neighbor donated a rocking chair so parents could rock while reading to small children. Friends and congregation members joined us for a dedication ceremony several months later where love generated by the entire experience overcame the sadness and brought joy.

Anthony's legacy goes on. Marla and I have chosen to be open about what happened and try at every turn to make the world a better place as a result of Anthony's brief life so that he is not forgotten. We painted the outdoor playhouse at the preschool Anthony would have attended, using the brightest colors we could find. We have shared his story with many people, regardless of whether they hold faith beliefs or endorse no beliefs. We have consoled many other bereaved parents. To express my grief, and to help inform and empower other death professionals, I published an account of my experience in the periodical literature (Gamino, 1999). Later, I accepted an invitation to write a comfort book on miscarriage and stillbirth together with nurse colleague Ann Cooney (Gamino & Cooney, 2002). Proceeds from sales of the book have been used to provide complimentary copies to anyone who may benefit. Each time a book goes to a grieving parent or grandparent, we honor Anthony and hope our experience will ease the journey for another bereaved parent.

Epilogue

I like to think my personal experience of losing a son has constructively informed how I approach bereaved parents and added to my reservoir of empathy for them. A sign in my office reads, "The difference between ordinary and extra-ordinary is that little 'extra.'" I hope my personal experience becomes that "little extra" that authenticates and enriches my efforts to help grieving families. I can think of no better way to honor Anthony than to empathize accurately with the suffering of bereaved parents and model the resilience I am trying to instill—something beneficial coming from something so painful.

Also hanging in my office is a framed family tree I received one Father's Day. The brown trunk represents Marla and me as parents, signified by our initials encircled with a heart. Green handprints of our three living children form the foliage of the tree, new growth generated from our married love. Above the tree is a small bluebird, a silent but clear reminder of the fourth child in the picture who flies in a different realm but is unmistakably present. This metaphorical image depicts both my personal life where Anthony is never forgotten and my professional life where his influence is never absent. Sometimes I tell patients I am a bereaved parent. Yet regardless of whether I disclose that Marla and I lost a child, Anthony's story innervates my work in myriad ways both conscious and unconscious.

Anthony's death is not the only form of child loss Marla and I have endured. Our oldest son, Gabriel, is intellectually disabled and hampered by intractable epilepsy. The extent of his impairments gradually unfolded during his developmental years. Coming to grips with his condition was a tortuous process of serial disappointments, begrudging concessions, and redoubled compensatory efforts. Raising a disabled son who still lives at home—an instance of nonfinite loss (see Chapter 12, "Non-Death Loss")—has brought parental grief such as loss of dreams and loss of possibilities. Yet these laments are punctuated with moments of celebration when Gabriel says something sagacious, does something uncanny or eminently functional, or is simply himself. Grappling with his limitations makes the ascendancy of our two able-bodied children—Claire and Dominic—all the sweeter and more rewarding. I like to think that contending with Gabriel's disabilities has matured me as an individual and as a practitioner by deepening my existential awareness of what can be controlled and what cannot be controlled—lessons I hope to pass on to others.

This writing occurs 27 years after my son Anthony's birth and death. That experience remains one of the major turning points in my life. No doubt the pain was greatest in the early months of bereavement. Seeking solace took several forms: turning to our faith beliefs, performing important rituals of leave-taking and remembrance, relying on each other and the generous support of family and friends, using my own knowledge of thanatology, and striving to create a legacy for Anthony both in my professional work and in the community.

Sometimes people ask how many children we have. Like other bereaved parents, I do not want to exclude Anthony. Typically, I respond with a statement such as, "We have three living children, and we lost one." If the listener expresses compassion or genuine interest, I elaborate. When they change the subject or move on with the conversation, so do I.

Like all bereaved parents, we are subject to grief upsurges. Around Anthony's birthday and death anniversary, we are likely to get misty eyed and forlorn. Some upsurges are unpredictable, brought on by encountering someone else's baby or noticing what other young adults with similar birthdays are doing. I recently attended a Catholic funeral service for a miscarried baby and was nearly overcome by déjà vu emotions and images. These times are bittersweet—a sour pill to swallow but also a welcome reminder of Anthony's presence in our lives. When bereaved parents report similar experiences and describe consternation, I pose a simple question: "If you could engineer that day over again, would you choose to live it with or without the upsurge?" Invariably, they opt for the upsurge. Just like them, I would rather embrace those mixed emotions than miss an opportunity to remember my son.

With time, legacy efforts and meaning making have become our most prominent ways of honoring and remembering Anthony. Journaling helps me record instances where Anthony comes to mind. I also journal certain highlight events from my clinical work when the wonders and triumphs of the human spirit move me or humble me. That is one way of reinforcing those interactions that make mental health practice so rewarding—what Norcross and VandenBos (2018) call "focusing on the good" as a mental discipline exercised by resilient practitioners. The power of a good story to illustrate a teaching point and bend the narrative in a meaningful direction cannot be overestimated.

In closing, I share three vignettes about how Marla and I continue to create meaning in the aftermath of Anthony's death and honor his legacy. I trust the metaphors they contain will speak for themselves about the ongoing journey of parental grief.

Statue

Around the time Marla was pregnant with Anthony, we purchased three pieces of Christian art from a prominent local sculptor who portrayed biblical scenes. We intended to give one piece to each of our (then) three children once they were old enough. Anthony's piece represented the "weeping woman" who washed the feet of Jesus with her tears and dried them with her hair (Luke 7:38). After Anthony's death, we placed that piece on a table in the entryway of our home.

One day the following autumn around the first anniversary of Anthony's death, Marla and I were both home from work in the late afternoon. The southern sun's last rays came through the window at just the right angle to illuminate the weeping woman statue but nothing else. Cast from white marble dust, it glowed radiantly in the waning light while the rest of the entryway was dark. We sat and watched in stunned awe. Anthony was okay, we concluded. That signal from beyond was silent and brief—just like Anthony's short life after birth—but real and heartwarming. We called it our Stonehenge moment. Other bereaved parents call such phenomena "celestial smiles" or "heart winks."

Unfortunately, a few years later, while Marla was mopping the entryway, she accidentally knocked the statue off the table. It shattered into so many pieces even a skilled Japanese kintsugi artist could not have reassembled it. She was greatly dismayed. The art piece so emblematic of Anthony was gone and could not be restored. The physical did not remain, only the recollection and the timeless love attached to it.

Baptistry

Several years ago, our church underwent extensive renovation requiring a capital campaign. Because Anthony would have been preparing for college around that time had he lived, we planned to make a contribution in his memory with funds we would have used for his education. We wanted to sponsor the new baptistry because it was the only Catholic sacrament Anthony received. However, the required donation for those naming rights was far beyond our means.

I mentioned this dilemma to some church friends. They must have talked among themselves because, over the next few weeks, four different couples approached us and proposed combining their intended contributions with ours to reach the criterion amount. Their generosity astounded us. We felt love for Anthony multiplying exponentially. Upon hearing what happened, our parents and siblings joined in the fundraising. Anthony's cause galvanized this group of contributors, and soon the needed amount was pledged.

When the new baptistry was installed, the contractor allowed us to place tiny crosses bearing the names of each donor in a special niche sealed beneath the last flagstone. As a family, we participated in laying that final stone and giving our blessing in Anthony's memory—a moving ritual of remembrance. Each time I enter and leave the church, I touch that stone and remember. Touchstone.

Tree

At the 25th anniversary of Anthony's birth and death, we again wanted to do some kind of memorial. We decided to plant a tree in one of the city parks along a walking trail I frequent. We found what seemed an ideal spot to memorialize our "forever child" between a playground and a running creek where laughter and water would be plentiful.

The city's crew leader agreed to plant Anthony's memorial tree at a time when I could personally attend and observe the proceedings. He came with an assistant named Richard who did most of the heavy lifting. Richard was a young Hispanic man wearing work boots and leather gloves who went about his task quietly but attentively. Once the tree was in place, I watched him spread and pat the mulch with deliberate care.

Due to a mix-up, the memorial marker was not finished at the time of the planting, but the crew leader promised to let me know when it was ready for installation. A week or so later, a friend who was walking the trail texted me a photo of the marker already in place beneath the tree. In addition, the crew leader called and left a voicemail saying he had some "information" about the tree.

When I returned the call, I expected the crew leader to explain why he had installed the marker without me, but his "information" was not what I anticipated. Although he was aware the tree had been donated in memory of our deceased son, his assistant Richard had not known. Richard had only commented to him that he had "a special feeling" about the tree as he planted it. When Richard saw the marker, he knew why. His birthday and Anthony's birthday were the exact same day and year.

The serendipity overwhelmed me. I sat in silence, soaking up what seemed like a sacred moment. Two infant boys born on the very same day. One lived, and one died. Now, 25 years later, the living child returned to plant a memorial tree for the deceased child. The circle of life. Unbelievable. No wonder Richard patted the mulch with such tender loving care, responding as he did out of an intuitive sense of connection. When I told Marla, we both cried. Just as a parent's love never ends, the search for meaning after a child's death never ends.

REFERENCES

Andreassan, C. S. (2014). Workaholism: An overview and current status of the research. *Journal of Behavioral Addictions*, *3*(1), 1–11. https://doi.org/10.1556/JBA.2.2013.017

Figley, C. R. (1995). *Compassion fatigue as secondary traumatic stress*. Brunner/Mazel.

Figley, C. R. (2002). Compassion fatigue: Psychotherapists' chronic lack of self care. *JCLP/In Session: Psychotherapy in Practice*, *58*(11), 1433–1441. https://doi.org/10.1002/jclp.10090

Gamino, L. A. (1999, January/February). A father's experience of neonatal loss. *Association for Death Education and Counseling: The Forum Newsletter*, *25*(3), 14–15.

Gamino, L. A., & Cooney, A. T. (2002). *When you lose a child through miscarriage or stillbirth*. Minneapolis, MN: Augsburg Fortress. (ISBN 978-0-8066-4355-7). Also published in Italian, *Quando Si Perde Un Bimbo* (2011, Edizioni Messaggero Padova) and Chinese (2012, Taosheng Publishing House, Kowloon, Hong Kong).

Gamino, L. A., & Ritter, R. H., Jr. (2009). *Ethical practice in grief counseling*. Springer Publishing Company.

Gamino, L. A., & Ritter, R. H., Jr. (2012). Death competence: An ethical imperative. *Death Studies*, *36*, 23–40.

Grollman, E. (2013, April). *Remarks after receiving lifetime achievement award*. Presented at Annual Meeting of Association for Death Education and Counseling, Hollywood, CA.

Haugen, M. (1982). *Eye has not seen [song]*. GIA Publications.

Larson, D. G. (2020). *The helper's journey: Empathy, compassion, and the challenge of caring* (2nd ed.). Research Press.

Naert, M. N., Pruitt, C., Sarosi, A., Berkin, J., Stone, J., & Weintraub, A. S. (2023). A cross-sectional analysis of compassion fatigue, burnout, and compassion satisfaction in maternal-fetal medicine physicians in the United States. *American Journal of Obstetrics and Gynecology MFM, 5*(7), 100989. https://doi.org/10.1016/j.ajogmf.2023.100989

Nikel, C., & Gildenblatt, L. (2023). Finding compassion when compassion fatigued. *International Journal of Psychiatry in Medicine.* Advance online publication. https://doi.org/10.1177/00912174231215923

Norcross, J. C., & VandenBos, G. R. (2018). *Leaving it at the office: A guide to psychotherapist self-care* (2nd ed.). Guilford.

Redinger, M. J., & Gibb, T. S. (2020). Counter-transference and the clinical ethics encounter: What, why and how we feel during consultations. *Cambridge Quarterly of Healthcare Ethics, 29*, 317–326. https://doi.org/10.1017/S0963180119001105

Saakvitne, K. W., & Pearlman, L. A. (1996). *Transforming the pain: A workbook on vicarious traumatization.* W. W. Norton.

Skovholt, T. M., & Trotter-Mathison, M. (2016). *The resilient practitioner: Burnout and compassion fatigue prevention and self-care strategies for the helping professions* (3rd ed.). Routledge.

Slocum-Gori, S., Hemsworth, D., Chan, W. W. Y., Carson, A., & Kazanjian, A. (2013). Understanding compassion satisfaction, compassion fatigue and burnout: A survey of hospice palliative care workforce. *Palliative Medicine, 27*(2), 172–178. https://doi.org/10.1177/0269216311431311

Sprang, G., Gusler, S., Eslinger, J., & Gottfried, R. (2024). The relationship between secondary traumatic stress and compassion satisfaction: A systematic literature review. *Trauma, Violence, & Abuse, 25*(3), 2282–2296. https://doi.org/10.1177/15248380231209438

Stamm, B. (2002). Measuring compassion satisfaction as well as fatigue: Developmental history of the compassion satisfaction and fatigue test. In C. Figley (Ed.), *Treating compassion fatigue* (pp. 107–119). Routledge.

Wampold, B. E., & Imel, Z. E. (2015). *The great psychotherapy debate: The evidence for what makes psychotherapy work.* Routledge.

Wogrin, C. (2013). Professional issues and thanatology. In D. A. Meagher & D. E. Balk (Eds.), *Handbook of thanatology: The essential body of knowledge for the study of death, dying and bereavement* (2nd ed., pp. 395–409). Association for Death Education and Counseling, The Thanatology Association.

Index

90 % rule 238

abandonment and rejection 147, 153
absence into presence 118–119
addiction 203–204, 230–231
adoption: loss 209–211; open 210–211
adverse childhood events 21
advocating 37–39, 170–171
Al-Anon 204
Alcoholics Anonymous (AA) 220
allocution 170; see also victim impact statements
ambiguous loss 198–199
ambivalent relationship 19–20, 156
American Academy of Pediatrics 84, 96
American Psychiatric Association 24
anniversaries and holidays 118–119, 174
assumptive world 12–14, 226
Attachment-Informed Grief Therapy 60–61
avocational pursuits 237

back sleeping 84
bed sharing 84
belabored acceptance 232
Bereaved Parents of the USA 21, 97
bereavement camps 105; see also sibling grief
body jettison 151

Boelen, P. A. 54–55, 62, 99
Boss, P. 198–200, 202, 205, 211
Breitbart, W. S. 51
burnout 239–240
Bureau of Justice Statistics 205
Byock, I. R. 32

Calhoun, L. G. 13, 40–41, 59, 63–64, 119, 138, 156, 202, 207, 225–226
Canadian Alliance for Children's Grief 105
capacity to act on a desire for death 154–155, 191–192
care tenor 56, 58
caregiving system 60–61
Casualty Assistance Officer 188
Centers for Disease Control and Prevention 174
changed address book 42
chair work 121–123, 168, 212–214
Child Bereavement Network 105
Chochinov, H. M. 55–56, 58
Cognitive Behavioral Therapy for Grief (CBT) 54–55, 99
coincidancing 104
collective coping 172; see also social support (positive)
compassion: fatigue 241–242; satisfaction 241–242
(The) Compassionate Friends 21, 97

INDEX

complicated grief 23
concealment 172
confidentiality 148
conflictual relationship 111; *see also* ambivalent relationship
continuing bonds 36–37, 57, 101, 172, 227, 230
continuing connection *see* continuing bonds
conversations with the deceased child 37; *see also* chair work; imaginal conversation
counterfactual thinking 64, 111–112, 148, 167–168
countertransference 4, 241
Courageous Parents Network 207
criticizing the deceased child 18–19, 168
culpability 133, 150, 159; *see also* criticizing the deceased child
cultural attunement 6–9, 63, 146, 158, 172, 176
cultural humility 7; *see also* cultural attunement
culturally informed practice 7–8; *see also* cultural attunement

Davies, B. 102–103
Davis, C. G. 40
death competence 4–6, 166, 237
death notification 188–189
death spiral 137
deconstruction and revision 53, 85, 121–124
desaparacido 206
Dignity Therapy 55–56
Doka, K. J. 34, 199
dosing 62, 66, 213
double death 137
disability 207–208
disenfranchised grief 199
DSM-5-TR 24, 48
Dual Process Model 35, 48–49, 55, 174
durable narrative 134, 154
dying with honor 186–188

early pregnancy loss 73–77
elective abortion for fetal anomaly 86–89

emotion-based coping 206
emotional leadership 41–42
empathic failure 75
empty track 14, 21, 34, 94
estate matters 115–116
estrangement 200–203
exile metaphor 63, 100, 223
expert companionship model 63–64, 202
explanatory framework 22–23
extraordinary experiences 100

Family Focused Grief Therapy (FFGT) 103–104
father grief 82–83
Figley, C. R. 241
finding meaning *see* meaning making
First Candle 85
forgiveness 85, 122, 158, 221; decisional 176; emotional 176–177
foster parents 9
Freud, S. 19, 36

Gamino, L. A. 4–6, 25, 31, 40, 57, 237
Gold Star families 183
goodbye 32–33, 57, 65, 80, 112, 121–123
grandparents 9, 14, 117–118, 175
Grief Recovery After Substance Passing (GRASP) 139
grief story 65–66
grief tax 11–12
Grollman, E. 236
guilt 88, 167–168; survivor 103

hardiness 29–30, 87, 112, 164, 228–229
helper secrets 240–241
helpful factors 146, 164, 231–232
Hogan Grief Reaction Checklist (HGRC) 224–225
homicide (mass) 174–175
hope 57, 67, 146
Hoskins, M. L. 6
Hoy, W. G. 32

idealization of deceased child 103; *see also* sibling grief
identification 5–6

253

INDEX

imaginal conversation 49, 85–86, 120–122, 156; *see also* chair work
imaginal revisiting 49
incarceration 204–205
inconvenience of death 113
infant death 79
infertility 208–209
injury deaths (unintentional) 130
(The) Injury Prevention Program (TIPP) 96
inner representation of the deceased child 100–101
inquest into the death 151–153
insecure attachment 60
intentional parents 209
International Classification of Diseases (ICD-11) 23–24
intuitive grief 121
intrinsic spirituality 30–31, 77, 112, 157, 164, 227, 228–229

Janoff-Bulman, R. 13
Joiner, T. E., Jr. 154, 191
Jordan, J. R. 60–63, 146–154

Kass, J. 31
kintsugi 232–233
Kissane, D. W. 104–105
Klass, D. 14, 36–37, 100–101
Knapp, R. J. 99, 209
Kobasa, S. C. 30
Kosminsky, P. S. 60–61
Kushner, H. S. 13

LaGrand, L. E. 100
Larson, D. G. 240–241
leave taking *see* goodbye
legacy and continuation 15–16, 86, 119
letter to deceased child 52, 85, 87–89, 129–130; *see also* chair work
Lichtenthal, W. G. 51–52, 57, 59, 99, 119, 129
lifespans worldwide 111
life story 65–66
living legacy project 52
living link 117–118
living will 155

loss of self 16
Lynch, T. 11–12, 73

Marris, R. W. 194
McIntosh, J. L. 61, 148–149
Meaning-Centered Grief Therapy (MCGT) 51–52, 86, 99, 119, 129
meaning making 39–40, 52, 86, 89, 104–105, 133–135, 172, 227
memories (positive) 33–34, 80, 96
military burial 189–191; *see also* goodbye
military culture 184–186
military protocol 188–191
milk donation 81
miscarriage 73–77
missing in action 188
missing or kidnapped children 205–207
Mitima-Verloop, H. B. 37, 115
Mothers Against Drunk Driving (MADD) 95–96
mother blame 75
motor vehicle crashes 131–135
mourner liabilities 21
Murray-Garcia, J. 7

Nadeau, J. W. 104–105
National Alliance for Children's Grief 105
National Center for Injury Prevention and Control 95, 111, 130
National Center for Missing & Exploited Children 206
National Crime Information Center 206
neonatal death 77–83
Neugarten, B. 13
Nietzsche, F. 51
Norcross, J. C. 58, 237–240

off time death 12–13, 94, 111, 184
Operation Here We Are 183
opioids (synthetic) 137
overdose (unintentional) 136–137
over identification 241

parental competence 61
parental identity 79, 99–101
parentified child 103; *see also* sibling grief
perceived burdensomeness 154, 191

personal disaster 5
personal experience 242–243
perpetual connection 156; see also continuing bonds
photographs 63, 80
positive outcomes 40–44
possessions of the deceased child 128
post-bereavement personal growth 223–225, 233
post-neonatal death 79, 83
posttraumatic growth 225–227, 233
post traumatic stress 226
powerlessness 148
preventability 18–19, 84, 94–95, 111, 132, 164
products of the deceased child 152–153; see also possessions of deceased child
professional will 6
prolonged grief disorder 23–25, 137
Prolonged Grief Disorder-13-Revised Scale 137
Prolonged Grief Treatment (PTG) 48–51, 99, 120
protective factors 146; see also helpful factors
psychache 150–151, 155

Rando, T. A. 21, 164
Raphael, B. 5
Redmond, L. M. 162, 164
Reed, M. L. 14
reenactment imagery 33, 52–53, 121–124, 179, 227
reflexive narrative mode 213
relational repair 153–154, 168
religious rituals 80
remembrance rituals 34–36, 77, 82, 97, 113–115
reprisal fantasies 165–167, 177
resilience 224–225, 227–233
Resilience Scale 228
Restorative Retelling 52–53, 99, 121–124, 177–179, 227
retrospective narrative 153–156
return channel 37
righteous anger 165–167, 205, 225
risk factors (general) 17–23, 145, 164

Ritter, R. H., Jr. 4–6, 25, 237
room of the deceased child 98–99; see also possessions of the deceased child
room sharing 84
Roos, S. 200, 208, 213
Rynearson, E. K. 17–18, 52–53, 58, 85, 99, 121, 177

Schut, H. 35–36
self-care (practitioner) 237–239
separation distress 17, 52
seppuku 158
shadow grief 209
Share Pregnancy and Infant Loss Support 77
Sharpe, T. L. 172–173
Shear, M. K. 48–51, 53, 57, 85, 99, 120
Shidu parents 15–16
Shneidman, E. S. 150, 155
sibling grief 101–103
situational revisiting 49, 62, 156
social support: lack 20–21, 79, 112; positive 41–42, 62–63, 100–101, 139, 146, 149, 224
sorrow (chronic) 200, 208
stepparents 9
student position 7–8
stigma 137–138, 147–149, 172
stillbirth 77–83
still-open door 202
Stroebe, M. 35–36
Substance Abuse and Mental Health Services Administration (SAMHSA) 203
Sudden Infant Death Syndrome (SIDS) 83–86
suicide bereavement model 61–63
suicide (military) 191–194
suicidogenic relationships 194; see also ambivalent relationship
suttee 157
symbolic mastery 34

task-based model of grief 66
Tedeschi, R. G. 13, 40–41, 59, 63–64, 119, 138, 156, 202, 207, 225–226
Tervalon, M. 7

theory-research-practice triangle 242–243
therapeutic justice 169, 172
thwarted belongingness 154, 191
transformation (personal) 42–43, 223;
    see also post-bereavement personal
    growth; posttraumatic growth
Tragedy Assistance Program for Survivors
    (TAPS) 183
trauma distress 17–18, 52
traumatic death 94, 130, 184
turning points 66

unanswered questions 152–153
unexpectedness 17, 94

VandenBos, G. R. 58, 237–240
vicarious traumatization 241–242
victim impact statements 170–171, 177;
    see also allocution

victim-perpetrator paradox 149–151
viewing the body 112–113, 132, 168–169
Virgilio, N. 190–191
vocation 236

Wagnild, G. M. 228
warrior ethos 184–186
Weiner, S. J. 75
Wogrin, C. 5, 241
Wolterstorff, N. 127
Worden, W. R. 66–67
workaholism 239
World Health Organization (WHO) 24, 137
Worthington, E. L., Jr. 176–177
wrongful death 37–39, 133

Xiong, J. 15–16

Young, H. M. 228

For Product Safety Concerns and Information please contact our EU representative GPSR@taylorandfrancis.com
Taylor & Francis Verlag GmbH, Kaufingerstraße 24, 80331 München, Germany

www.ingramcontent.com/pod-product-compliance
Lightning Source LLC
Chambersburg PA
CBHW050530300426
44113CB00012B/2027